Black Market Beatles:
The Story Behind The Lost Recordings

Jim Berkenstadt and Belmo

Published by Collector's Guide Publishing, Box 62034, Burlington, Ontario, Canada, L7R 4K2
Editor - Carl Krach

Manufactured in Canada
Black Market Beatles: The Story Behind The Lost Recordings / Jim Berkenstadt & Belmo
First Edition
ISBN 0-9695736-9-3

DEDICATION

This book is dedicated to the memory of master artist Aaron Bohrod (1907–1992). Aaron was not only the premier American still-life artist of the Twentieth Century, but he also was a family man, humorist, a die-hard Cubs' fan and a keen observer of popular culture. His work continues to be exhibited and celebrated throughout the United States.

Aaron understood and appreciated my fascination with artists' "rough drafts" (be they his own or those of The Beatles) and the evolution of creative expression. I know Aaron would have enjoyed this book. I dedicate my portion of this book to you Aaron.

—*Jim Berkenstadt*

John Ono Lennon (1940–1980) was an artist, musician, author, humorist, humanitarian, family man and a free spirit who lived his life publicly and with no apologies. He was also a collector of unreleased recordings (especially of the Beatles), so I know he would have enjoyed this book.

Ralph Edward Belmer (1916–1974) was a promising young cartoonist who, having had to abandon his art so he could raise his family, became a loving husband and father. He encouraged me to write, to follow my own path, and to know the importance of humor in life. It is to these two men I dedicate my portion of this book. I miss them both.

—*Belmo*

ACKNOWLEDGEMENTS

Nobody writes a book without a little help from their friends. This book is no exception. The authors would like to acknowledge their sincere gratitude and appreciation for the assistance received from family and friends, without whom…Please hold your applause for these nice folks until the end.

Jim's thank you list...

Thanks to mom and dad (Lois and Ed). My mom *turned me on* (to The Beatles) and *tuned me in* (to Ed Sullivan in February, 1964) and bought me my first Beatles' album. She has always encouraged my interest and love for music and The Beatles. She's a hep cat! My dad finally admitted in 1989 that "the Beatles did make *some* good music." Dad taught me truth, honesty, when to change the car's oil and some big fancy words to use when I write.

To my brother Gene, thanks for *Sgt. Pepper* and the *White Album* and for bailing out your little brother whenever he got into trouble over the years. To my sister Joy, thanks for *Rubber Soul* and for sharing so much wisdom, love, concern and affection.

To my mother and father-in-law, Helen and Garvin, who still love, support and accept me, even though they think The Beatles were noisy rubbish. Of course, that's what I think about Lawrence Welk's music. So we're even!

A special thanks to our wonderful draft editors Gary "Mal" Schumacher and Kate Lyster. You both helped make this book a reality and discovered that I never took grammar in grade school. Your assistance was invaluable. Many thanks also go to Bob Walker for his editing, fact checking, and words of wisdom!

Kudos are also in order for Adrian Belew, who so graciously accepted the task of writing a forward for the book. Adrian has been a fan of The Beatles since his youth. His recollections of The Beatles' influences on him come directly from the heart.

To Allen J. Wiener, a great friend and the world's premier Beatles historian. Thank you for freely sharing your data base, knowledge, recording information, resources, contacts, faxes, and for imparting advice about the publishing industry.

To my fellow co-workers at TWC, thanks for your help and for demonstrating that *anybody* can use a computer: Carol Koslo (computers 101), Helen George, Gerri Stanczk & the Network (see Appendix B!), Dave Butcher (see Appendix D!), Yukiko Felper (translation), Darcy Little and Dale Dull.

Saving the best for last, I would like to thank my wonderful wife Holly, who has endured my endless late hours typing and my weird fascination with preserving the musical history of The Beatles over the last 19 years. Thank you for your love, understanding and patience while I endlessly worked on this book. And finally to my two beautiful kids, Rebecca and Bradley who dance to the "Wilbury Twist" and represent a new generation of Beatles fanatics!

Belmo's thank you list...

A huge thank you goes to my wife, Terri. Without her patience, encouragement, love, suggestions and hugs, the writing of this book would have been a lot more difficult and a lot less fun. I love you.

To Jeff Jerdon, a pre-eminent collector and good friend who shared his collection with me, as well as contributing many helpful ideas and valuable information.

To Tom Jones for all the music and invaluable data which I would not have had access to otherwise.

To Allen J. Wiener for his friendship and unselfish assistance in the preparation of this book. I appreciate you and the work you've done for the cause of Beatledom.

To Jeffrey Ressner for his encouragement, suggestions and especially for the Paul McCartney World Tour (1989) Press Pass. I finally got to meet a Beatle.

And finally, a heartfelt thank you goes to my mother. She put up with years of having to listen to me play my Beatles records over and over again. And though she didn't approve of me spending my allowance on records, she never kept me from the music I loved. And with the publication of this book, I can now say to her, "See, mom, there was a reason why I spent all my money on those records!"

The authors gratefully acknowledge the efforts of the following people who assisted us either directly or indirectly in our preparation of this book: Bob Walker and Hot Wacks Press for believing in the success of this book!, Tess J. Welch, Esq. for her legal review of the book and the Stroud law firm; Mike Westcott, Esq., Dan Hardy, Esq. and the Axley, Brynelson law firm; Boris and Natasha Badinoff (on the inside of the Bureau), Jeff Tamarkin and Bonni J. Miller, *Goldmine*'s super editors, *Rolling Stone* Magazine, Pete Howard, Eric Flanagan, *ICE the Monthly CD Newsletter*, Oliver Dziggel, Charles Rosenay!!! and Good Day Sunshine, Michael Meshew, Peter C. Palmiere, Allen Kozinn, Dave Stein B.V.A., Marshall Terrill, Jay Olsen (award-winning documentary producer) at CBS-TV, Dave Benton, Butch Vig, Lord Buddha, Rinaldo Tagliabue, The Mal Evans Fan Club, Nurk Twin, L.R.E. King, Sandy Maris Esq. (Attorney for Boz and Mick!!), Leanne Martin and Darcie Wilson (super nannys!), Roxy (you dog), The New York Opera News, New York Public Library, Northwestern University Library, University of Wisconsin Library, Madison Public Library, Frank Badenius, Dr. Mike Beller, Michael Church, Renato Facconi, Arno Guzek, Michael J. Papelian, Mark Sokolski, Mike Hawkinson, Paul Inks, Steve Loveless, Mike Moon, James McNally, Russ & Denice, Ted Pastuszak Jr., Tony Wedeking, Janet Wilson, Thom Whetston, Denny Shields, the Beatle Gals, Beatlefan, and finally, Dr. Winston O'Boogie, Paul Ramone, Hari Georgeson & Ognir Rrats without whom...

CONTENTS

Dedication v

Acknowlegdements vi

Foreword by Adrian Belew 3

Preface 5

Chapter One
In The Studio With The Beatles 9

Chapter Two
A New Industry Is Created Around The Big Three 18

Chapter Three
Bootleggers Reunite The Beatles:
The Most Significant Black Market Releases 1958–1970 50

Chapter Four
The Beatles On Bootlegs: In Their Own Words 107

Chapter Five
Inside Interviews With The Beatles' Bootleggers 123
  Mr. Nurk Twin (1972–1982) 123
  Mr. Lord Buddha (1975–1977) 146
  Mr. Rinaldo Tagliabue (1988–present) 155

Chapter Six
The Beatles' Underground Discography 159

Appendix A
Glossary of Terms 215

Appendix B
List of Beatles' Bootlegs Organized By Major Manufacturer 217

Appendix C
Photo Survey of Bootleg Trademarks and Logos 226

Appendix D
Bootleggers' Family Tree 231

Reference Books/Periodicals 236

About The Authors 238

FOREWORD

By Adrian Belew

Not everyone is fortunate enough to have lived through the hurricane known as "Beatlemania" when it first struck the shores of America. Let me tell you what it was like.

At the time I was a 14-year-old drummer in the junior high school marching band. There was a radio in the hallway of my parents' house and it was always tuned to a "popular" music station, but I never paid much attention to it. I couldn't relate to songs about cars and surfboards as I didn't have a car and was several states away from the nearest beach. But one day as I walked through the hallway the radio suddenly blurted out "Well she was just seventeen...you know what I mean. And the way she looked was way beyond compare..." I was galvanized.

To this day I don't know why that moment had such a stunning effect on me. It couldn't have been the massive media blitz; I had never even heard their odd name, "Beatles." It wasn't the amazing new hairstyles, collarless suits and Beatle boots or their British wit and collective charisma; I hadn't even seen a "Beatle." I simply heard their music and it stopped me in the hallway and turned my life around in a different direction. From that day forward I dreamed of making records.

Call it obsessive behavior but it sure was fun. I joined my first band as a singing drummer. We mimicked The Beatles right down to their English accents. We had our own Beatle-like bass drum logo, the military suits, and Vox SuperBeatle amps. I learned to play guitar and became consumed with figuring out the smallest detail of every Beatle album, spending hours a day in front of a record player.

For the MTV generation it might be difficult to imagine the pure electric anticipation of anything to do with The Beatles—their television appearances and hilarious press conferences, the thrill of hearing a new Beatle single on the radio for the first time. I remember skipping school to ride the bus downtown to sit in a theatre all day watching *Help!* over and over. When they played in Cincinnati I spent the night in the Crosley Field parking lot waiting in line to get a ticket. The next day The Beatles played for 30 minutes in the middle of a base-ball field while all 26,000 of us stood up the entire time screaming with wild excitement. Later someone supposedly sold one-inch squares of their bed sheets from the Vernon Manor Hotel. Such was the power of The Beatles.

They made records together for a mere seven years, but they changed the world. They were so prodigious and innovative they left behind a trail of golden musical thoughts the rest of us continue to mine. Not all of it made it onto offi-cial Beatle albums. Some of their ideas live on in the form of bootlegs which vary greatly in quality and content but can at times be as exciting as hearing a new release. For example, I recently acquired a collection called *Artifacts* which fea-tures five discs in a well-designed package. I was thrilled with its 12 minute 30 second chronicle of "Strawberry Fields Forever" which begins with John's home demos and traces the songs' development right through to a version of George Martin's brilliant orchestra by itself. Terrific.

There are, however, bootlegs which may not be worth having. And so at last we arrive at the purpose of this publication; an informative look at bootlegged music available from the minds of John, Paul, George and Ringo. Read on and you'll see why they still hold such fascination for people like me. They were young, attractive, rich, and famous. But that wasn't what floored me in the hall-way…it was the music.

Adrian Belew
April 1994

PREFACE

When Neil Armstrong descended the steps of his Apollo lunar module to the moon's surface in July of 1969, he uttered the now famous words, "That's one small step for a man, one giant leap for mankind." These profound words might aptly describe the musical and cultural path of The Beatles as their Pan American Yankee Clipper touched down at Idlewild Airport in New York on February 7, 1964. On that day, four young men stepped off their plane to conquer America and the world of popular entertainment would be forever changed. Never before, and not since that time, has any musical group had such a profound influence on the musical, social, political and economic environment, as did this quartet of renaissance minstrels.

This book traces the historic audio footsteps left behind by the Beatles through the exploration of their rarest unreleased recordings. These recordings, unheard by the general public, have been historically preserved and commercially exploited by groups of people known simply as bootleggers. The book reveals the untold story behind the release of the Beatles' lost recordings.

Unauthorized sound recordings, or bootlegs, have been a part of rock and roll music since 1969. Over the last twenty-plus years, bootleggers have thrilled music fans with previously unheard releases, while simultaneously angering music companies and their artists who claim financial and artistic hardship. Today the recording industry's biggest names, from Beatles and Rolling Stones to Madonna and Nirvana, are being bootlegged onto compact disc. The recordings, sold at record stores, trade shows, flea markets, fan conventions and through mail order, make up a multimillion dollar black market industry which has for two decades remained a mystery to most people...until now!

The book also provides a brief historic overview of the underground recording industry that began as a turn-of-the-century experiment, then developed as a lucrative hobby for most of its participants at the end of the 1960s, all while riding on the coattails of The Beatles' break up. The illicit record trade began as a small cottage industry. However, the advent of digital technology in the 1980s helped expand it into a worldwide "big bucks" industry, which in some ways parallels its legitimate counterpart.

While The Beatles toured and recorded as a group in the sixties, they were far too busy to collect, record or document their many rehearsals, performances and appearances. The people working for the group were either too careless or busy to realize the immense historical value of the many impromptu performances that took place in the studio, at concert halls, backstage, in hotel rooms and on radio and TV. Thus, it was the fans, collectors and music scholars who became archivists and curators of the audio treasures left behind by The Beatles. These rare tapes, leaked by recording studio personnel, staffers and even friends of The Beatles, have been passed along or sold from one person to another until they found their way into the hands of bootleggers. These lost tapes complete the last piece of puzzle behind the musical mystique that personified the Fab Four.

This assemblage compiles for the first time ever, from numerous interviews and press conferences, the quoted personal opinions of the individual former Beatles, on the subject of their many unofficial releases. Additionally, a detailed narrative history highlighting the most significant *unreleased* Beatles recordings is provided, spanning their earliest known demonstration discs and rehearsals to their final recording sessions for the *Abbey Road* album.

For collectors, music scholars and historians, the book contains the most complete reference discography ever published on the group, listing all of the unauthorized Beatles releases from the United States, Europe, the Far East and Down Under. The staggering number approximates more than *1,600* titles! The discography contains all bootleg formats: long-play records, compact discs, cassettes, 45-rpm singles, seven and twelve inch extended-play records, flexi discs, colored vinyl, picture discs and box sets.

Included are first-hand, insider interviews with past and present bootleggers of The Beatles' unreleased music. The veil of secrecy concerning this clandestine trade is finally lifted in these revealing admissions. Lavish photographic illustrations documenting the rarely seen, unique and creative artwork designed for album covers, help to round out the profile on The Beatles' black marketeers.

All in all, the authors believe this book will appeal to fans, collectors, record retailers, disc jockeys, music and cultural scholars, historians, commercial record industry executives, and yes, even The Beatles themselves. Although The Beatles disbanded as a group in 1970, their unreleased works have continued to escape for more than twenty years, with more still to come. It is the hope of the authors that this book captures and forever preserves the story behind the most important unreleased musical performances of this century...the door to the studio vaults is now open. Please step inside and discover the hidden treasures of The Beatles.

1

In The Studio With The Beatles

*T*hree *Abbey Road.* Perhaps the most famous musical address of this century. *Abbey House.* Formerly a private residence more than 100 years old, nestled within the comfortable London suburb of St. John's Wood. It is today one of the most visited tourist sites in England. *Abbey Road Studios.* Situated within the EMI (Electronic & Music Industries) Records Limited Abbey House, along tree-lined Abbey Road.

Originally opened on November 12, 1931, Abbey Road Studios was custom-designed to serve the recording needs of a diverse spectrum of musical and non-musical styles and genres. If the walls of this building could speak, they would describe a rich history of recorded sounds by the leading recording artists of the century, ranging from classical and comedy to popular rock and rap. However, only one musical group consisting of four young men is responsible for immortalizing Abbey Road's reputation. It is this group's recorded output over a nine-year period from 1962 to 1970 that has bestowed legendary landmark status on Abbey Road. The group's name is of course, The Beatles.

It was an unseasonably warm 58 degree evening on Monday, November 8, 1965, when the four Beatles ascended the nine steps leading them through the glass double doors housing Abbey Road Studios. They had assembled for yet another recording session. John, Paul, George and Ringo were running out of time to complete their next album in order to make the Christmas release deadline. The Beatles and their producer, George Martin, had two projects in mind for this 9 p.m. session that would eventually end at 3 a.m. the next day.

The primary goal was to finish rehearsing and recording George Harrison's song, "Think For Yourself," for their forthcoming album entitled *Rubber Soul.*

9

The song contained some difficult three-part harmonies to be sung live in the studio by George Harrison, John Lennon and Paul McCartney. The Beatles made several unsuccessful attempts at completing the song during the rehearsal.

Producer George Martin had a secondary purpose for this November 8th session. He knew that The Beatles needed to produce their annual *Fan Club Christmas Record* in the near future. Beginning in 1963, The Beatles had annually made a special record to be distributed free of charge to their *Beatles Fan Club* members. The 45 rpm flexi disc singles contained statements of appreciation to fans, season's greetings, silly dialogues and short bits of mostly unreleased songs. Knowing that the group always provided a constant source of humorous, spontaneous banter in the studio, Martin decided to record and preserve all of the between-song discussions that evening. His hope was to capture a sufficient number of charming, anecdotal sound bites to produce the Christmas Fan Club single, while finishing the song "Think For Yourself."

The Beatles were well aware that their between-song comments were being recorded that night. As a result, they made a concentrated effort to talk in their own unique "Beatle-speak." Their sound bites ran the gamut from crude toilet humor and movie satire, to religious rambling, all while flexing their famous vocal chords in Scouse, Indian and Bronx accents. The fun, frustration and interpersonal dynamics of the group was clearly illustrated by this unique session dialogue.

Ultimately, none of the recorded rambling from the "Think For Yourself" rehearsal was appropriate for use on the Fan Club Christmas Record. Only a brief snippet of harmony recorded amidst the chatter was included on the soundtrack of the animated film *Yellow Submarine*. The rest of the non-musical banter was relegated to EMI's studio vault, seemingly to be left unheard by the public's ears for eternity.

The following narrative takes you back to a time in 1965 when The Beatles were a huge worldwide phenomenon. They had just completed their second successful World Tour and were finally back home doing what they liked doing best…making records. It was in the studio, away from screaming girls, stuffy dignitaries, flash bulbs and news cameras, that the group was able to relax and create their musical artistry. The sanctity of the recording studio meant more to this group than merely making records, however. It was their private boy's club, whose inner circle consisted of John, Paul, George, Ringo and a few confidants. The Beatles spoke in an uncensored, disjointed, metaphoric, comic language that was only understood by them. It served as a unifying protective barrier which shielded the group from the endless tornado of outsiders always trying to get inside the "club."

The comradery between all four members and their producer was still quite congenial in 1965. John Lennon was married to his first wife Cynthia. Ringo Starr had recently married Maureen Cox. Paul McCartney and George Harrison were still the world's most eligible bachelors. Beatles' manager Brian Epstein was alive and well, guiding their continuing rise to unprecedented superstardom. The group was in good spirits and in full command of their vocal and playing abilities as they began to rehearse the intricate phrasing and harmonies of "Think For Yourself." The doors to Abbey Road Studio Number Two are now open. Welcome to The Beatles' musical laboratory...

"THINK FOR YOURSELF" RECORDING SESSION
NOV. 8, 1965—9 p.m.

Inside the cavernous, vaulted ceiling room of studio number two, John, Paul and George gather around a single microphone to rehearse and record the first take of harmony vocals. The song's working title at this point is "Won't Be There For You." Ringo Starr and Beatle assistants Neil Aspinall and Mal Evans are probably sitting in their usual corner of the studio, quietly playing cards on a stool. Their services would not be necessary for quite a while.

As the cue for take one is given from the control booth, the three Beatles begin to sing in unison: "About the good things that we can have if we close our eyes..." The singers stop, immediately realizing that their first run-through is flawed.

From the first attempt to record this song, John Lennon sings the wrong notes to the three part harmony, causing a dissonant vocal sound. As producer George Martin prepares for a second take, Paul rehearses his part singing, "And go where you're going to..." Meanwhile, John tries to explain his mistake to George Harrison. "'Cause I only did it once wrong on the first take you know. Now I got it in my bleeding mind for remembering it...(singing) 'About the good things that we can have if we'..." At this point, George cuts in, reminding John, "No. Play (the note in the) major (key)." After rehearsing the harmony together in unison and pretending to choke on the words, they both break up laughing. The atmosphere in the studio is relaxed and jovial.

As John, Paul and George ready themselves for take two, producer George Martin calls down to them from the control booth. "Waiting here then lads." On both of the next two recording attempts, Lennon repeats the same singing mistake.

While The Beatles await their opportunity to do the fourth take, John feels *this one* will be right. "Okay" he says, "I think I might have it now." Producer Martin jokes with John about his repetitive faux pas, trying to lighten up the session. He is also attempting to encourage John and Paul to begin a humorous dialogue, with an eye toward obtaining some Christmas Fan Club material between formal song takes. Martin calls down to Lennon, "...Oh, you're a right particular one today." John laughingly responds, "I know. I get something in me head, you know, and all the walls of Rome couldn't stop me." Martin's ploy works to a degree, loosening up the band members. However, the discussion between John and Paul quickly degenerates. The ensuing dialogue is deemed unfit for release to the fan club, as McCartney enters into a "school boy" personal hygiene exchange, playing off of John's remark:

PAUL: "You're right, pickled onion."
JOHN: "Pooh, and I stink too. I'm waiting for somebody to say something about it."
PAUL: "It's that deodorant you use."
JOHN: "It isn't."
PAUL: "It is!"
JOHN: "Cynthia licked it clean before we left."
PAUL: "Let me tell you, it's that B.O...odorant, that B.O.dorant you're using..."
JOHN: "Here's some...pickles." (Sings some notes.)
GEORGE: "B.O.-dorant." (Laughs.)
PAUL: (Sings) "That great big B.O.-dorant. It's great big B.O.-dorant."

John quickly tires of the banter and begins to practice his part in serious preparation for the fourth attempt at the song. However, after flubbing the fourth take, Lennon jokingly blames Paul for distracting him during the attempt. This leads the two songwriting partners into a mock argument and finally, a discussion of the previous night's television programming.

JOHN: (To Paul) "Why do you keep pointing up there every time?"
PAUL: "I was doing it as a joke, because every time we came to there, you pointed it out."
JOHN: "Well, you know that was the first time that I went wrong when you started doing that, and ever since then, we've had this trouble."
PAUL: (Joking) "Do you want to fight?"
JOHN: "No."
PAUL: "OK. Let's settle it other ways!"

JOHN: "You play snooker?"
PAUL: "Yeah."
JOHN: "I don't."
PAUL: "Did you see Rocky Marciano last night?"
JOHN: "Yeah."
PAUL: (Imitates Rocky) "Duh! Duh!" (Laughter.)
JOHN: "The whole conversation was about everything else and he goes, (In Bronx accent) 'I remember da great Joe Louis'."
PAUL: (Also in Bronx accent) "He was a great fighta'."
JOHN: (Imitating a news reporter) "And what do you attribute it to, Rocky?" (Answers as Rocky) "Training."
PAUL: (In Bronx accent) "Da conditioning. No, I had a good condition."

While waiting for take five to begin, John suddenly and humorously finds religion! He shouts out in a fanatical evangelist accent, "Somebody up there likes me. Jeez! That's Jesus, our Lord and Savior. Oh, baby, he's only begotten bread for us to live and die on. And that's why we're all here. And I'll tell you, brethren, there's more of them than there are of us. And that's why there are so few of us left."

George Harrison plays along, asking John, "What is this wrath that beholds you?" Paul, in his best Scottish brogue chimes in, "Why such fervor? Why such fervor?" John finally steps away from this fictitious character and laughs at the group's silly digression from recording. He pleads to the others laughing, "I can't go on. I really can't. Come on, let's do this bleeding record."

Take number five is no better than its predecessors, as John's redundant miscues begin to accumulate. George Martin asks John to try it again. Keeping the session relaxed, The Beatles enter into yet another disjointed exchange before their sixth try at the song.

JOHN: (To Martin) "Hey, you can't do (*record*) it in bits, can you?"
MARTIN: "Could do…Let's have one more go."
JOHN: "Well, we'll have one more try. You know and then if not, you know then I concede…"
PAUL: (To John) "Try. It looks like supercar is getting out of control. (Sings) 'Marina, aqua marina'!"
JOHN: "Yeah, we'll do one of them for Christmas."
GEORGE: "Yeah."
PAUL: (Sings to John) "How come you fuck up everything that you do?

Marina?"

JOHN: (In answer to Paul) "I will be pleased to see the earthmen disintegrated."

The haunting error returns again on takes six and seven. Still sounding relaxed however, John offers a semi-serious apology to the others. "I'm sorry. Sometimes I feel less than useless at these sessions. I really do. 'Course, Cynthia understands. I often talk to her about it when we get home. I say, 'Sometimes you know Cynthia, I just can't get the note'." Paul's simple response demonstrates his understanding at his partner's frustration. "Yeah," he sighs, "Oh well."

Once again, Lennon misses the note on take eight, which propels John and Paul into *another* make-believe argument. This time however, their silly dialogue mocks amateur thespians who can't get their lines straight in a theatre production. The satire here may have been a personal, yet playful poke at their manager Brian Epstein, who was at the time a frustrated actor himself.

PAUL: "That's wrong."
JOHN: "Oh, I'm so sorry. I feel so stupid. I don't know what to do."
PAUL: "Look, Terence, if you want to resign from the amateur dramatics, do!"
JOHN: "It's not that, I put a lot of money and thought into the whole thing."
PAUL: "Yeah, but let's face it. You're crap. Aren't you?"
JOHN: "Well...all right! All right!"
PAUL: "I mean you're only doing walk-on's."
JOHN: "Who's father was it got the hall in the first place, eh?"
PAUL: "...Yes, well you're only doing walk on's and you're farting those up."

The anguish of John's mental block *finally* lifts during a rehearsal between takes nine and ten, allowing him to correctly sing his part of the harmony. The three harmonize together, "And you got time to rectify all the things that you should." Paul joyously tells the others, "Magic...that was it!" John, in his best imitation of his friend, comedian Peter Sellers, informs George Martin, "You should've gotten (*recorded*) me there. I was moved. And tell that Norm (the sound balance engineer) to get back in here. He's kind of groovin' out the place, you know...Oh, I got it now. Listen to this. I'm gonna give expression as well."

On take number ten, The Beatles record the three part harmony correctly, however, their phrasing of the words is not quite together. Thus, they must try to perfect the line yet another time. Having shaken off the jinx of singing the harmony part, Lennon is unfazed by the prospect of yet another take. He is relaxed and breaks into song while waiting for George Martin to rewind the master tape. John sings to the tune of "Do You Want To Know A Secret?" a crude, explicit version. (singing) "Do you want to hold a penis? Doo wah ooh." Just then, George Martin cuts him off and warns that the eleventh take is about to begin.

The three vocalists are successful on takes eleven and twelve. John sings the notes perfectly and the phrasing comes together quite nicely. There is a sense of creative nirvana in the studio. But success is short lived and frustration quickly sets in, as the boys discover that George Martin has accidently erased the correct portion of the tape. George Harrison mildly scolds Martin. Once again, John and the others must return to the microphones to sing the part for a thirteenth time!

MARTIN: "I'm sorry. I made a boo boo."
GEORGE: "Ah, but that was it."
PAUL: "Right."
MARTIN: "Okay, but then we need John again."
PAUL: "Come on John."
GEORGE: "Why?"
MARTIN: "Because I started wiping (*erasing*) it, before I should have done."
GEORGE: (To the producer) "…Ahh, naughty!" (Calling for Lennon to return to the vocal booth) "John? John, love?"
MARTIN: "Jonathan, what are you doing?"
PAUL: "He's just messing behind…I'll get him."
GEORGE: (Whistles a circus tune.)
(Footsteps approach.)
JOHN: "What is it?"
GEORGE: "He rubbed (*erased*) that bit that you did *right*…off."
JOHN: "I was just thinking in the toilet, so I think I should get it."
GEORGE: "Paul?"
MARTIN: "We're going from where 'the future looks good'."
GEORGE: "Oh, I see."

Before the start of take number fourteen, John briefly looses his cool and airs his frustration to George Martin, who is offering to cue up the words which must be sung yet again. Harrison whispers off microphone in school boy fashion to John, suggesting that they try recording the song with Martin's assistant (instead of Martin) on the next day. This causes the lads to laugh out loud.

JOHN: (In a hushed tone to himself) "…hardly got a breath left."

MARTIN: "Do you want to hear the words to it?"
JOHN: "No, God, we have never heard them once, you fool. No wonder we've been getting it wrong."
MARTIN: "I'm hearing 'em up here."
JOHN: "Wonderful for you."
MARTIN: "Very lovely."
GEORGE: (Whispers) "I wonder if Ron Richards (George Martin's production assistant) is free tomorrow?"
JOHN & PAUL: (laughing.)
MARTIN: "Okay. Here it comes."

The session tape ends abruptly, without our ever hearing the finished product and clearly demonstrates the difficulty, tedium and frustration inherent in making good recordings. However, later that evening, the tired group would successfully complete the recording of "Think For Yourself." On the next day, the song was mixed and mastered in both mono and stereo, in preparation for the forthcoming album.

In the 1990s, this uncensored rehearsal session (along with many other previously unreleased Beatles recordings) was released on compact disc and distributed throughout Europe, Japan and the United States, all *without* the blessing of the group or their record company. The "Think For Yourself" rehearsals were manufactured and distributed in 1992 (*Unsurpassed Masters Vol. 7, YD-013, CD*) by a Luxembourg company called Yellow Dog Records, as part of a series called, *The Beatles' Unsurpassed Masters*. Yellow Dog, which today has a number of subsidiary labels, is merely one of many record companies that release unauthorized recordings of The Beatles, (commonly known as bootlegs in the United States) in an ever-expanding worldwide underground marketplace.

By the middle 1980s, a significant number of European and Far Eastern record companies had formed, in order to take advantage of loopholes in international copyright laws. The relaxed copyright standards, they argued, permitted these plundering music barons to release contraband compact discs containing material more than twenty years old by major artists and to exploit them for commercial gain. In the United States and elsewhere, these recordings are considered illegal since they are protected and have been released and distributed without the consent of either the artist or their record label. These black market music purveyors are referred to as bootleggers.

A number of questions have arisen in light of the bootleg record industry's meteoric rise from a college kid hobby of the 1960s, to its present global, multimillion dollar status. In the first place, how did so many unreleased hours of material fall into the hands of bootleggers? Who were the pioneers of bootlegging? What factors contributed to the growing popularity of bootlegs from the late sixties to the present?

There are additional issues which concern the impact of black market music sales on artists, specifically The Beatles. For instance, how did bootleggers obtain The Beatles' unreleased music? What types of music are contained within the more than 1,600 Beatles bootleg albums? Does the release of illicit recordings of live shows and often below par studio performances pose a threat of overexposure or embarrassment to The Beatles and other artists? What are the implications of taking an artist's work out of his or her control? And how do The Beatles themselves feel about the unauthorized release of their discarded musical "rough drafts"? Finally, do bootleg recordings serve any historical or cultural purpose? If so, is this a valid justification for exploiting artists?

This book attempts to explore these questions, and to solve mysteries previously obscured from public scrutiny. We will examine these issues by uncovering the *Black Market Beatles: The Story Behind The Lost Recordings*. The following chapters *get back* to where bootlegs, bootleggers and bootlegging of The Beatles once began.

A New Industry Is Created
Around The Big Three

As the sixties drew to a close, many of its beloved icons and musical heroes began to fade away, retire, change careers, burn out, or die from their own excessive experimentation with drugs. Ironically, many first generation rock 'n' roll bootleggers jump-started their careers underground, due to these pop culture personnel transitions. However, the most dramatic change came with the sudden announcement on April 10, 1970, that The Beatles had broken up, never to work together again. Of the "Big Three" (Bob Dylan, The Beatles and The Rolling Stones), The Beatles' following was unquestionably the strongest, considering record sales alone at the time. Bob Dylan's two-year absence from music in the late 1960s helped fuel a demand for his unreleased music. The Rolling Stones record label moved quickly to fight bootleg concert albums which started to multiply like rabbits in 1969 and 1970. The Stones gave fans what they wanted, namely a legitimate release of a great live concert in superb sound quality. The album *Get Yer Ya Ya's Out* helped to refocus record bootleggers away from The Stones, albeit temporarily. And of course, The Rolling Stones remained intact as a group and continued to release new material for their legion of followers. However, The Beatles were a special case. Beatles fans would no longer be able to purchase newly created musical product once their group had disbanded in 1970. Thus a cottage industry developed, centered around the unauthorized music of The Beatles, Bob Dylan and The Rolling Stones.

GREAT WHITE WONDER

By the end of the 1960s, Bob Dylan's legend had grown to mythical proportions. Dylan's poetic songs of protest mirrored the disenchanted feelings of a young, rebellious generation for its establishment. Fueled by his feared retirement from the music scene (due to a near fatal motorcycle accident) and his extended absence from the recording studio and concert stage, a craving arose for new Dylan material by his legion of followers.

This "new" music arrived on a humid day in July 1969, in the form of a bootleg record entitled *Great White Wonder* (No Label, GF-001/2/3/4, 2LP). Considered by many to be the first and most notorious rock 'n' roll bootleg ever produced, this collection of songs featured, among other things, performances by Bob Dylan and The Band. The "Basement Tapes Sessions" (as they became known) were originally packaged as a double album in a plain white jacket without any further labeling or title. The first pressing produced 8,000 copies secretly manufactured in California. According to Dylan's record label at the time, a man with the nickname of "Dub" was purportedly the first person to manufacture *Great White Wonder*.

After the initial run of 8,000 *Great White Wonder* bootlegs quickly sold out, another group of entrepreneurs jumped aboard the robber's ship in September 1969, to copy, manufacture and distribute thousands more. However, on December 16, 1970, Columbia Records won a temporary restraining order in Los Angeles Federal District Court against Mr. "Dub," two other men and a California pressing plant, to prevent the further manufacture and sale of *Great White Wonder*. A similar successful action was also instituted in Canada against another questionable "record" company. Columbia Records might not have ever found the perpetrators, had they not received an anonymous tip from a woman who knew the bootleggers and didn't appreciate their "bad mouthing" her friends.

The "Basement Tapes" were recorded by Dylan and The Band in the basement of a house called Big Pink. The house had been rented by members of The Band and was located in West Saugerties, New York. Approximately twenty-four songs were recorded in the basement between June and October 1967. The tracks were recorded live on a home, reel-to-reel tape recorder, using several microphones.

The success of *Great White Wonder* was unparalleled for its day. This was fueled in part by extensive reporting and commentary in *Rolling Stone* magazine. Sales of this bootleg were reported in the underground press—roughly estimated at between 75,000 and 250,000 copies. Although these figures may well have been exaggerated, the cultural impact of this early black market release reverberated around the United States. Of course, there was no reliable way to calculate bootleg sales or to verify the sales figures. Nevertheless, the success of these illicit recordings undoubtedly influenced Columbia Records to release a legitimate version on two records in 1975, entitled *The Basement Tapes* (Columbia, C2 33682).

As a bootleg, *Great White Wonder* has continued to survive and sell under a myriad of titles and formats. This set has been copied and reissued so many times over the past twenty-plus years that it would probably qualify for R.I.A.A. gold record award status if it were a commercial release. Perhaps more importantly, *Great White Wonder* served as a catalyst to other would-be bootleggers, illustrating the potential profit associated with this enterprise. The result was a sustained wave of Beatles, Rolling Stones, Dylan and other superstar bootleg releases containing live concerts, studio rehearsals, jams, outtakes and radio/TV appearances not otherwise available to the general public.

BOOTLEGGING BEFORE THE BEATLES

Long before John, Paul, George and Ringo became famous, record robbers were sailing the high seas, pillaging and plundering the treasure trove of unreleased concert and recording sessions produced by famous, yet unsuspecting artists. Tracing the history of the underground cottage industry that has stealthily released Beatles bootlegs is an arduous task given the obvious lack of first-hand information and documentation. By necessity, this is an oral history devoid of written documentation. There is no "Underground Recording Industry Association of America" to tap for historical data. All of the manufacturing, marketing and distribution is handled covertly and haphazardly. This market is after all another form of criminal activity, intended to make a profit. Additionally, none of the unauthorized recordings receive regular airplay on the radio, nor are these discs charted on the "Top 100" countdown. The emergence and disappearance of the many underground record labels specializing in The Beatles is never covered in commercial entertainment magazines such as *Billboard* and *Variety*. The conventional media rarely, if ever, presents a story on bootlegging, save for the occasional confiscation of contraband recordings. Until now, no one has ever attempted to document this particular underbelly of the record industry. What began as an experiment in 1901, progressed as a simple way to support a hobby for a select few music fanatics in the late 1960s. Today, with the advent of digital technology, the contraband music trade has mushroomed into a multi-million dollar enterprise. The focus of this history primarily centers on the circumstances and people involved in releasing the Beatles' bootleg recordings.

The research presented here must by necessity come from a variety of forms and sources. This account is based upon more than ten years of reporting, including scores of interviews, the review of news articles, bootleg publications, FBI Freedom of Information Act records, music industry books, album cover liner notes, the bootlegs themselves and other sources to present this story. Wherever possible, the authors have chosen to rely upon first-hand information gleaned from interviews with the people who have or had some contact with this illegal profession. This collective includes Beatles' bootleg manufacturers, tapers, album cover artists, wholesalers, retailers, recording artists, FBI agents and others in the know. The authors have attempted to authenticate the factual history presented here from multiple sources. In an era that glorifies free-market capitalism, this narrative clearly illustrates the principle by uncovering the rise of an underground enterprise clearly based upon supply and demand.

WHAT IS A BOOTLEG?

It is important at the outset to distinguish between the terms *bootleg*, *pirate* and *counterfeit* recordings. Recording artists, journalists and industry spokesmen often confuse the terminology of these three distinct forms of unauthorized recordings. This book deals mainly with bootleg recordings.

Bootlegs or underground recordings include the body of unreleased material of a given artist such as demonstration and rehearsal tapes, studio outtakes and alternate takes, TV/radio performances, and concerts. People who purchase bootlegs, generally speaking, are aware of what they are buying because they are often completists who already own all of the artist's commercial releases. The people involved in the taping, manufacturing or distribution of bootlegs are often referred to as either pirates or bootleggers.

Pirate recordings are those made by copying *legitimate* records and tapes. In the case of a pirate release, no attempt is made to reproduce the legitimate album cover or record label.

Counterfeits make up the third class of unauthorized recordings. These records attempt to completely reproduce an officially released album, including the music, album artwork and label graphics. Only the best selling albums of a famous artist are selected for counterfeiting purposes. Counterfeits are considered more economically damaging to the record industry, as consumers are duped into purchasing the bogus version of a highly successful album, at a lower cost, instead of the authorized version.

THE EVOLUTION OF BOOTLEGGING

The concept of bootlegging got its start quite innocently at the turn of the twentieth century with the aide of a New York librarian. Lionel Mapleson is thought by many to be a pioneer of the first "live" recording. In 1901, Mapleson received a gift of a cylinder recorder from inventor Thomas Edison. The audio cylinders were limited by their short running time of a few minutes. Of course, they also lacked the sonic and tonal qualities of today's modern recording technology. A drawing of Edison's cylinder phonograph is illustrated herein, and is quite similar to the recordable version used by Mapleson.

During the 1901–1903 operatic seasons, Lionel Mapleson took his prized gift from Edison high up into the loft of the Metropolitan Opera Hall. It was here, in this bastian of musical culture, that the concept of bootlegging was born. Mapleson, a devoted fan of the opera, experimentally recorded and preserved a number of performance pieces from these programs. Although his recording apparatus was located quite a long distance from the singers on stage, the voices could be heard well enough for the listener to gain an insight into the unique quality and style of these turn-of-the-century performers.

The historical significance of these aural snapshots cannot be underscored. Mapleson's early crude recordings have given opera fans and historians the only opportunity to hear some of the world's best singers of this era. Most of the opera stars of the early 1900s have never appeared on commercial recordings. If not for Lionel Mapleson's experiment, many of these rare historical pieces would have been lost forever. According to the *New York Opera News*, there is no historical data available to suggest that Mapleson was ever given permission by the Metropolitan Opera to make these recordings.

This audio pioneer probably had no intention to market his operatic recordings for profit. However, during the early years of 78 rpm and long-play records, there were numerous aficionados who were eager to purchase copies of these types of "collector" recordings. For years, fans of opera, jazz and classical music privately pressed concerts, jam sessions, and radio broadcasts onto vinyl disc for sale or trade to fellow collectors. As for Mapleson's 1901–1903 recordings, they were finally published officially on disc in 1985 by the New York Public Library.

Mapelson's innovation was soon followed by others. Bootleggers have been credited with (or have taken credit for) releasing the first complete recordings of several operas. They have also boasted of offering the first "budget" labels, forcing the commercial labels to create their own. Home taping of live radio performances has been a common practice for decades. In fact, many of the great jazz reissues and several rock concerts that have surfaced commercially in recent years, were recorded from radio broadcasts.

In the 1950s the Jolly Roger label appeared. It specialized in manufacturing copies of records that were no longer in print and in pressing a few radio broad-

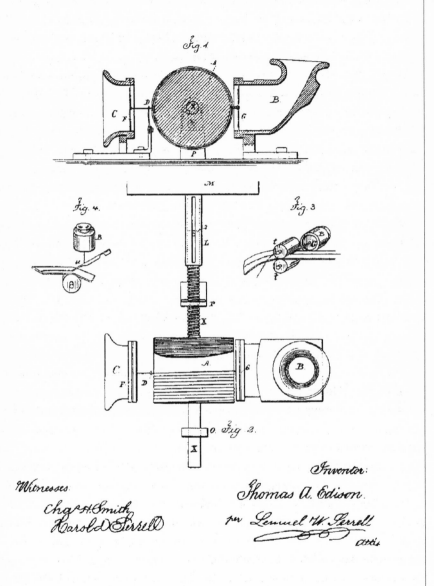

T. A. EDISON.
Phonograph or Speaking Machine.

No. 200,521   Patented Feb. 19, 1878.

Illustration of Edison's cylinder phonograph

casts of live performances as well. The former activity was technically defined as *pirating*, while the latter was considered *bootlegging*. Jolly Roger was promptly taken to court by the publishers of the songs and charged with theft of property and unfair competition. Jolly Roger's defense was that its owner was merely a jazz enthusiast who could not tolerate classic performances being lost forever. Indeed, this argument has been proffered by bootleggers for decades as a justification for their unlawful activities. Jolly Roger, whose fictional name was appropriate for his pirate activities, finally settled with the publishers and ceased his operations.

There are yet other examples where black marketeers have, in some instances, served the public by bringing them closer to the performing artist. To their credit, bootleggers have inspired the commercial record industry to leave the studio and move into the concert and recital halls to preserve and document live performances. The incentive to the above-ground industry to release live albums was no doubt due to the potential loss of profits and the perceived harm to their artists from inferior quality bootleg releases. Rock and roll fans can certainly appreciate this "contribution" when they are reminded of such legitimate, popular album titles as *Live At Leeds* (The Who); *Woodstock* (various artists); *Get Yer Ya Ya's Out* (The Rolling Stones); *Four-Way Street* (Crosby, Stills, Nash & Young); and *The Beatles Live At Hollywood Bowl* (The Beatles).

The recent success of commercial "box sets" containing previously unreleased concerts, outtakes and alternate takes owes much to the underground market. Bootleggers have been supplying these types of recordings to collectors and music historians for decades. It is only since the late 1980s that the legitimate music industry has realized the potential market value of their own archives.

For all of their alleged innovations, these illicit music purveyors were little more than hobbyists for the first 60-odd years of the twentieth century. It took more than six decades to transform Lionel Mapleson's experiment into a profit-making industry—an industry that now rakes in millions of dollars per year by illegally usurping the artist's control over the release of his or her own "rough drafts" and live performances.

FROM A COTTAGE INDUSTRY TO A BUSINESS

Bootlegging exists primarily because of the basic economic principle of supply and demand. Regardless of the method employed, bootleggers cut through the legal red tape and sell their illegal recordings because fans of a given artist or group demand it. Fans desire more material than their favorite artist is willing to release; or, the artist or group ceases to record, creating a void of new products.

Bootleggers have traditionally filled the gaps and reaped the profits.

At the end of the 1960s, rock and roll's "superstar triad" was comprised of The Beatles, The Rolling Stones and Bob Dylan. The Beatles were in the process of breaking up, and had not toured since 1966. In 1969, The Rolling Stones were content to produce fewer albums with each passing year, and had not toured the U.S. since 1966. Bob Dylan had been seriously injured in a motorcycle accident in July 1966. For the next two years, Dylan's recovery made him a recluse, removing him from the music circuit. In essence, the "Big Three" was failing to nourish its music-starved fans with the new music they craved.

These were not merely the three most popular artists at the time. Collectively, this elite trio represented more than just good music and good times. They were perceived as a transcendent cultural force—a sustaining line of communication to a new generation of young people. These bands were rebel leaders to an often alienated, extended family of followers. (It is important to note that there were far fewer "blue chip" recording artists in the late sixties than there are today.) The lack of new and continuing music messages from the "Big Three" caused a culture gap of sorts to this generation.

New bands like Led Zeppelin and Crosby, Stills & Nash began emerging to fill the void for young music fans. However, many die-hard fans held out for their "old" favorites. As the seventies began, this demand for more music from The Beatles, Rolling Stones and Bob Dylan went largely unnoticed by the commercial recording industry, which merely found new ways to package previously released material into "Greatest Hits" compilations.

The recording industry expanded technically, economically and artistically in the late 1960s, due in part to the increased popularity of rock and roll music. This factor, coupled with new low-cost tape recorders available on the consumer market, gave rise to tape piracy as a profitable and viable underground enterprise.

Initially, small groups of college-age collectors and enterprising businessmen recognized that profits could be made by continuing to supply the insatiable demand of fans, music scholars and collectors with "new" unreleased recordings. The obvious move was to produce bootlegs of previously unreleased material primarily by The Beatles, The Rolling Stones, Bob Dylan and other superstars. ("One-hit wonder" groups were rarely singled out for bootlegging.) This would virtually guarantee a low risk sell-out of their limited run issues, helping bootleggers cover their production costs while making modest profits. Record bootlegging was also attractive due to the anonymity of its producers. Early black market discs contained no information traceable to its creators.

It was intoxicating and addicting for fans in the late 1960s and early 1970s to actually hear, for the first time, their musical heroes in concert or in rehearsal. Now they could listen to performances which had previously been off limits. The shroud of creative secrecy was starting to lift.

In October of 1967, the first issue of *Rolling Stone* magazine rolled off the press in San Francisco, California. Few people at the time would have predicted the long term survival of this underground publication. In the late sixties, there were literally thousands of regional underground magazines, newsletters and comic books circulating throughout the United States. The enduring success of this fledgling publication was due in large part to Jann Wenner's (founding editor/ publisher) vision to honestly cover the music, attitudes and issues relevant to the "Baby Boom" generation. At the time of its inception, none of the conventional media were adequately covering the music scene or this unique generation like *Rolling Stone*. It was this magazine that served as a bi-monthly communal newsletter to the youth of the nation.

From time to time, *Rolling Stone* provided news of the underground recording industry, usually in its record reviews section. This served to inform its readership of important bootleg releases. Many bootleggers no doubt owe a debt of gratitude for their initial success to the free publicity and encouraging record reviews printed in *Rolling Stone* magazine. The "honeymoon" period experienced by bootleggers and *Rolling Stone* would dissolve in the late 1970s as the magazine began to court the commercial industry for advertising revenues in order to survive. As more record industry money poured into *Rolling Stone*'s advertising coffers, their philosophical alignment appeared to quickly shift away from bootleggers and to their new benefactors.

Indeed, while still sympathetic to the underground, *Rolling Stone* magazine (September 17, 1970) went so far as to publish a fascinating (albeit fictional) account of The Beatles' "master tape" for the unreleased album *Hot As Sun* getting "kidnapped," held for ransom and ultimately erased by accident. The myth-filled article entitled, "The Beatles Album No One Will Ever Hear," served to fuel the fertile minds of bootleggers, fans and collectors worldwide. Several early bootleggers even borrowed the title *Hot As Sun* for their own Beatles underground releases, successfully capitalizing on the "buzz" created by the *Rolling Stone* article.

Perhaps unknowingly, *Rolling Stone* was an important vehicle for the sustained existence of early bootleggers. Many bootleggers and middlemen routinely advertised their catalogs in the back pages of *Rolling Stone*'s classified advertisements. This conduit helped bootleggers reach the largest segment of market population most interested in purchasing underground recordings. From *Rolling*

Stone's pages, the existence and distribution of bootleg recordings grew and prospered as it was disseminated throughout the United States and parts of Europe.

THE EARLY BEATLES BOOTLEGGERS

By and large, the first illicit Beatles' recordings were mostly inaudible concert performances and a few studio recordings. The tape sources were usually several generations removed from the master and were copied on primitive equipment. In most cases the sound was terrible. However, the opportunity to hear an early acoustic version of "While My Guitar Gently Weeps" (sans the electric guitars of George Harrison and guest Eric Clapton) with its haunting, forlorn vocals, or the excitement of a live, manic concert by The Fab Four, was undeniably worth the "price of admission."

The first Beatles bootleg to demonstrate the value of this illicit rock medium was called *Kum Back*. From this 1969 release, collectors realized that there might be a potentially large stash of unreleased Beatles studio recordings. The promise of good quality, rare outtakes hooked many collectors in the late 1960s. *Kum Back* was a rough version of the aborted *Get Back* album The Beatles had begun in January 1969.

The first Beatles bootleg albums were heavy, thick, scratchy, and poorly pressed black vinyl discs with blank labels that neglected to indicate side A or B. The early album covers, mostly blank white, made no attempt to disguise the illicit nature of the recordings, nor did they provide the listener with much in the way of historical data. Bootleggers that did provide information on these early releases often gave their audience inaccurate information. One reason for this practice may have been to prevent the legitimate copyright owners from following the trail of a tape back to the perpetrators. Most often, it resulted from bootleggers failing to carefully research the correct historical source for a given recording. This practice, which occasionally continues even today, has proven frustrating to collectors and music historians alike.

Only a few of the early bootlegs attempted to credit a company name for its production. Early Beatles bootleggers used fictitious business names such as Avocado, Lemon, Pinetree, Michael & Allyson, Kustom and Dittolino. All of these companies were based in America, though none of them continue to do business today.

Later generation Beatles bootleggers would frequently use legitimate record company names for their black market products, such as Apple, Capitol, Parlophone, and EMI. This was an attempt to disguise the bootlegs sitting in record store racks next to their legitimate counterparts. (Throughout the book, the authors distinguish these bootlegs by placing the word "bogus" before a legitimate record company name where it has been used illegally by bootleggers to identify their underground albums.)

Many early bootleggers justified their practices as catering to the legitimate demands of collectors. In the early stages of the illegal album trade, these entrepreneurs rarely sold more than 500-1,000 copies of a given title—certainly not enough to harm an artist or record label, they reasoned. In fact, some artists were more flattered than outraged by the "outlaw" notoriety of being bootlegged. Many artists realized they were not losing profits, since the illicit recordings were never planned for release, and that collectors of boots already owned their entire commercial catalog.

As early as 1970, the ethical debate between bootleggers and legitimate industry members started to heat up. One Rolling Stones bootlegger justified his trade succinctly, "Do you really think the Stones miss the money we're making? Whatever we take out of their pockets, we're doing as much for them in terms of publicity and interest in their music. The word moral doesn't apply."

Another anonymous thief of Bob Dylan recordings took a more pious position in talking with a *Rolling Stone* magazine reporter, "Some of these (unreleased) songs are better than the shit that Columbia has released…they just keep sitting on them, so you might say, in a sense, we're just liberating the records and bringing them to all the people, not just the chosen few."

Of course, legitimate industry representatives of the time held a different perspective. While perhaps mildly concerned with the potential loss of sales, they felt that bootlegs hurt performers and composers because of lost royalty revenues, fear of overexposure and poor-sounding performances. The right of the artist and its label to determine what material was fit for release was yet another argument against bootlegging. This debate would shift from the trade papers to the courtrooms in the latter part of the 1970s.

Bootlegging, like any business, carried its share of expenses. Record bandits had to invest their own money into recording and purchasing rare performances, mastering, pressing, packaging, printing labels and cover art, and for marketing and distribution. Early bootleggers took advantage of classified magazine print advertising, and they also relied upon coverage or reviews in "underground" journals. Sales were made through used-record stores, mail-order brochures, flea markets, trade shows, conventions, and "head" shops. (Examples of early mail-order brochures are reproduced on the following pages.) In the late sixties and early seventies, a number of notorious retail stores surfaced in Greenwich Village (New York), Old Town (Chicago), Harvard Square (Boston), and Height-

Ashbury (San Francisco), that catered to underground record buyers' insatiable "needs."

Some of the early bootleggers were quite humorous and sarcastic in their approach to the business. Contra Band Music (CBM), for example, boldly used a drawing of a pirate with a knife between his teeth to illustrate its activities and promote identification with its label. (See illustrations of various bootleggers' logos in Appendix C).

Others poked fun at the U.S. copyright laws with a statement on the album cover which read, "All rights reserved, all wrongs *reversed*." The Amazing Kornyphone Record Label (TAKRL) illustrated its back album covers with a photograph of Dr. Terrence H. "Telly" Fone, the fictional founder of TAKRL, along with a long humorous explanation of the evolution of the phonograph record. Several other bootleggers openly taunted the authorities by burying a message in the record disc's run-out wax. Epithets such as, "You can't catch us!" were not uncommon—all good fun in a day in the life of a record bootlegger.

In Canada, the publication *Hot Wacks* was born in 1974. This quarterly and annual publication (which continues today) served collectors, music historians and retailers by reviewing and detailing the bootleg releases of all major rock music artists. Historic sources for recordings were accurately described, and descriptions of sound and graphic qualities were also provided. Meanwhile, newsletters, collector magazines and tape trading networks developed around the most popular artists, carrying news, reviews and advertisements of the newest bootleg releases. All of these publications attempted to lend scholarship and credibility to this new black market business. What had once been merely a profitable hobby was beginning to evolve into a formidable industry.

THE RAW MATERIAL

Bootleggers drew upon a number of sources to obtain their recordings. Security at concert halls and recording studios in the 1960s and 1970s was lax to say the least. In fact, many studios were the scene of all-night parties with many unauthorized guests coming and going. At the conclusion of a session, the artists would either obtain acetates of the songs recorded at the session, or (in later years) ask the recording engineer to run dubs (copies) onto tape to take home. At that point, many of these tapes were given away to friends and relatives or stolen by insiders.

Legitimate record companies were often careless in the security of their recording archives. One recording artist told the authors how the general security system for rehearsal and outtake tapes works in a commercial setting today:

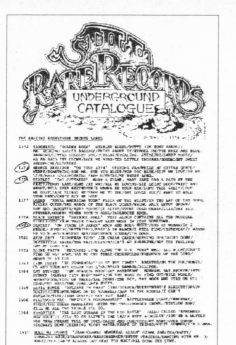

STILL RARE RECORDS
UNDERGROUND CATALOGUE

THE AMAZING EVERYTHING RECORD LABEL

1172 YARDBIRDS "GOLDEN EGGS" STEELAWAY BLUES/PUTTY (IN YOUR HANDS)/
MR. ZERO/NO GREATER BAGGAGE/TRICKY JIMMY IT/STROLL ON/TEN YEARS ARE BLUE/
DRINKING LITTLE SOLDIER BOY/PLEASE/STEALING, STEELING/SHAPE MUSIC/
HA HA SAID THE CLOWN/BACK WO NINE/TEN LITTLE INDIANS/GOODNIGHT SWEET
JOSEPHINE/GLIMPSES

1173 GEORGE HARRISON "ON TOUR 1974" OPENING JAM/WHILE MY GUITAR GENTLY
WEEPS/SOMETHING/SUE ME . SUE YOU BLUES/FOR YOU BLUE/GIVE ME LOVE/IN MY
LIFE/MAYA LOVE/NOTHIN/FAR NORTH/DARK HORSE/MY SWEET LORD.

1175 BEATLES "OH! DARLING" MARY A JUDGE, MARY JANE HAD A PATH AT THE
PARTY/PENNY LANE/JOAN (AS WAS)/ALL MY LOVING/SHE SAID I DROP/TWIST AND
SHOUT/ROLL OVER BEETHOVEN/I WANNA BE YOUR MAN/LOVE ME DO/SELL IT/SAVE
ME DO/PLEASE PLEASE ME/THANK ME TO YOU/SHE LOVES YOU/I WANT TO HOLD
YOUR HAND/CAN'T BUY ME LOVE.

1177 QUEEN "ROYAL AMERICAN TOUR" FLICK OF THE WRIST/IN THE LAP OF THE GODS,
KILLER QUEEN/THE MARCH OF THE BLACK QUEEN/BRING BACK LEROY BROWN/
SON AND DAUGHTER/KEEP YOURSELF ALIVE/STONE COLD CRAZY/LIAR/BOY SHE/
STEALER/MODERN TIMES ROCK N ROLL/JAILHOUSE ROCK.

1178 BLACK SABBATH "GREEDEE POLL" THIS ALBUM CONTAINS ALL THE MUSICAL
INTERVIEWS/VIEW THEIR CONCERT LAST WEEK IN YOUR HOMETOWN.

1180 BEATLES "ON STAGE IN JAPAN" ROCK AND ROLL MUSIC/BABY IS MUSAK/IF I
NEEDED SOMEONE/BATTLE BOYS/BABY'S IN BLACK/I FEEL FINE/YESTERDAY/I WANNA
BE YOUR MAN/NOWHERE MAN/PAPERBACK RIDER/I'M DOWN.

1181 JEFF BECK "EUROPEAN TOUR" ICE CREAM CAKES/MORNING DEW/BLUES DOWN/
DEFINITELY MAYBE/YOU WAIT/PLENTY/AIN'T MY SUPERSTAR/NOT THE FEELING/
LET IT LING IN.

1182 BLIND FAITH "RECORDED LIVE ALONG THE U.S. TOUR" WELL ALL RIGHT/CAN'T
FIND MY WAY HOME, HAD TO CRY TODAY/CROSSROADS/PRESENCE OF THE LORD/
MEANS TO AN END.

1183 JIMI HENDRIX "IN COMMEMORATION OF JIMI HENDRIX" MASTER/OH THE MONEY/
YE ALL FREEDOM HEY COULD YOU STAR/WAIT/LAST DANCE/EELIPSE.

1184 CAT STEVENS "THE HEAVENS MIDNIGHT BANDSTAND" MONDAY, WAS BROKEN/1970
PRINCE CASPAR/CITY NIGHTCAPS/ON THE ROAD TO FIND OUT/WILD WORLD/
MORNING HAS RISEN/OH TREES/SAD LISA/PEG'S SON/THE MOON AND STARS ON HIS
SHADOW/HARD/THE HURT/LIFE JUST.

1185 DAVID BOWIE "DOLLARS 'N DRAG" 1984/SCREEN/EVERYTHING'S ALRIGHT/DRAPE
SUITS/DIFFERENT/HANG ON TO YOURSELF/JEAN IN THE MIDDLE/I CAN'T
EXPLAIN/TIME/JEAN GENIE/I SAY YOU. SANE.

1186 FLEETWOOD MAC "SMELL A KISSMASTERS" BATTLESNAKE SHAKE/WHEREVAT/
FIRE/THE GREEN MANALISHI (WITH THE TWO PRONGED CROWN)/STATION MAN/
TELL ME ALL THE THINGS YOU DO.

1214 VARIOUS "THE LAST STREAM IN THE BIG APPLE" (ALSO CALLED "REMEMBER
HOW GOOD IT USED TO BE/ALIVE") THE TRAIN KEPT A ROLLIN'/FOR ME A MATTER
FOR THEM/HEART FULL OF SOUL/CAGED AND CHAINED/BABY SOUL CHIN DOWN
WEDNESDAY BOMB/BLESSING OF/OFF WATER/KNAVE OF THINGS/WITH SHAKER/OCR 2 MAN.

1915 ROLLING STONES "JEAN-CLAUDE MEMORIAL ALBUM" (JEAN ANKETA)/HAPPY/
STARFUCKER/HEARTBREAKER/SWEET VIRGINIA/DANCING WITH MR. D/
SOLES/YOU CAN'T ALWAYS GET WHAT YOU WANT/ALL DOWN THE LINE.

ORDERING PROCEDURES

Order only LP's that are in our catalogs & updates and listed as still
available. List alternates. We will use them only if we have to.

    Single LP's: $ 3.80, unless otherwise noted.
    Double LP's: $ 7.90, unless otherwise noted.
    Triple LP's: $11.40, unless otherwise noted.
    Boxed Sets : $15.00, unless otherwise noted.
Please include $1.00 per order (not record) for postage and handling.

CANADIANS, add $1.00 postage & handling, plus $1.75 for the first two
    discs (doubles are two discs, triples are three) and $0.50 for
    each additional two or less.

OVERSEAS - Surface Mail - Add $1.40 for the first two discs (doubles
    count as two, triples as three), and $0.60 for each additional
    two discs or less.

    Air Mail - Prices with the Post Office have increased, sor-
    ry. Please send $6.00 for the first disc, and $4.00 for each
    additional disc. (Doubles count as two discs, triples as three.)
    Any excess postage sent will be credited to you.

SPECIAL HANDLING: $0.70 per order (not record). Gives speed priority
    through the U.S. Postal Service.
INSURANCE: $0.60 per order (not record).

REMIT ONLY IN U.S. FUNDS. Money orders, certified checks & cash are
processed immediately. Checks take at least 20 days to clear.

        Still Rare Records

Catalogs are $0.50 with a self-addressed stamped envelope.

Dealer rates are available for stores and wholesalers.

WE HAVE NOTHING TO DO DIRECTLY OR INDIRECTLY WITH THE MANUFACTURING
OF THESE ALBUMS. WE OBTAIN THEM FROM INTERNATIONAL DISTRIBUTORS.

NOTE: Import #1, _Five Nites In A Judo Arena_ is $6.00.

ABOUT US AND OUR UNDERGROUNDS

    None of our albums are meant to compete with regularly released
albums by the same artists. (Bootlegs compete with regular albums because they are counterfeit copies of regularly released records.) Our
records are meant for the collector who desires to add dimension to his collection not offered by the major record companies. Most of our albums are
concert recordings by today's popular artists, and while most artists issue
only one or two concert recordings in their career, none are able to offer
one or more from each of their concert tours. In fact, the Beatles never
released an official live recording; Bob Dylan has issued only one, and
The Rolling Stones only two. Even when an artist does release a regular
live album, he usually omits many of the songs on the tour. The rest
of our albums are made up of unreleased studio recordings and studio outtakes. (Different from versions officially released). To the true collector, these albums offer a perspective of their favorite artists not
otherwise available. Without these records much of the studio and concert
recordings of artists such as Bob Dylan, The Beatles, and The Rolling Stones
would not be heard.

    Utmost care has been taken to insure the best possible recording
quality on all these records. In most cases the albums are stereo and live
recordings are recorded either from FM broadcasts or off the PA system. In
some cases, especially with the earlier, more obscure recordings, fidelity
and sound will not equal most albums, but the mere existence of the recordings rather than the quality is what is important to the collector.

    All our albums are guaranteed against physical defects and will gladly
be replaced by good copies of the same album if defective.

Excerpts from a Still Rare catalogue

History of The Amazing Kornyphone Record Label (TAKRL)

THE BEATLES' "UNFINISHED MUSIC" VOLUME NUMBER ONE (STEREO)

SIDE ONE: Mothers and Dollars* (Ringo 1968); I'll Stay With You* (John & Paul 1964); Kali California* (John, Paul, & George 1967); Guru* (John 1967); Trance of Sorrows* (All, "Sgt. Pepper" outake); You Never Give Me Your Money (Version from No. 3 Abbey Road bootleg).

SIDE TWO: I'm In Love* (George 1964); A Different Girl* (John & Paul 1965); Living* (John 1966); Love You Too* (Alternate version, George 1966); My Story* (Paul 1966); Different Thoughts* (John 1967); Something (Version from No. 3 Abbey Road bootleg).

THE BEATLES' "UNFINISHED MUSIC" VOLUME NUMBER TWO (STEREO)

SIDE ONE: Ballad of Sir Winston* (John & Ringo 1968); Another Song* (Paul, 1966); See How They Run Like Pigs From A Gun* (Alternate version of "I Am The Walrus"); The One We're Looking For* (Paul 1968); Sole Survivor* (Paul, 1968); A Song For Peace* (John & Yoko 1968).

SIDE TWO: Happy and Free* (John & Paul 1969); So Much With You* (Paul, 1968); Maxwell's Silver Hammer (Version from No. 3 Abbey Road bootleg); Dreams Come True* (Paul 1967); A Rainy Day* (John 1968); Twickenham Studios Outake Medley* (Five short numbers from 1969).

*Tracks marked with an asterisk were previously unavailable, having NEVER BEFORE appeared on ANY bootleg.

THE BEATLES' "RARE OUTAKES FROM THE LET IT BE SESSIONS :
THE BEATLES PLAY OLD ROCK AND ROLL" (STEREO/MONO)

SIDE ONE: Why Don't We Do It In The Road?; Memphis; Good Golly Miss Molly; Pentua; Carol; Hitchhike; Miss Ann; Maybelline; Right String, Wrong Yo Yo.

SIDE TWO: Three Cool Cats; Rock Island Line; Bad Boy; All Along The Watchtower; True Love; Da Doo Run Run; Lucille; Little Queenie; Why Don't We Do It In The Road Number Two.

Flyers featuring Beatles bootlegs

Each studio has a vault, like banks have, where the tapes go when they are not being used. It is the artist or the person who is paying for the studio time who owns the rehearsal tapes, and that person decides what happens to them. Today, studios check for cameras and tape recorders, so that they don't get inside...But, I don't think that this additional security over the past ten years has had any effect on bootlegs.

Careless storage, discarding of rehearsal and outtake recordings, and employee theft have led to many underground releases. Rare Beatles' recordings have been found in a number of different locations by bootleggers. Some were found hanging in a garage and later auctioned off, while others were pilfered from radio and TV archives taped off the air and at concerts, or taken by friends and former employees of the group.

Rare tapes were aggressively pursued by bootleggers in the seventies. Early on, tapes were purchased by bootleggers from people who had inside connections with a given group. Others hired concert-goers or sound equipment personnel to tape the important tours of the era. Syndicated radio concert broadcasts (such as *King Biscuit Flower Hour*) and televised programs (such as *Midnight Special* and *In Concert*) were yet another inexpensive way for bootleggers to acquire excellent soundboard concert recordings. Many of the live Beatles' concerts were obtained from radio and television station archives or taped directly off-air.

Later in the 1980s and 1990s, rare rock recordings were often purchased through high profile auctions at Sotheby's and Christie's. Prices paid for tapes ranged from $300 in 1973 for a copy of the famous Beatles rehearsal tape (privately purchased from a former Beatles employee) later bootlegged as *Sweet Apple Trax*, to nearly $5,000 paid in the early 1990s (at Sotheby's London) for another hour's worth of *Get Back* album rehearsals. Historic value, sound quality and uniqueness of performance were all important factors to the musical thieves.

But, regardless of *how* these rare recordings leaked out over the years, there was always someone ready and able to plunder the historic audio treasure and release it.

MANUFACTURING AND DISTRIBUTION

The manufacture and distribution of Beatles' bootleg records in the 1970s involved a simple process. Bootleggers bypassed many of the traditional mechanisms of the commercial industry, and most of the associated costs. And of course, the tapes they obtained had already been recorded by the artist.

A large majority of underground Beatles records made in the 1970s and 1980s were pressed in Philadelphia, Pennsylvania; The Bronx, New York; and in Los

Angeles, California. In fact, the illegal tapes were often sent to the *same* pressing plants that were also pressing commercial releases for major record companies.

Reports from those working in the underground estimate that Beatles releases in the 1970s were pressed in numbers ranging from 500 to 15,000 copies. However, the average first run was usually in the range of 1,000 copies. As a general rule, a significant portion of the copies of each U.S. release were immediately shipped to distributors in European countries and Japan, with the remaining copies distributed throughout America. The apparent reason for this division was that most foreign countries at this time had either weak copyright protection laws or gave enforcement of the laws a low priority.

In the early 1970s, an album, the jacket, insert sheet, and plastic sleeve (the finished product) cost bootleggers $0.50–.60 each to manufacture. The manufacturers (through their representatives) would sell the LPs to dealers for approximately $0.90–.99 each. Retailers then sold the albums to their customers for $3–4.50. The retail cost of vinyl bootlegs increased to a range of $5–10 in the late 1970s, due to the higher cost of production as competition caused the emergence of full-color covers, picture discs, and colored vinyl albums. Another reason for bootleg inflation was the increased pressures applied by the commercial industry on bootleggers and record plants.

In 1976, bolstered by a stronger Federal Copyright Law, the record industry finally began taking notice of some particularly large bootleg sales, with the momentous underground release of live concert albums by Bruce Springsteen and Paul McCartney. The legitimate industry started to keep a closer eye on nearby record plants, hoping to intimidate and discourage those plants that might be involved with the underground. Recognizing the increased risk of serving bootleggers' needs, while retaining their legitimate customers, several plants chose to increase the pressing costs assessed to bootleggers in order to cover the increased risk. This new cost was, of course, passed on to the consumer. However, the $5–10 retail price range was still far removed from the high cost of bootleg compact discs which would retail at $25–30 each in the nineties.

Most of the underground record companies paid little attention to documenting their catalog of albums (e.g., tracking catalog numbers, numbers of copies pressed, record sales by artist, region, demographics, etc.). Few, if any, paid royalties or reported income tax on bootleg record sales, for obvious reasons. The people manufacturing these records in the early 1970s were either college students or recent graduates. For this group, bootlegging was merely a way to subsidize their tuition as well as their hobby of collecting rare music. For many it even became a vocation, an enjoyable alternative to getting up early each day and wearing a tie.

Underground distribution has been, and perhaps always will be, a hit-or-miss, haphazard system. The reason is obvious: Distributors must operate covertly to keep from being arrested. They were more likely to be visible by making regular and systematic sales to retailers and customers. Wholesalers and retailers who dealt directly with bootleg manufacturers rarely, if ever, were allowed to know the last name of the person with whom they did business. Postal boxes became the "office" of choice where many transactions were handled.

Some enterprising "jobbers" would travel an entire region of the United States with bootlegs stuffed in their car trunks, calling on used record stores and "head" or paraphernalia shops, and attending regional record conventions. Availability on any specific album title was (and still is today) a hit-or-miss proposition. Mail order was seen as the safest way to market underground releases. Many brochures conveniently offered "one-stop" shopping for albums, 8mm concert films, posters and other pop culture relics of the era. (Examples of these early catalogs are illustrated in the book.)

Record stores that chose to carry bootlegs often kept them safely stowed behind the counter or in the back room, to hinder the job of the local law enforcement agency. Paraphernalia shops were usually more brazen in displaying the albums out front and on the walls next to their "black light" posters.

Given the lack of record-keeping and the haphazard distribution system of bootleggers in the 1970s, it is understandable why few documents exist today on illicit record manufacturing and distribution. Most documents that did exist were either confiscated by law enforcement authorities or the R.I.A.A. through litigation, or thrown away by producers to avoid leaving a paper trail. Therefore, the only true artifacts illustrating and documenting the early days of this fledgling underground system are the memories of former bootleggers, and the end products themselves—the bootlegs!

THE MIDDLE 1970s

The appearance of new Beatles' bootlegs slowed to a virtual stand-still in the mid-seventies. Many of the old familiar releases were recycled with different titles or artwork by companies such as Berkeley, Wizardo, Newsound, Wonder Land, De Weintraub, The Amazing Kornyphone Record Label (TAKRL), Pig's Eye, Mushroom, Zap, SODD, and An Aftermath.

Several of the first generation companies went out of business during this time. Some lost interest, while others found different careers. A few quit or sold their businesses after experiencing a close brush with law enforcement agencies.

The fact that "new" illicit Beatles' material temporarily dried up may have influenced some to get out of the business. The lack of any "new" and significant studio recordings spawned a rash of Beatles booleg repackages, containing familiar material carrying new names and covers. Material taken from *Get Back*, The Ed Sullivan Shows, Hollywood Bowl and Shea Stadium were recycled almost monthly. Immediately, a second generation of bootleggers began to arrive on the scene as the legitimate record industry failed to see the potential market for rare, previously unreleased archival recordings.

Two significant changes that did occur in the middle of the decade were the improved quality of vinyl used for album pressing, and the development of elaborate color artwork on the jacket covers. Though much of the music remained the same, retail prices of individual albums rose from the $3 range up to the $8–10 range. The increase reflected not only improved packaging and product quality, but it also covered the new risk of pressing plants producing illegal discs behind the backs of the watchful commercial record industry.

Prior to 1976, bootleggers went about their business without much concern for criminal and civil enforcement. According to one former Federal Bureau of Investigation (FBI) agent interviewed by the authors, the Bureau did not place a high priority on the copyright infringement of sound recordings in the 1970s. Somehow, a bunch of college kids selling a few hundred bad-sounding copies of a rock concert did not carry the enforcement priority of more pressing crimes, like drug and weapon sales, money laundering and monitoring the mafia. Several news reports in the late seventies credited the FBI with bootleg record busts, when in fact, the arrests were focused on record counterfeiters or were effected by local authorities using information supplied from the Recording Industry Association of America.

The authors' response (in the 1990s) to requests from the FBI concerning record bootleggers, under a Freedom of Information Act (F.O.I.A.) request, bears out the FBI's lack of substantial involvement throughout most of the 1970s. The authors requested information on seven of the most notorious Beatles bootleg companies of the decade. The names Trade Mark of Quality, The Amazing Kornyfone Records Label, Audifon Records/Ruthless Rhymes, Contra Band Music, Wizardo Records Music Business, Tobe Milo Productions, and Melvin Records were provided to the FBI. Their response stated that "a search of the indices to our central records system files at FBI Headquarters revealed no record responsive to your F.O.I.A. requests…" Their position on bootlegs seemed similar to former director, J. Edgar Hoover's view of organized crime…it simply did not exist, because they choose not to focus resources on it.

Of course, the FBI may well have arrested or indicted bootleggers on an individual basis rather than under an "assumed" company name. This might explain why the authors' F.O.I.A. request yielded very little information under the bootleg company names submitted. It might also explain why, after finding "one cross-reference which mentions all three subjects" (Trade Mark of Quality, Contra Band Music, and Wizardo Records), our request was denied, pursuant to:

> *Title 5, United States Code, Section 552, subsection: (b) (7) (d)* records or information compiled for law enforcement purposes, but only to the extent that the production of such law enforcement records or information could reasonably be expected to disclose the identity of a *confidential* source...

In 1976, superb sounding live multi-disc albums appeared, containing bootlegged performances by "blue chip" artists Paul McCartney and Bruce Springsteen. At the time, neither artist had released a commercial live album. These underground releases filled a huge demand for live material by these popular artists and sold extremely well.

Once the legitimate record industry discovered how well the live bootlegs were selling at swap meets, trade shows and through mail order, they began to step up pressure to combat bootleggers and counterfeiters. The pressure was organized through the R.I.A.A. Record pressing plants were warned not to accept orders from bootleggers. (See interviews with Nurk Twin and Lord Buddha). Record conventions and swap meets were frequently raided. Music magazines which courted legitimate advertising from the industry were subtly warned not to glorify or review any more bootleg releases.

The combination of these actions had a substantial impact on the once casual underground. Bootleggers were forced to take their endeavors more seriously and become even more covert. The legitimate industry sent bootleggers a strong message that it would no longer look the other way. In 1976, bootleggers were finally perceived as a serious commercial threat to their legitimate counterparts. A few bootleggers, caught in the late seventies enforcement web, were fined heavily and lost their black market product. Those who remained in the unlawful enterprise merely raised prices to compensate for their increased risks, and used subsidiary "assumed" label names to disguise the source of ownership. (See Appendix D – Bootlegger's Family Trees.)

THE END OF THE DECADE

The 1970s gave rise to a hobby of collecting unreleased rock and roll recordings by the "Big Three"—Beatles, Dylan, and The Rolling Stones—which soon grew into a cottage industry business. Every major recording artist in the 1970s, from the Allman Brothers to Frank Zappa, was bootlegged and the music was sold through a pervasive yet simplistic system of haphazard manufacture, distribution and record keeping. As a result, a vast amount of rare musical performances came out of the studio and concert "closet." The fact that many of rock and roll's musical heroes died early gives the historic preservation of these recordings even greater significance. Certainly, Lionel Mapleson could never have imagined the degree of popularity that unauthorized recordings would achieve in the seventies when he performed his first successful recording experiments at the turn of the century.

In 1977, two East Coast Beatles fanatics paid a handsome price of about $4,500 to obtain The Beatles' Decca Audition Tapes. Though the group (with then-drummer Pete Best) failed the tryout, the tape was historically important. The release of the 1962 Decca Tapes was to be the last significant piece of musical treasure mined by Beatles Bootleggers in the 1970s.

As we shall see in the 1980s and 1990s, the musical "booty" of the past amounted to only a few doubloons in the treasure chest of unreleased music, especially with respect to The Beatles. The quality of the bootleg product continued to witness improvement both in packaging and in sonic clarity. Costs of discs continued to rise, but so did the consumers' level of expectation as to sound quality, professional packaging and distribution. College bootleggers supporting their hobbies were replaced by more sophisticated, covert and profit-minded entrepreneurs. Perhaps most significant is the incredible number of musically historical discoveries that continued to be plundered and released by a new generation of bandits sailing the seas of the underground music industry.

THE DEMISE OF VINYL BOOTLEGS AND THE BIRTH OF BEATLES' BOOTLEGS ON COMPACT DISC, 1980–PRESENT

In 1980 few people could have forecast the great outpouring of "new" black market Beatles' music which would surface at the end of that decade. Nor could they foresee the advent of the compact disc (CD). Compact discs would have a rejuvenating and transforming effect on both the black market and commercial record industry. So, while the early years of the decade were lean for bootleggers and collectors alike, the end of the eighties would find bootleg aficionados in the midst of a Golden Age.

The 1980s bore witness to a great many changes in the underground music scene including: the birth of new digital recording technologies; the rise and fall of numerous bootleg labels; a significant trend in covert manufacturing and distribution akin to the legitimate music industry; the release of landmark Beatles bootleg albums of master tape studio quality; an increased public awareness of what music was actually locked away in record company vaults; the R.I.A.A.'s continued crackdown on bootlegging; and the buying public's increased expectation for a better sounding underground product.

The popular and prolific bootleg labels of the seventies had, for all practical purposes, disappeared by the beginning of the Reagan Presidency. Gone were names like Wizardo, Instant Analysis, Contra Band Music, TAKRL, Trademark of Quality, ZAP, Old Glory, and King Kong. Gone for the most part were the tacky white label albums with stamped covers, and vinyl which sounded like your grandparents' old 78 rpm records. They were gone because these "Mom and Pop" operations had run out of material; their product was lackluster, distribution was poor, and the recession had forced many to change careers (as did a few arrests and civil suits).

DIGITAL BEATLES: GOODBYE TO VINYL BOOTLEGS

Nineteen hundred and eighty-eight was the year the dam burst open for collectors and bootleggers alike. Just as compact discs were taking over the market share in legitimate releases throughout the music industry, so too were bootleg CDs in the underground market.

The advent of digital compact discs saved the record business from a serious economic decline in the 1980s, from which many thought it would never recover. The record buying public was growing dissatisfied with much of the music of the eighties and had turned to so-called "classic rock" radio stations, as well as to nostalgia acts of the sixties and early seventies. Record sales were down and live concert tours were scaled back. The digital technology of compact disc, however, breathed new life into the record business by making available superb sounding releases of old "classic rock" favorites, as well as presenting new artists in a better sounding medium. The CD revolution had made perhaps a greater impact on the music consumers than even the advent of stereo phonograph record players. Again, the face of music had been forever altered.

Likewise, thanks to this new recording format, bootleggers struck gold in the late eighties. Advanced digital technology (with no loss of sound quality for each tape generation), loopholes in Euro-copyright laws, and the unending quest for the almighty dollar (in a world whose economy was in recession) helped create the right conditions for a black market industry resurgence. As this innovative, brighter-sounding format for storing recorded music opened up a new (and highly profitable) market for a slumping record industry, it was inevitable that it

TOP: *An original CD* from *The Swingin' Pig's* Ultra Rare Trax *series*
ABOVE: *A two vinyl set on Stash Records*

would have a parallel affect on the bootlegging underground. With the aid of computerization, noise reduction, and "declicking," the sub-par vinyl bootleg records of old could now be revitalized and remastered into professional sounding releases. The advent of portable digital audio tape (DAT) recorders enabled improved-sounding live concert recordings of current rock stars to be bootlegged as well. Suddenly, those often horrid-sounding bootlegs of the 1970s were a forgotten memory. Black market music enjoyed a rebirth which brought with it a new generation and a wider audience than its predecessors.

For whatever reason, collectors who had been sitting on rare Beatles' tapes suddenly started selling them to European CD bootleggers. In 1988, the first releases of "new" and pristine-sounding EMI studio outtakes of The Beatles were released on compact disc, called The Swingin' Pig's *Ultra Rare Trax* series. The release of these discs did not go unnoticed by the mass media. Articles describing these amazing releases began to appear in *Rolling Stone* magazine and major newspapers such as the *Chicago Tribune*, *The Washington Post* and the *New York Times*. This above-ground news served to dramatically expand the normally small base of bootleg collectors. A much larger audience of intrigued baby boomers who had plenty of discretionary income to spend on CDs, became aware of "new" (albeit illicit) Beatles recordings containing all the flubs, mistakes and wrong notes they had never heard before.

The renewed attention to the old art of music bootlegging also caused the commercial record industry to stand up and take note. However, this time the record executives were up against more savvy and sophisticated black market competitors—competitors who were more organized than their brethren of the seventies, and who were selling professionally packaged good sounding recordings of forbidden musical fruits.

While popularity of compact discs and the virtual demise of vinyl took place in the late eighties, retail prices soared. Bootleg CD's sold for between $20–35 apiece. Some double CDs even retailed for as much as $75! For the first time, bootleg recordings had become twice as expensive as commercial recordings.

Collectors were initially bewildered by the high price of the "grey area" CDs. Compact discs, including the disc, case and printing generally cost approximately $4 each to manufacture. However, supply and demand, as always, ruled the day with bootleg sales. Most of the CDs were being pressed in Europe in limited quantities. Both the Japanese and U.S. markets hungered for these same limited quantity releases. Additional distribution costs were pumped into the discs covering shipment to other continents and for alleged payoffs to customs agents, to move the contraband material into the respective countries. Still, even at the inflated prices, fans hungry for new, forbidden music were only too willing to pay the price—even if they didn't like it. At the time of this writing, retail bootleg prices in the United States have, on average, remained the same (around $25 each) as when they first entered the market in 1988. The same cannot be said for commercial CDs which entered the retail market at $10–12 each. Today, these discs sell for $17–18.

BOOTLEG MANUFACTURING RELOCATES TO EUROPE

By the middle 1980s, the manufacture of bootlegs in the United States had slowed to a trickle. This was due to the successful efforts of the Recording Industry Association of America and various Federal and State law enforcement agencies. Compact disc manufacturers in America were made to press identifying codes onto the CDs which revealed the location of the plant where the disc was manufactured. Obviously, no U.S. pressing plant wanted to lose its livelihood by taking the risk of producing bootleg discs that could be traced back to their facility. Likewise, bootleggers did not wish to be arrested when they showed up at the pressing plant to pick up their prohibited merchandise. In this way, the R.I.A.A. was able to virtually cut off all black market music production in the United States.

Vinyl bootleg records are still being made in America, in small numbers. However, the demand for vinyl is so limited that most companies have ceased high-volume operations. Only the West Coast's Vigatone label (with its Beatles' albums, *Nothing But Aging* and *Arrive Without Travelling*) and Bag Records (*Lost Lennon Tapes* series) seem to have had some moderate success with their vinyl albums. Vigotone eventually switched to CD manufacturing outside the U.S. Starlight Records (*The Real Early Beatles*) attempted a vinyl resurgence in 1988, but poor quality pressings and the indictment of the principals put them permanently out of business in 1991.

The successful CD bootleggers rely upon various sources for their materi-

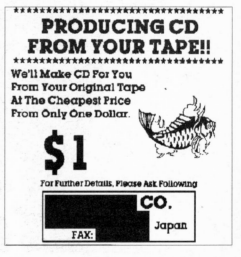

al. Often, it comes from collectors who possess tapes of concerts or videos that they have recorded themselves. Bootleggers in both Europe and Japan boldly

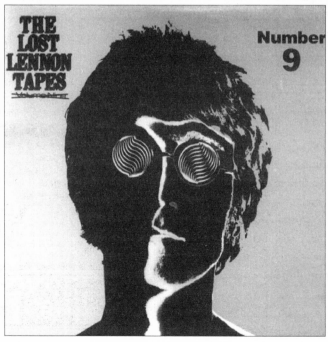

TOP: *Vigotone's* Nothing But Aging *vinyl*
ABOVE: *Bag Records'* Lost Lennon Tapes *vinyl*

advertise in U.S. publications seeking "new" rare material by major artists, in exchange for copies of the subsequent CD release.

Sometimes bootleggers purchase recordings offered for sale privately or at British and American auction houses (such as The Beatles' "Garage Tapes" containing impromptu recordings of Beatles' songs made in hotel rooms and in the back of their limo during the tour years). Or, as in the case of the *Ultra Rare Trax* and *Unsurpassed Masters* Beatles series, they have acquired copies of tapes taken or dubbed from masters that once rested safely in the EMI Records company vaults. These tapes rest in the hands of the very few and are highly valued.

The next step after the tape is obtained, is to master it for pressing. Tapes are digitally "cleaned up" to maximize sound quality. The equipment and technology needed to do this is readily available and is not expensive (although some European Beatles bootleggers like Bulldog Records and Adam VIII would transfer poorly-made recordings onto disc without attempting to "brighten" the sound.) After the tape is prepared it is taken to a pressing plant familiar to the bootlegger. Historically, many plants located in Europe or the Far East cared little about the content of what they pressed, so long as they got paid. However, as a safeguard during distribution into foreign countries, the bootleggers often misrepresent their material by placing bogus artist names on the discs (such as "Paul Ramone" for Paul McCartney). These phony names have assisted underground distributors in smuggling Beatles bootlegs past the Customs Agents. Generally, 1,500–5,000 copies of a title are made at a cost of about four dollars apiece (including the manufacture of the disc and the accompanying package).

The final step is marketing and distribution. Much of the distribution is done through a wholesale/retail network. This network, though more organized than its 1970s predecessor, still lacks the cohesive structure of its commercial counterpart. Only the largest bootleg manufacturers maintain a formal distribution system in the North America. Their responsibility is to smuggle the contraband into the country and distribute it to dealers across North America. Usually, the discs are shipped *separately* from the jewel boxes and printed material in order to escape detection. Ports of entry are carefully researched in order to locate the safest and "friendliest" harbor.

By the fall of 1993, the bootleggers' covert distribution into America began to resemble football's "end-run" play. One example included an extensive eight-disc Beatles box set of January 1969 rehearsals, called the *Get Back Journals*, issued underground in the United States. All of the liner notes and printing materials for the set were researched, written and printed within the United States. The master tapes for the set were sequenced and prepared in America as well, before being sent to Europe. Compact discs were then pressed in Europe. Once all of the components were complete, the discs were purportedly shipped first to Canada rather than directly into the U.S. From there, the discs were sent by private overnight express carrier to a secret destination within the United States. The packages containing The Beatles' contraband discs were declared to have a customs duty value of *only* one dollar! In this way, no suspicion was aroused when passing by the unsuspecting U.S. Customs agents on the border.

East and West Coast distributors, charged with the responsibility of pre-selling all of their new product, also had the chore of assembling the black market discs into jewel boxes, along with all of the appropriate printed material. Once the *Journals* set was complete, it was ready to swiftly travel interstate without detection to music dealers via common carrier, private delivery and even U.S. Mail. The *Journals* box sets sold in retail record stores for a staggering $250 to $300.

Today, the world of underground music distribution has been made smaller and more efficient due to advances in telecommunication. Bootleggers' press releases announcing upcoming titles are now routinely faxed or transmitted by computer modem to U.S. magazines and retailers direct from Europe and the Far East.

Problems can and do arise for foreign manufacturers and for those who seek to import the bootlegs into the United States. While the laws governing these compact discs are more lax in Europe and Japan (though this is changing), when these discs enter the United States, importers take a big risk smuggling musical contraband into the country. According to Steven D'Onofrio of the R.I.A.A., there were just a handful of bootleg CDs confiscated in 1988 as compared to 38,000 in 1989, 95,000 in 1990 and 120,000 in 1991. In addition, a number of individuals importing these goods have been arrested and/or fined for their participation in this illegal activity, not to mention having all of their previously prepaid goods confiscated. The number of confiscations is merely the tip of a rather large musical iceberg. The majority of bootleggers, because they are white-collar criminals, have rarely seen the inside of a jail cell. Instead, they are punished economically by having their contraband confiscated and fined large sums. (See interview with bootlegger Lord Buddha.)

It is unlikely that a few arrests and confiscations will deter the persistent black market purveyors because the potential for large cash profits is so great. Currently, as this book is being published, there are hundreds of *new* compact disc titles being marketed each month, covering the most important rock artists of the 1960s through the 1990s. According to one U.S. CD bootleg dealer's print

Bulldog Records advertisement

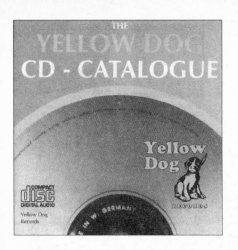

YD 001
THE BEATLES - 1962-63 outtakes
UNSURPASSED MASTERS VOL. 1
Incl.: Besame Mucho - How Do
You Do It ? - One After 909

YD 002
THE BEATLES - 1964-65 outtakes
UNSURPASSED MASTERS VOL. 2
Incl.: Leave My Kitten Alone -
That Means A Lot - 12-Bar Original

YD 003
THE BEATLES - 1966-67 outtakes
UNSURPASSED MASTERS VOL. 3
Incl.: Mark 1 - Strawberry Fields
Forever - Aerial Tour Instrumental

YD 004
THE BEATLES - 1968 outtakes
UNSURPASSED MASTERS VOL. 4
Incl.: Brian Epstein Blues - I Hate To
See The Evening Sun Go Down

YD 005
THE BEATLES - 1969 outtakes
UNSURPASSED MASTERS VOL. 5
Incl.: Something (take 37) - A Huge
Melody (part 1 & 2) - Stand By Me

YD 006
THE BEATLES - 1969 outtakes
CELLULOID ROCK
Incl.: Shake, Rattle And Roll - Blue
Suede Shoes - Teddy Boy

YD 007
THE WHO - 1969 outtakes
THE TOMMY DEMOS
Incl.: Overture - Pinball Wizard -
Tommy, Can You Hear Me ?

YD 008
THE BEATLES - 1968 outtakes
UNSURPASSED DEMOS
Incl.: Singalong Junk - Sour Milk
Sea - Child Of Nature

YD 009
THE BEATLES - 1963-69 outtakes
ACETATES
Incl.: Bad To Me - One And One Is
Two - Christmas Time (Is Here Again)

YD 010
BOB DYLAN - 1962
LIVE FINJAN CLUB
Incl.: The Death Of Emmett Till -
Blowin' In The Wind

YD 011
THE SILVER BEATLES - 1962 live
THE DECCA TAPES & CAVERN TAPES
Incl.: Like Dreamers Do - Hello Little
Girl - Love Of The Loved - Catswalk

YD 012
THE BEATLES - 1963-69 outtakes
UNSURPASSED MASTERS VOL. 6
Incl.: I You've Got Trouble - Not
Guilty - What's The New Mary Jane

YD 013
THE BEATLES - 1963-69 outtakes
UNSURPASSED MASTERS VOL. 7
Incl.: Can't Buy Me Love - Think For
Yourself (studio talk) - Come And
Get It

YD 014
THE BEATLES - 1969 outtakes
GET BACK AND 22 OTHER SONGS
Incl.: Save The Last Dance For Me -
I Lost My Little Girl - Schooldays /
Hail Hail Rock And Roll

UPCOMING RELEASES:

THE BEATLES -
ALL THINGS MUST PASS 1969
Harrison songs by The Beatles

THE BEATLES -
COMPLETE ROOFTOP CONCERT
plus more Let It Be outtakes1969

THE ROLLING STONES -
BLACK BOX COLLECTION VOL.1
Decca outtakes

THE ROLLING STONES -
KARAOKE
Backing Tracks without Vocals

THE ROLLING STONES -
BLACK BOX COLLECTION VOL.2
Decca outtakes

ELTON JOHN -
DICK JAMES COLLECTION VOL. 1
Unreleased outtakes and demos

THE ROLLING STONES -
BLACK BOX COLLECTION VOL. 3
Decca outtakes

ELTON JOHN -
DICK JAMES COLLECTION VOL. 2
Unreleased outtakes and demos

AVAILABLE AT :

Yellow Dog CD catalogue

advertisement, "It is getting nearly impossible for us to keep up with all the new releases *pouring* out of Europe. Hundreds of new titles are popping up each month from just as many companies." Profits can be enormous (between $25,000 and $50,000 for a single successful CD title). Bootlegging, therefore, has become a risky yet highly profitable business, with no end in sight!

BOOTLEGGERS VS. ARTISTS:
THE DEBATE OVER UNRELEASED MUSIC

As CD bootlegging progressed from a cottage industry to a bonafide competitor of its above-ground counterpart, the renewed moral debate over this illegal enterprise began to escalate. Members of the black market trade have been quick to provide moral justification for obtaining the rare tapes and releasing them without permission of the artist or his record label. Dieter Schubert (owner of Perfect Beat/The Swingin' Pig and a purveyor of unreleased Beatles albums) explained the underground's position to the U.S. CD newsletter *ICE*:

> The basic philosophy of Swingin' Pig is to make available historically important, previously unreleased recordings which would otherwise never see the light of day. Take, for example, *Ultra Rare Trax* by the Beatles. EMI keeps them in their vaults for so many years, with no intention to release them. Even the Beatles themselves say they don't want them out because they feel the outtakes are not up to normal standards. The public obviously has a totally different opinion, claiming that…in many cases…these recordings match or even surpass the well-known versions because they sound fresher. But the tapes are over twenty years old now, some nearly thirty. Twenty more years in the archives would possibly destroy the tapes, like many outtakes from the fifties…and they'll be lost forever.

The artists within the commercial recording industry debate the view taken by bootleggers such as Dieter Schubert. Historically, artists of every genre prefer not to release any product unless it is their best performance. The artist often does not feel there is any value to their "rough drafts." Understandably, artists and their record company's want to control everything they might wish to release, in order to prevent overexposure and embarrassment over sub-par performances. Representing the commercial recording artists and their labels, Steven D'Onofrio provides this counterpoint:

> There are artists out there that are very concerned about this bootlegging. Over the years, they would literally write me personally, saying they saw an ad for a bootleg and it bothered the hell out of them. They hear their voice

not as flattering as it is in the studio and they don't necessarily like that. Although they may have sounded that way in concert, they don't want that to be memorialized. You have to understand the perfectionism that some of these artist have.

By 1991, CD bootlegging had become so profitable and prolific, that artists and their record labels began to fight back by releasing their own rare music. Additionally, they began a campaign aimed at pressuring European pressing plants to turn down orders for the manufacture of underground discs.

"I think it's up to artists to do whatever they can to stand up for their rights," said the late composer/artist Frank Zappa. The above-ground recording industry had adopted a new position in its fight against record bootlegging. "If you can't beat them...join them." Thus, they have finally begun to release albums (and extended play singles) containing rare live songs, demos and outtakes, to feed the insatiable music-buying public, while cutting into the bootlegger's bottom line.

The debate however, between the bootleggers and their commercial counterparts continues. The battle lines are drawn and neither side is likely to back down. However, one thing is certain, bootlegging is no longer the harmless romantic hobby of rebellious college students taping their favorite artist's concert and selling a copy to the local bootlegger for pressing onto vinyl. It has, in the late eighties and early nineties, become an economic competitor and a significant threat to the commercial record industry.

The following chapter highlights and presents, in chronological order of recording, the most significant unauthorized record and compact disc recordings of The Beatles. By no means is this treatise on unauthorized recordings an endorsement of the illicit record trade's activities. Rather, it serves as an overview of the most significant lost recordings of this supergroup. The study reveals a more complete and interesting historical picture of the recording artists themselves than was afforded merely by their commercial releases. It also demonstrates the bootleggers' impact on our popular culture and musical history. This, is the story behind the lost Beatles' recordings that the general public was never supposed to hear.

3

Bootleggers Reunite The Beatles: The Most Significant Black Market Releases 1958–1970

In their brief, yet prolific recording career, The Beatles recorded thirteen long-playing albums and twenty-two singles between June 6, 1962 and January 4, 1970. The total sum of this music clocks in at ten-and-a-half hours. This figure represents a mere three percent of the more than four hundred hours of Beatles recordings currently sitting in the vaults of EMI Records in England—a rather small tip of the group's musical iceberg. The remainder of these irreplaceable historic recordings contain alternate attempts at familiar songs, jam sessions, Beatles banter, jokes, creative discussions, arguments and a handful of finished outtake songs. These outtakes are songs which, for one reason or another, were deemed unfit for release at the time.

Additionally, The Beatles made hundreds or perhaps thousands of public appearances on radio, television and in concert throughout the world during their career. Many, if not most, of these performances and appearances were recorded for posterity. Add to that the many boxes of composing and demo tapes recorded by the group's three principal songwriters, John, Paul and George and one quickly realizes the vast treasure trove of musical booty that bootleggers had to choose from.

This chapter recounts in chronological fashion the most significant unreleased works by The Beatles which have been hijacked and exploited by bootleggers since 1969. The chronicle is by no means a complete account, but rather, serves as an overview highlighting the most significant *lost* recordings of the group, from their earliest work as The Quarry Men, to their last sessions of 1970. These are the songs that the world was never meant to hear…

1958
LIVERPOOL, ENGLAND

The first group John Lennon formed was called The Quarry Men, named after his school, Quarry Bank High School. The group was formed by a 16-year-old Lennon in 1956. However, the earliest known recording of the group occurred in the middle of 1958. The nucleus of the band that would become The Beatles was already in place as John Lennon, Paul McCartney and George Harrison were joined by fellow Quarry Men Colin Hanton and John "Duff" Lowe for what is believed to be their first attempt at recording proper studio songs.

The young men, with their primitive skiffle instruments in tow, hoofed it down to Liverpool's Kensington Recording Studio and plunked down a mere 25 shillings to record a two sided shellac disc. On that day, the five lads squeezed into a small recording booth to record two songs, "That'll Be The Day" and "In Spite Of All The Danger." Only The Quarry Men's cover of Buddy Holly's "That'll Be The Day" has been bootlegged from a radio broadcast. The bootleg has appeared in its best sounding (yet edited) quality on a 1993 boxed set of rarities called *Artifacts* (Big Music, 4018-4022, 5CD, 1993).

The song features a confident John Lennon attempting to copy the vocal stylization of Buddy Holly, as he imitates and stutters, "…'cause that'll be the day-hey-hey when I die." It appears that Paul McCartney is actually heard singing a high harmony part of "ahhhhs" throughout the song. However, due to the record's primitive sound quality, it is difficult to verify.

Paul McCartney is, in fact, the proud owner of what is believed to be the only original copy of this historic pre-Beatles recording. The appearance of Ringo Starr and the beginnings of Beatlemania were still several years away.

1960
HAMBURG, GERMANY

Another underground recording of historic import was titled *Liverpool May 1960* (Indra, M5-6001, 2LP). This two-record set consisted of early Beatles rehearsals that the group had recorded of themselves during the fall of 1960 in Germany (not in May, nor in Liverpool as the bootleg's liner notes mistakenly claim). The bootleggers came by these historic rehearsals in the late 1980s by way of their sale at a major auction, consigned by an anonymous European collector. Although these recordings were attributed by bootleggers to be The Quarry Men, they are in fact, The Beatles. The group had already changed their name to "The Beatles" on or about August 12, 1960, prior to the making of these recordings.

This bootleg preserves some of the earliest known recordings made by John,

51

QUARRYMEN REHEARSE
WITH STU SUTCLIFF
SPRING 1960

Quarry Men bootlegs

Paul, George and Stuart Sutcliff (on bass) without any drummer. Considering the age of the original tape (over thirty years old) and the technology used to make the recording, the sound is of surprisingly good fidelity. To hear the embryonic "Beatles-sound" on rough versions of songs they would return to later in their career such as, "I'll Follow The Sun," "The One After 909," "Matchbox," "Hello Little Girl" and "Hallelujah I Love Her So," is quite remarkable.

Perhaps the most fascinating gem culled from this session is an instrumental which has been credited to Lennon/McCartney/Harrison entitled, "Thinking of Linking." One of the very few instrumentals recorded by The Beatles, the song features a Spanish sounding, moody, somewhat rambling melody. Stuart Sutcliff plays a one-note bass part, whenever he feels that it will fit. George's attempt at a lead solo is quite interesting as he utilizes what appears to be a partial chromatic scale exercise, climbing and descending to finish off the song.

Another gem from these rehearsals is the Lennon/McCartney original "I'll Follow The Sun." The song would eventually be properly recorded some four years later in 1964 for their *Beatles For Sale* album (*Beatles '65* in the United States). The song begins with John uttering some unintelligible gibberish in German to spur his partner on. McCartney's voice is relaxed as he sings to a speedy skiffle rhythm which occasionally falls off the beat due to the lack of a drummer to hold it together. A most interesting aspect of this early version is the attempt at creating the middle portion of the song ("middle eight") which had yet to develop into the one they would formally record at Abbey Road Studios in 1964. George's guitar solo, though filled with some rough notes, begins to formulate what would eventually become the official melody of the lead part.

If one compares these recordings to the later official versions, the results might seem disappointing to the unseasoned ear. Yet this rehearsal highlights just how far The Beatles had come from their Quarry Men days and how far they still had to go in fine-tuning their songwriting and instrumental skills. The road to success was paved with many more performances and practice sessions before the Fab Four would strike gold four years later with a tight, tough "Mersey-beat" sound.

1962
THE DECCA AUDITION TAPES

Throughout the 1970s, a number of bootlegs purported to contain the Beatles' legendary 1962 audition tapes for Decca Records. However, most of the mislabeled material was, in reality, recordings of the group's appearances on the British Broadcasting Company (BBC). By 1973, only one Decca audition song had surfaced, called "Love of The Loved," on a bootleg entitled *L.S. Bumblebee* (CBM, 3626, LP). The other Decca songs remained secure in the vaults until the end of the seventies.

Understanding the background of how the early Decca audition tapes were originally created helps one to appreciate the historic significance of these recordings. Late in 1961, Brian Epstein, the Beatles' newly appointed manager, was attempting to generate interest in the group which was not yet signed to a record label. On January 1, 1962, Epstein secured a try-out with Mike Smith, Artists & Repertoire man for Decca Records in West Hampstead, North London. On that date, John Lennon, Paul McCartney, George Harrison and drummer Pete Best performed fifteen confirmed songs at their audition, namely: "To Know Her Is To Love Her," "Memphis," "The Sheik Of Araby," "Three Cool Cats," "Till There Was You," "Like Dreamers Do," "Hello Little Girl," "Love Of The Loved," "September In The Rain," "Money," "Besame Mucho," "Searchin'," "Sure To Fall," "Take Good Care Of My Baby," and "Crying, Waiting, Hoping."

The music was raw and unpolished. At times, The Beatles sounded nervous, yet practiced. The fact that the songs revealed the group's potential future success went unnoticed by Decca's Mike Smith on that cold January morning. Smith turned the Beatles down on the basis of this audition and history will probably never allow Smith or Decca Records to forget!

The song "Like Dreamers Do" featured Paul singing in a style that seemed to combine the early Elvis Presley with Ricky Ricardo. This Lennon/McCartney composition illustrates their early, simple teenage daydream style of songwriting. After George's nine-note guitar lead-in, Paul begins the song singing, "I...I saw a girl in my dreams / and so it seems that I will love her / Oh you, you are that girl in my dreams / and so it seems that I will love you..." Later at a climatic point in the song, McCartney is forced to stretch out one word several bars for want of more lyrics. He sings, "Oh, I'll be there yeah / waitin' for you-you-you-you-you-you-you-you / you came just one dream ago..." The song's drumming, performed by Pete Best, gives an early indication of why he would later be fired in favor of Ringo Starr some eight months later. Best seems to have trouble staying with Paul, often getting ahead of his singing.

The Decca songs were finally assembled together and released in bootleg form on three different formats in the late seventies. In 1977, a series of colored vinyl singles were first released by a Beatles' fan magazine. Several different picture disc albums (in both color and black & white) were also released with the same material. However, the most well known (and best sounding) bootleg of this material was *The Decca Tapes* (Circuit Records, LK 4438-1, LP). *The Decca*

The Decca Tapes *albums*

Tapes, released in 1979, was made to look like a legitimate release and included extensive, yet inaccurate, historical liner notes about the group on the album sleeve.

In the early 1980s, a couple of quasi-legal, good sounding releases of the *Decca* material appeared. These distributors realized that at the time the Decca tapes were recorded (January 1, 1962), the Beatles had not yet been signed to an exclusive recording contract with EMI. They believed this loophole permitted them to legitimately release the Decca material. Thus, the legality of these releases was open to question. The albums were titled, *Dawn Of The Silver Beatles* (PAC Records, VDL 2333, LP) and *Silver Beatles–Like Dreamers Do* (Backstage Records, BSR 1111, 2LP). The tracks on these releases appear to contain some artificial modifications such as changes in speed and song length.

In 1988, lawyers for The Beatles filed a claim against a European record company for manufacturing and selling an album of Decca sessions, entitled *The Beatles: The Decca Sessions*. Again, the question of who properly owned the performance rights to the recordings was at issue. The record company ultimately agreed to cease and desist from manufacturing and distributing the album pending a proposed settlement.

Finally in 1991, the best sounding release of this original *Decca* material appeared on a bootleg compact disc entitled, *The Decca Audition Tapes 1962 and The Cavern Club Rehearsals* (Yellow Dog, YD 011, CD). All fifteen songs from this historic session were digitally enhanced, yet left in their original form.

The Decca audition tapes were a significant discovery to fans, scholars and collectors for a number of reasons. First, the audition was one which The Beatles failed to pass! That fact has given these recordings a humorous juxtaposition to John Lennon's remarks on the rooftop of Apple Corps, Ltd. after The Beatles' last live performance, when he said, "Thank you on behalf of the group and myself…and I hope we passed the audition!" A second aspect of the auditions is the presence of one-time Beatle Pete Best on drums. These recordings forever preserve the interim sound of The Beatles, with a drummer who would not be making the journey with the group to the top of the world's entertainment ladder, a mere eight months later. Third, many of these songs were yet more "new," albeit illegal musical discoveries (in the late 1970s) which scholars could use to study the musical progress, style, and taste of the early Beatles.

MARCH 7, 1962–JUNE 7, 1965
THE BEATLES BBC RADIO SESSIONS

The Beatles' long and mutually beneficial relationship with the BBC began when they stepped into The Playhouse Theatre on St. John's Road in Manchester, England on March 7, 1962. Pete Best was still the group's drummer and EMI's recording contract offer to The Beatles was still three months away. The group's manager was looking for exposure—and what better way to accomplish his goal then to broadcast his proteges on radio to eager teenagers.

The Beatles began their work on the BBC by recording four songs before a live audience. The show, broadcast the next day (March 8, 1962), was called "Here We Go," hosted by Ray Peters. The Beatles recorded "Hello Little Girl," "Memphis, Tennessee," "Dream Baby" and "Please Mr. Postman." Of special interest was Paul's lead vocal on "Dream Baby," a Roy Orbison hit that had been climbing the American charts only a few weeks before The Beatles' performance. Paul's version is another attempt to copy a unique American pop vocal style. This is a technique McCartney relied upon quite early as he honed and practiced the vocal stylings of Little Richard, Elvis Presley, Roy Orbison and Buddy Holly. Paul's own unique style today is often described as an amalgam of the above-mentioned influences.

The early 1970s marked the first appearance of bootlegs containing The Beatles' in-studio performances for the British Broadcasting Corporation. These recordings represented yet another revelation to fans, collectors, and music scholars because they contained many Beatle performances of songs that were *never* commercially released on record. Roughly one-third of the ninety different songs recorded for BBC radio over a three year period were never pressed onto Beatles records. Most of these gems were cover versions of songs performed by groups that influenced The Beatles early on. The BBC tapes also contained alternate versions of commercially released Beatles songs. The performances were recorded at various radio studios around England. Most importantly, the radio performances did *not* contain the screaming that accompanied live concerts. Bootleggers mostly obtained these historic recordings from British fans, who, in the 1960s had recorded the radio performances directly off the airwaves.

There are many rarities scattered across the three years of BBC broadcasts. On May 24, 1963, for example, the theme for The Beatles' radio series titled "Pop Goes The Beatles" was recorded. The Lorne Gibson Trio performed the song, which was knocked off from the traditional arrangement of "Pop Goes The Weasel." The Beatles provided the instrumental backing for the song, but never sang it, leaving that job to the Trio. Then on December 17, 1963, The Beatles

BBC sessions albums

recorded for the "Saturday Club." After reading some dedications from their fans and wishing them a Christmas greeting, they broke into spontaneous song, "All I Want For Christmas Is A Bottle..." The group's ability to parody themselves was quite evident at they performed a silly medley of one line from each of the songs: "Love Me Do," "Please Please Me," "From Me To You," "She Loves You," "I Want To Hold Your Hand," and "Rudolph The Red Nosed Reindeer." A single guitar is heard, playing a repetitive line as the Beatles' medley fades out with the group singing and laughing to the line "Crimble." "Crimble" was, of course, The Beatles' word for Christmas.

"Clarabella" is another "lost" diamond in the rough that The Beatles never formally recorded. However, on July 2, 1963, they preserved their version of this obscure rhythm and blues number for "Pop Goes The Beatles." The song was introduced by John Lennon in response to a request from some fans for "a beaty song and swingin' voice." John in his off-the-cuff witty style responds, "So here's Paul whistling Clarabella." With that, Paul takes his cue and jumps in screaming..."Well I've got a baby, crazy for me. Yea, I've got a baby (screaming even louder) won't let me be. Oh baby, baby Clarabella..." Suddenly, the rest of the band joins into the R & B backing which features a great harmonica part played by John Lennon. Lennon had been greatly influenced by Bruce Channel's harmonica player Delbert McClinton when the two groups appeared on the same bill at the Tower Ballroom in New Brighton, England the previous summer. McClinton's influence and style are evident on Lennon's early experiment with blue harp which helped to shape the unique sound of several early Beatles hit songs such as "Love Me Do" and "I Should Have Known Better."

The earliest releases of BBC material were bootlegged onto albums entitled, *As Sweet As You Are* (Dittolino Discs, D-1, LP), *Yellow Matter Custard* (TMOQ, 71032, LP), *Studio Sessions One* (CBM, WEC-3640, LP) and *Studio Sessions Two* (CBM, WEC-3641, LP). At the time, most collectors were duped into believing that the BBC songs were actual outtakes from proper studio recording sessions. In this instance, bootleggers purposely misled their consumers in order to sell records, unconcerned with providing accurate documentation about the correct source of the recordings.

Most of these early BBC bootlegs carried the same collection of songs which were culled from British radio between the summer and fall of 1963 for the show "Pop Go The Beatles." The songs reflected the Beatles' biggest musical influences at the time. Included were titles such as: "I Got A Woman" (Ray Charles), "Slow Down" (Larry Williams), "Please Don't Ever Change" (Goffin-King), "Sure To Fall" (Carl Perkins, et. al.), "Crying, Waiting, Hoping" (Buddy Holly), and "To Know Her Is To Love Her" (Phil Spector).

It was not until the late 1980s and early 1990s that the majority of Beatles' BBC performances was bootlegged in excellent sound. The source of the bootlegs came from radio broadcasts. However, these were new radio specials that aired The Beatles' performances retrospectively in the 1980s. Unauthorized compact discs of these radio shows were manufactured by such European companies as Beeb Transcription Records and Pyramid.

The Complete BBC Sessions, released by Great Dane Records in 1994, usurped all previous black market compilations of The Beatles' radio archives. The nine CD set (with a tenth disc released months later) came packaged in a large twelve-inch square box with a thirty-six page color booklet. The original set contained 257 Beatles songs. According to *ICE, The Monthly CD Newsletter* that reviewed the set, "...*The Complete BBC Sessions* is a five star, hall-of-fame package that, frankly, EMI/Capitol (The Beatles' record company) stands little chance of equaling." High praise indeed, for an illicit collection that sold on the streets to collectors for $200-$250 a piece.

The BBC performances enabled the quartet to have fun playing a number of cover tunes by their favorite artists such as Chuck Berry, Little Richard, Buddy Holly, Carl Perkins and others. Since many of the cover songs were never released by the group on albums, the radio shows served as a surprise to most fans. It also allowed the group to freely promote their latest hit singles to all of England without having to pay for advertisement. From a performance standpoint, the repertoire resembled their live shows, yet without all of the screaming. And finally, the banter between the announcers and The Beatles illustrated that the four lads were funny, and most importantly, human.

Finally, on December 6, 1994 (in the U.S.), The Beatles and their record companies released an official double CD set entitled, *The Beatles: Live at the BBC*. The historic package contained 56 songs culled from the vaults of the BBC (as well as those of some private collectors) compiled by George Martin and digitally remastered by Abbey Road's Peter Mew. Though the set was "old news" to hard core collectors who owned the Great Dane box set, it became a worldwide multi-platinum seller to the mass music markets. The package included a 48-page booklet with track-by-track annotation and literally dozens of rare photos of The Beatles at the BBC. Of course, the songs on the official set were generally of superior sound quality to their unofficial counterparts.

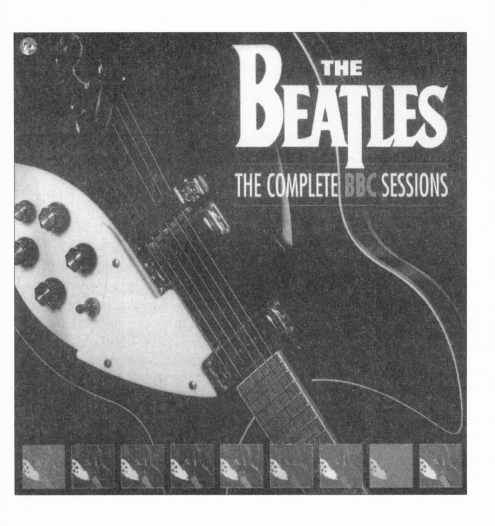

CD booklet cover for Great Dane's acclaimed The Complete BBC Sessions

MARCH 5, 1963
LONDON, ENGLAND

On this day, The Beatles assembled at Abbey Road Studios to work on three songs, namely: "From Me To You," "Thank You Girl" and "One After 909" (which remains unissued in this form). The privileged visitor to Abbey Road that day would have heard take after take of attempts to build the basic musical ideas into finished songs. Following the evolution of these songs from raw beginnings to their ultimate completion is a facinating experience.

In 1994, an unofficial album entitled *March 5, 1963—The Complete Session Tape* was released by Vigotone (VT-123, CD), which contained the entire master reel tape of this session. Apparently, the tape had been stolen from EMI's vaults years before. This disc is significant, not only for its history, but for taking the listener into the studio for the first time to hear continuous takes and edit pieces of the Fab Four at work on a complete single day of their recording career.

OCTOBER 24, 1963
STOCKHOLM, SWEDEN

To the sound of whistles and polite applause, The Beatles are introduced by the Swedish announcer who welcomes the teenagers into the Karlaplan Studio for the recording of a radio show called, "Pop '63." He states very simply, "John, Paul, George 'o Ringo, The Beatles!" With that cue, Paul counts off the now famous "1, 2, 3, 4..." and The Beatles surge forward into a raw, hard-rocking version of "I Saw Her Standing There." After a near-perfect rendition of the song, driven by Ringo Starr's powerful back beat, Paul introduces the next song, "From Me To You."

Paul provides another introduction for the follow up song "...from our new LP released in November." Just then, a confident George mocks Paul's ongoing record promotion, mimicking his words, "New LP." Paul laughs, but doesn't miss a beat. Repeating the upcoming release date, Paul says, "Released in November, the song is called, 'Money'." Lennon lets out a whoop, propelling the song forward with a barrage of electric guitar riffs that would make the heavy metal rockers of today sit up and take note. Paul and George supply strong vocal backing to John, singing "That's what I want" in response to John's exhortation for "Money." Finally, the previously polite crowd wakes up and starts screaming. Yet another country of kids won over by the spread of Beatlemania. George takes his solo with "Roll Over Beethoven" and turns in a performance topped only by the amazing drumming of Ringo who flies all over the kit in a frenzied flurry. The show finishes up with three more songs, "You Really Got A Hold On Me," "She

Loves You," and "Twist & Shout."

This concert, a favorite of John Lennon's, is perhaps the best live performance document of The Beatles ever recorded. The near-perfect show features the group at the height of their powers, with strong, tight harmony vocals and raw, precise guitar playing. Ringo Starr, who had been with the group at this point for approximately one year, was the final piece to the puzzle catapulting the group to "the toppermost of the poppermost."

The show was recorded for later broadcast throughout Sweden. From there it was no doubt taped off the air, before making its way into the hands of bootleggers. The best sounding copy of this concert appeared in 1988, on a compact disc entitled, *Stars Of '63*. The disc was released by The Swingin' Pig Records, whose purported copyrights to the recording were "Realized somewhere over the rainbow" according to the album's sleeve notes.

The confidence exhibited by the group on this show marked a turning point in their careers. From this point forward, it certainly must have been clear to the Fab Four that they were indeed about to conquer the world.

FEBRUARY 1964
THE ED SULLIVAN SHOW PERFORMANCES—NEW YORK CITY

During the 1972–1973 time period, portions of the Beatles' "Ed Sullivan Show" performances started to circulate in bootleg form. For many American fans, these releases were significant, marking the moment when millions of people were first exposed to The Beatles. The Beatles' Ed Sullivan performances of 1964 also represented at the time, a pleasant diversion which lifted the spirits of a grieving nation that had recently lost its president to assassination.

The first underground appearance of the "Sullivan" material was released in 1972, on the album *Renaissance Minstrels 1* (TMOQ 71025, LP). The source of the "Sullivan" songs came from the television videotape soundtrack of February 9, 16, and 23, 1964. The Trade Mark of Quality people performed extensive audio surgery on the *Sullivan* tracks, adding applause, edits and echo, to create a fake concert setting. In 1988, Living Legend Records in Europe released a CD named *Conquer America* which captures all of the 1964 and 1965 Sullivan performances in excellent sound quality.

The excitement and hysteria generated on Ed Sullivan's show by The Beatles when they first arrived in America was clearly another milestone in their career. The quartet represented the first popular British music group to break through commercially, in a then closed-knit U.S. music industry. Their success paved the way for an entire British invasion of music and other entertainment to follow in

Albums featuring The Beatles' February 1964 performances,
including "The Ed Sullivan Show"

the 1960s.

As he introduced The Beatles to a live television audience of approximately 73 million American viewers for the first time, Ed Sullivan aptly summed up the fever of Beatlemania that had swept New York upon their arrival. "Now yesterday and today, our theatre has been jammed with newspapermen and hundreds of photographers from all over the nation. And these veterans agree with me that the city never has witnessed the excitement stirred by these youngsters from Liverpool, who call themselves The Beatles. Now tonight you're going to twice be entertained by them. Right now and again in the second half of our show…Ladies and Gentlemen, The Beatles!" At this point, the din of screaming is so loud that a jet could have landed on the theatre and no one would have heard it. The Beatles performed "All My Loving," "Till There Was You," "She Loves You," and "I Want To Hold Your Hand" on that historic evening. Practically every American alive in 1964 (regardless of their age) claims to have seen this first ever U.S. performance of the "gear" guys from Liverpool.

In the fall of 1991, Apple Corps Ltd. and MPI Home Video released an extraordinary documentary of this time period entitled, *The Beatles: The First U.S. Visit* (Apple Corps/MPI, 6218, VHS/Laser Disc). The film chronicles the Beatles' arrival in America as well as the first Ed Sullivan performances. Today, this video release eclipses any comparable bootleg material. However, back in the early seventies, bootleggers had found a way to capitalize on the pleasant nostalgia of a war-torn generation of youth, by selling them an illegal piece of 1964 audio innocence.

1964
THE BEATLES IN CONCERT—HOLLYWOOD BOWL AND PHILADELPHIA

The early seventies witnessed the unauthorized release of numerous live Beatles concert recordings. Fans, collectors and music scholars welcomed this "new" and exciting material, despite the barely audible sound quality. The majority of The Beatles' concert recordings were audience tapes recorded among the throngs of screaming teens and journalists. Combining the less-than-ideal recording environment of a frantic Beatles show with primitive 1960s recording technology yielded some very noisy, yet important, performances. These performances documented the group's world tour repertoire during the years of 1964 through 1966. The tapes captured the essence of Beatlemania hysteria at its height— something that has never been reproduced to the same degree in the entertainment world since The Beatles stopped touring in 1966.

In July 1970, *Rolling Stone* magazine reviewed an early unidentified bootleg disc entitled simply *Beatles "Live"* (No Label, BE-1001-A/B, LP). Though critical of the manufacturers, reviewer Ed Ward was enthralled with the release. "This one's such a shoddy number that the people responsible didn't even bother putting the label on the record…all that is quite forgivable though…this is an immensely likeable album." This review exemplified the seventies phenomenon of instant acceptance of "new" underground Beatles releases combined with very low expectations of sound quality.

Live Concert At The Whiskey Flats (TMOQ-70418F, TMOQ-71007, OPD 67-2, CBM-1001, LP) was an early example of bootleggers simply not knowing the correct historical source of a tape and misleading consumers. For several years after its initial underground release, many fans believed the *Whiskey Flats* show had been recorded in Atlanta, Georgia. In fact, this show was actually recorded on September 2, 1964, at the Philadelphia Convention Center. As later generations of bootleggers reissued this show, they retained the incorrect title. The track listing is as follows:

Side One	*Side Two*
1. Twist And Shout	1. Can't Buy Me Love
2. You Can't Do That	2. If I Fell
3. All My Loving	3. I Want To Hold Your Hand
4. She Loves You	4. Boys
5. Things We Said Today	5. A Hard Day's Night
6. Roll Over Beethoven	6. Long Tall Sally

In 1993, Yellow Dog Records released the Philadelphia show on a double compact disc set of live shows called *The Ultimate Live Collection Vol. 1* (Yellow Dog, YD-038/39, 2CD). This disc contains the best sounding version of this typical set from the 1964 American leg of the world tour. *At The Hollywood Bowl* (TMOQ S-208, LP) was recorded August 23, 1964 at the Hollywood Bowl. This performance typified Beatlemania at its height of hysteria. The Beatles could hardly hear themselves above the droning din of screaming girls. Song line-ups, introductions, pacing and between-song patter had already fallen into a repetitive pattern for the group, by the summer of 1964. The continuous performance of the same basic show, day in and day out, was noticeable on these recordings. As live performers, the group was already starting to stagnate.

Portions of the 1964 show recorded at the Hollywood Bowl were later re-engineered and released commercially by Capitol Records in 1977. However, most Beatles scholars and collectors had obtained a bootleg copy of the 1964 show in complete, unedited form approximately five or six years before Capitol's official release. The Capitol Records release edited together the "best" portions of the 1964 and 1965 live performances at Hollywood Bowl. The bootleg version which captures the complete unedited 1964 show was a dub of Capitol's acetate recording of the show. This acetate, which years ago "walked out" of Capitol Records in the grips of a former employee, has changed hands among record collectors for nearly twenty years. In 1993, The Yellow Dog Company released *Hollywood Bowl Complete* (Yellow Dog, YD-034, CD) which contained the complete 1964 (mono) concert and for the first time, the complete 1965 (stereo) performance.

1965
THE BEATLES IN CONCERT—SHEA STADIUM

Another significant "lost" concert surfaced on bootleg in the early 1970s. This show documented the Beatles' historic outdoor performance at New York's Shea Stadium on August 15, 1965, before some 56,000 screaming fans. The performance served as a milestone in concert-going attendance and as a major cultural event for its time. The Shea concert bootleg was pilfered from a fifty minute film documentary soundtrack of the event.

The Beatles overdubbed some of the music for the film documentary in order to improve on their live performance. The group purportedly inserted the commercial studio recording of Ringo's "Act Naturally" for the original live version when preparing the film of this event.

One of the earliest known bootleg releases of the Shea Stadium show was entitled *Shea The Good Old Days* (CBM 2315, LP, 1972). Prior underground releases had come out, claiming to contain the *Shea* concert, with titles such as *Live at Shea 1964 1* and *Live at Shea 1964 2*. However, these bootlegs were actually extended play 7" records of the Beatles live at the Hollywood Bowl. Once again, the bootleggers were playing fast and loose with sloppy historical research. Reproduced below are the song titles from the Shea Stadium show and representative of the 1965 Beatles touring period:

Side One	Side Two
1. I'm Down	1. Can't Buy Me Love
2. Interview	2. Baby's In Black
3. Intro	3. A Hard Day's Night
4. Twist & Shout	4. I'm Down (repeat)
5. I Feel Fine	
6. Dizzy Miss Lizzy	
7. Ticket To Ride	

Live bootleg albums

1966
THE BEATLES IN CONCERT—TOKYO, JAPAN AND
SAN FRANCISCO, CALIFORNIA

The earliest release of the Tokyo, 1966 show appeared on two albums entitled *Tokyo '66* (CBM 1900, LP, 1974) and *On Stage in Japan—The 1966 Tour* (TAKRL 1900, LP, 1974). The source of *Tokyo '66* is the soundtrack to a television film of the event made in Japan on June 30, 1966; as a result, the sound quality is quite passable. The recording was the first of five performances by the group in Tokyo, made between June 30 and July 2, 1966. Though playing to ecstatic crowds, the Beatles sounded sluggish, hoarse and tired. At one point between songs, John Lennon mocks the Japanese fans with his gibberish version of their language. Surprisingly, the crowd roars its approval. Meanwhile, Paul McCartney, ever the "public relations" Beatle, thanks the crowd incessantly in their own language.

The June 30, 1966 performance has since been re-released underground a number of times under different titles and in different formats. Recent compact disc versions, such as the mistitled *Live In Japan 1964* (Document Records, DR-002, CD, 1987) have removed some of the crowd noise, improved the sound quality and have added another Beatles Tokyo show from July 2, 1966.

Reproduced below are the song titles from the Tokyo show which represent the group's 1966 repertoire:

Side One	*Side Two*
1. Rock 'n' Roll Music	1. Yesterday
2. She's A Woman	2. I Want To Be Your Man
3. If I Needed Someone	3. Nowhere Man
4. Daytripper	4. Paperback Writer
5. Baby's In Black	5. I'm Down
6. I Feel Fine	

Candlestick Park in San Francisco, California represented the passing of an era that will never return. To a stadium crowd of some twenty or thirty thousand fans, The Beatles played their last-ever rock concert. The group was fed up with living in hotels, flying in planes, running from fans, giving press conferences and singing the same songs every day. Beatles publicist Tony Barrow was asked by a knowing Paul McCartney, to preserve this last ever public concert with his tape recorder. Barrow's tape ran out before the show actually did, but managed to capture ten of the eleven tunes: "Rock And Roll Music," "She's A Woman," "If I Needed Someone," "Day Tripper," "Baby's In Black," "I Feel Fine," "Yesterday," "I Wanna Be Your Man," "Nowhere Man," and "Paperback Writer."

The final performance was uninspired, as the group hurried their show, due in part to the cold winds swirling through the park. John introduces a song in his usual flippant manner, yet perhaps also exhorting his fellow members to keep themselves together musically one last time…"Ah thank you. We'd like to carry on now, ah carry on together…at will, all together and all for one…with another number that used to be a single record back in ah…a long time ago…and this one's about the naughty lady called 'Day Tripper'."

Within just thirty short minutes, The Beatles were transformed from a touring ensemble to strictly a studio group. As the Italian company Bulldog Records described it on their compact disc *Candlestick Park—San Francisco—August 29, 1966* (Bulldog, BGCD-0016, CD, 1988), "No more desperate and shouting fans, no more teenagers praising at the airports, no more Beatlesmania. From that moment, only studio sessions." Bulldog further explains that they acquired the historic Tony Barrow tape at a London auction.

To collectors, scholars, and fans, these underground concert releases offered an opportunity to hear the progression (or in the opinion of some, the regression) of Beatles' stage performances during the worldwide tour years of 1964–1966. Listening to the performances today demonstrates the excitement and electricity that flowed through each live Beatles concert. It is perhaps the *only* way to explain the "mania" to younger generations who will never witness the phenomenon first hand. However, the shows collectively illustrate the disintegration of the Beatles as a live touring unit. In the sixties, there were no stage monitors which allowed the group to hear their voices or instruments above the ever-present noise of the screaming teenagers. Thus, out-of-tune vocals and instruments went uncorrected as the group ran through its live sets. The Beatles themselves were frustrated by the fact that they could no longer reproduce the sounds of their most recent studio records in the live medium. Nevertheless, these shows represent an unprecedented enthusiasm and an innocence that will not be soon forgotten. And once again bootleggers took credit for preserving an important piece of twentieth century musical history.

1967
THE PSYCHEDELIC ERA

Having placed touring behind them forever, The Beatles were finally free to spend more time in their favorite environment…the recording studio. The success achieved by the group at this point gave them the luxury of unlimited studio time and experimentation. The resulting work, *Sgt Pepper's Lonely Hearts Club Band*, stands as a cornerstone to the group's musical legacy.

"A Day In The Life" is perhaps the penultimate song of The Beatles' recording career. The song melded in equal parts the songwriting talents of John Lennon and Paul McCartney. On January 20, 1967, The Beatles recorded some early takes of the song. On take 5, John counts in, "Sugar plum fairy, sugar plum fairy," instead of a more conventional numeric count in. A single acoustic guitar starts off the song, followed by piano accompaniment and finally, John's haunting voice…"I heard the news today oh boy…"

The Beatles knew they wanted some sort of orchestral arrangement in the middle portion of the song, to divide John's part from Paul's. As a lonely piano marks rhythm for this space, Beatles' roadie Mal Evans dutifully counts off 24 bars to be filled in later. At the end of the count, Mal sets off an alarm clock to mark the end of the first passage. McCartney begins his first vocal attempt of his section in fine form. Yet, it is obvious he is still searching for the right feel to his portion of the song. Then Paul sings, "Made the bus in seconds flat / Made my way upstairs and had a smoke / and everybody smoked and I went into a dream (laughing)…oh shit!" Paul laughs as he realizes he's blown the lyrics on this take. John's part comes around again and his vocal performance soars to near perfect conclusion. This unreleased version ends with another bar count by Mal Evans and tumbles to a close without the familiar extended multiple piano chord of the finished version. This amazing alternate take first appeared in digital studio quality on the 1991 Yellow Dog release *Acetates*. The collection amassed a number of rare acetate recordings that had been sold at auction. This take of "A Day In The Life" not only demonstrated the behind-the-scenes, creative energy of The Beatles at work, but it also served to illustrate the genius of the Lennon/McCartney writing collaboration.

CHRISTMAS TIME (IS HERE AGAIN)

Sergeant Pepper was released in June of 1967 to worldwide popular and critical acclaim. With the holidays fast approaching, The Beatles entered the studio on November 28, 1967 to attempt something different. The obligation of another fan club record was looming, so the group decided to record a complete Christmas theme song. Unfortunately, they forgot to write some memorable lyrics for this song which has never seen a commercial release.

The song was "Christmas Time (Is Here Again)." On this date, the group recorded a full 6 minute 37 second version. John jokingly announces the intro as, "Take four hundred and forty-four." With that, Ringo leads off with a five-beat drum intro as Paul, George and John sing, "Christmas time is here again, Christmas time is here again." At the breaks, Paul sings a solo of "It ain't been

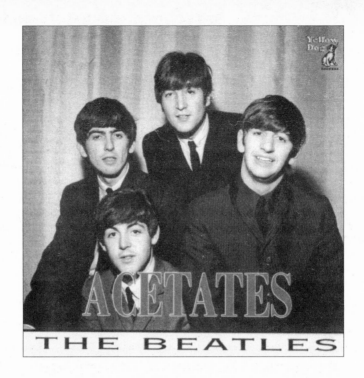

Sgt. Pepper's Lonely Hearts Club Band-*related bootlegs*

'round since you know when," and Ringo occasionally breaks in with, "O-U-T spells out!" This pattern repeats several times ad nauseum. The line up of guitar, bass, piano and drums churn out a repetitive rhythm and melody. At one point, Paul yells to the others over the music, what appears to be a self critique. "Lyrically, not the most convincing pop." This statement appears to loosen everyone up to add their own silly comments and noises. All in all, this musical frolic shows the foursome having fun together. The song has appeared on a number of underground releases, most notably on *Acetates*. A shorter version of the song (less than a minute in length) was prepared for release on the aborted 1985 EMI Records, *Sessions* album. Despite its shortcomings, the commercial release of this "lost" recording would probably guarantee annual radio airplay during the Christmas holidays.

1968
ON THE ROAD TO RISHIKESH, INDIA

In February of 1968, The Beatles and their wives/girlfriends took off on an adventure to Rishikesh, India to learn Transcendental Meditation from Maharishi Mahesh Yogi. Others, including Mike Love of The Beach Boys and Donovan came along for the spiritual "ride."

The amazing "Rishikesh Tape" recorded in February 1968 by an Italian TV crew preserved a musical jam session of The Beatles and friends while in India. This ten minute tape featured a fascinating aural snapshot of life within the Maharishi Yogi's camp during The Beatles' brief stay. Listeners are treated to The Beatles, Donovan and assorted friends singing their acoustic versions of "When The Saints Go Marching In," "You Are My Sunshine," "Blowing In The Wind," "Hare Krishna" and others. This behind-the-scenes glimpse of The Beatles and their celebrity friends relaxing in India offers a rare perspective on their brief respite away from the demands of Beatlemania. It also provides an interesting prelude to the May 1968, *White Album* demos, when placed into proper historical context. This time of spiritual regeneration yielded a barrel full of original songs written by Lennon, McCartney and Harrison. Thus, The Beatles decision to make one of rock music's first double albums. Though this tape, which ended up on a vinyl bootleg called *Nothing But Aging*, (Vigotone, VTLP-1968, LP, 1992) contained mostly cover tunes, three months after the return from India, it would yield a gold mine of original practice demos for an album which would simply be called, *The Beatles* (a.k.a. *The White Album*).

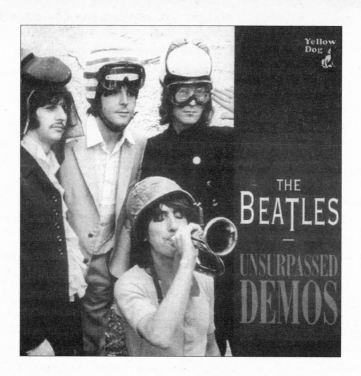

The White Album *demos*

THE WHITE ALBUM DEMOS

Upon their return from India, The Beatles were anxious to get their newly written songs and rough arrangements down on tape. So on May 20, 1968, the group met at George Harrison's Esher, Kinfauns, England home to record a cache of rehearsal demos for their upcoming album titled *The Beatles*, (better known as *The White Album*). *Unsurpassed Demos* (YD-008, CD) released on Yellow Dog Records in 1991, contained many of these mostly acoustic guitar-based demos. Listeners who obtained this rare disc were amazed to hear The Beatles sitting around, singing primitive, pre-studio arrangements of such songs as "Back In The U.S.S.R.," "Piggies," "Revolution," "Cry Baby Cry," "The Continuing Story of Bungalow Bill," "Sexy Sadie," "Yer Blues" and many more.

Two legendary "lost" songs recorded during the session were released for the first time anywhere on the Yellow Dog album. The two songs entitled "Circles" and "Sour Milk Sea" (written by George Harrison) never surfaced on a proper Beatles' album. However, "Sour Milk Sea" was subsequently recorded by Apple recording artist Jackie Lomax and produced by Harrison.

For years after the Beatles' break-up, rumors of an unreleased song called "Colliding Circles" circulated among collectors and music historians. In fact, the demo "Circles" from these sessions was probably the source for this speculation. The song begins with a very somber dirge-like organ solo, leading up to composer George Harrison's mystical introduction. The introspective spiritual nature of the lyrics reflected the very profound and lasting influence that Eastern religion and ideology would have on George for years to come. He sings, "Life goes and life goes / as we go 'round and 'round in circles / He who knows does not speak / he who speaks does no not know / As I go 'round in circles." None of the other Beatles appear to be playing or singing on the song, but instead, are heard chatting casually in the background as the song winds down with a meandering organ solo that finally loses steam on a long whole note. The eerie, unfinished tune which lasts for 2 minutes 16 seconds will probably never see a release in this form, due to the lack of finished lyrics and a musical bridge.

By contrast, the other unreleased Beatles tune, "Sour Milk Sea," sounds very much like a rehearsed demo that easily could have fit on The Beatles' *White Album*. As George begins his count-in to the song, "Ah one, two, three, four...," it appears as if Paul says, "I'm tired of..." The impression given is that The Beatles have been performing a number of takes prior to this one that survives on the tape. We can hear John's sluggish rhythm guitar, Paul's occasional bass, George's lead and Ringo on bongo drums. Tambourine and maracas can also be heard throughout, playing slightly off the beat. Despite George's enthusiasm for the song, it sounds like the others are not quite sure of the song's potential for the upcoming album. This may explain why it was ultimately given to Jackie Lomax.

Four songs from this session would not be formally released until after the groups' break up. John, who performed "Jealous Guy" on his *Imagine* album, first recorded an early version here called "Child of Nature." Paul would later include the song "Junk" on his first solo effort *McCartney*, but seemed to be using the name "Jubilee" at the time of this session. George returned to record improved, finished versions of "Not Guilty" and "Circles" for subsequent solo albums in the late 1970s.

1969
THE BEATLES GET BACK...TO TORONTO

Though *Abbey Road* was the last album recorded by the group, The Beatles' final official release was *Let It Be* (Apple, AR-34001, LP), issued on May 18, 1970. With the exception of *Let It Be, The Beatles At The Hollywood Bowl* (Capitol, SMAS-11638, LP, 1977) and the grey area release, *The Beatles Live! At The Star Club In Hamburg, Germany: 1962* (Lingasong/Atlantic LS-2-7001, LP, 1977), The Beatles did not release any other "new" product in the 1970s. This huge gap in the market place for such an insatiable, large, and loyal record-buying audience encouraged the emerging underground record business—all in the name of servicing the needs of Fab Four aficionados.

The first releases of "authentic" Beatle bootlegs seemed to come from the identical musical tape source, namely the ill-fated *Get Back* rehearsal sessions recorded in 1969. The *Get Back* sessions began as filmed rehearsals in Twickenham Studios, England at the beginning of January 1969. They were largely impromptu, unstructured rehearsals. The sessions consisted of numerous hours of tape that memorialize the group jamming, joking and singing mostly rock and roll standards recalled from their youth. The project would not be released in final form until more than a year later on the eve of the group's official break-up. The title of the album and film evolved into the now familiar *Let It Be*. On the eve of the commercial album release in May 1970, George Harrison summed up the project for the news media: "The whole album you see, is very spontaneous because all we were doing was rehearsing...you know, however we felt at the time. So there's little bits and pieces."

During the *Get Back* rehearsals, The Beatles became increasingly disillusioned with the project. However, on March 4, 1969, John and Paul asked their uncredited sound producer Glyn Johns to review the many hours of *Get Back* tapes and

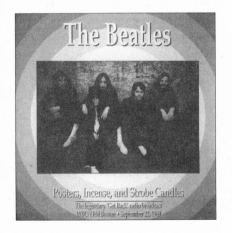

Get Back *bootlegs*

assemble an album from them. It appears that Johns ultimately prepared three mixes (over the course of a year) for the proposed album. They are referred to here as: 1) rough mix; 2) Get Back mix #1; and 3) Get Back mix #2.

Johns, as instructed, began preparing an early *unofficial* rough mix (undocumented in EMI company records and hereafter referred to as "rough mix") sometime between March 4, 1969 and May 28, 1969. During this period, Johns mixed the following song titles:

1. Get Back (two versions)
2. Teddy Boy
3. Two Of Us (two versions)
4. Dig A Pony
5. I've Got A Feeling (two versions)
6. The Long And Winding Road (three versions)
7. Let It Be (two versions)
8. Rocker
9. Save The Last Dance For Me
10. Don't Let Me Down
11. For You Blue
12. The Walk
13. Lady Madonna
14. Dig It (two versions)
15. Maggie May
16. *Medley*: Shake, Rattle and Roll / Kansas City / Miss Ann / You Really Got A Hold On Me

On or about March 10, 1969, Glynn Johns reportedly gave a working draft (acetate) of the rough mix for *Get Back* to the four Beatles to assess their reactions. The group rejected this rough mix. Johns had definite recall of making this rough mix at the request of the Beatles, in the book, *The Record Producers* (by John Tobler and Stuart Grundy, St. Martin's Press, 1983). The acetate contained eleven songs from the rough mix list above, namely:

1. Get Back
2. Teddy Boy
3. Two Of Us
4. Dig A Pony
5. I've Got A Feeling
6. The Long And Winding Road
7. Let It Be
8. Don't Let Me Down
9. For You Blue
10. Get Back (second version)
11. The Walk

According to Mark Lewisohn (*The Complete Beatles Chronicle*, Harmony Books, 1992), two documented *official*, banded album master tapes were subsequently completed by Johns on the *Get Back* material. The first one was delivered to the group on May 28, 1969 (hereafter "Get Back mix #1") and the second one was presented on January 5, 1970 (hereafter "Get Back mix #2"). These two versions of the ill-fated *Get Back* project were also rejected by The Beatles, who later hired legendary producer Phil Spector to finish the project.

The first Beatles' bootlegs came from Glyn Johns' rough mix of the *Get Back* sessions. There has been a great deal of speculation concerning how this March 1969 acetate fell into the hands of record bootleggers. Some have suggested that the acetate (or a tape copy) was given to a journalist by John Lennon on September 13, 1969, when he was in Toronto to perform at the Live Peace In Toronto Festival. The reporter, in turn, allegedly gave it to a New York disc jockey for subsequent airplay. The tape of the acetate was also reportedly aired by a number of other stations in New York and in St. Louis. Radio stations (which began rapidly trading the tape between cities) referred to it as an "official, advance copy" of the forthcoming Beatles' album *Get Back*. In fact, there was never an official, advance copy of the album released to radio stations anywhere.

However, John himself seems to contradict the "Lennon as unintentional bootleg source" theory. He was openly critical of the *Get Back* bootleg material shortly after The Beatles' breakup. In June of 1971, a New York disc jockey asked Lennon about the exciting rumor that some twelve hours of unreleased *Get Back* rehearsals lay in the vaults. Lennon shot back the following angry response:

> Well let's hear it…If anybody listens to the bootleg version which was pre-Spector…and listens to the version Spector did, they would shut up. If you really want to know the difference between what…The tapes are so lousy and so bad, that none of us (Beatles) would go near them to touch them. They'd been laying around for six months. None of us could face remixing them. It was the only album like that. It was terrifying! Spector did a fantastic job on them.

Given that the timing of this quote (June 1971) was subsequent to the release of the *Get Back* bootleg, one might logically conclude that Lennon would not have supplied an acetate or test pressing of the "rough" version to a journalist if he disliked it so. On the other hand, Lennon and McCartney were airing out dirty laundry with each other in 1971. McCartney had been openly critical of Spector's production on the finished *Let It Be* album, especially on Paul's song "The Long and Winding Road." In his December 1970 sworn legal affidavit to dissolve The Beatles partnership, Paul stated:

> I found that in the recording of my song "The Long and Winding Road"
> Spector had not only 'mixed' the recording, but had added strings, voices,
> horns and drums, and had changed the recording of my other songs con-
> siderably…and I regarded this as an intolerable interference with my work.

In as much as John Lennon was using Phil Spector as his producer in 1971
(for the upcoming *Imagine* album), he may have taken this opportunity to defend
Spector's remixing on the *Get Back* tapes and contradict McCartney at the same
time. Anyone who has followed Lennon's interviews over the course of his career
is aware of his penchant for changing his opinions on a given subject as often as
most of us change clothes. So we leave it up to the reader to discern whether
John Lennon was unknowingly responsible for the leak that led to one of the first
Beatles bootleg records.

While the details regarding the exact source remain vague, the acetate (or
taped copies) did find its way into radio station studios, and was broadcast to
bootleggers' waiting tape recorders as early as September 1969. *Kum Back* (Kum
Back #1, WCF, LP, 1969) appears to have been the first bootleg to release the
eleven tracks, all apparently taken from the radio broadcast of the rough mix
acetate. The album does not include any of the disc jockey's comments, interviews or commercials. *Kum Back* is a monaural recording and all of the songs
appear to have been speeded up. *Get Back To Toronto* (IPF-1, LP, 1969) and other
early bootleg titles contain several of the eleven songs broadcast from the first *Get
Back* acetate. The *Get Back To Toronto* album title, chosen by bootleggers, clev-
erly attempts to implicate the Toronto/Lennon connection as the source for the
bootleg. *Get Back To Toronto* contains nine of the eleven songs from the original
radio broadcasts, omitting "The Long And Winding Road" and "Get Back" (second version).

Similarly, Glyn Johns' mixing sessions of Spring 1969 are the source of the
oldies medley listed above, heard on several bootlegs, including *Celluloid Rock*
(Yellow Dog, YD-006, CD, 1991). Like many other compact disc bootlegs,
Celluloid Rock offers several tracks from the mixing sessions, but in improved
sound quality.

The album *Posters, Incense, and Strobe Candles* (Vigotone, VIGO-109, CD,
1993) is also taken from the early broadcast of the Johns rough mix acetate. The
Posters bootleg is recorded from an actual, documented broadcast purporting to
be made from a Boston radio station (WBCN-FM), on September 22, 1969.
This disc contains all eleven songs, but offers the interesting perspective of the
actual disc jockey broadcasting the recording that day! His observations, and the
actual commercials from that time period, provide a fascinating historical frame-

work for the *Get Back* acetate. To quote the bootlegger's liner notes, "This is an artifact of an era that won't come again."

The most interesting highlight of the rough mix bootlegs was the fact that the Beatles could be heard laughing and enjoying each others' company. Media reports had described the recording sessions as acrimonious, yet one can hear the laughs first hand as the Fab Four run through their material. On the song "For You Blue," George Harrison begins to strum the opening chords, only to get his fingers tangled and breakdown giggling. He takes a drink and starts over without a snag. Lennon and McCartney perform a complete run through of the song "Dig A Pony" with the laughs and giggles left in. The jocularity continues with the song "I've Got A Feeling." When Paul sings the line, "I've got a feeling, it keeps me on my toes...," John humorously shouts out, "On your what?" This counterpoint is clearly an effort by Lennon to crack up his partner. The listener is also treated to an unreleased Beatles version of "Teddy Boy" (which was later redone by McCartney and released on his first solo album) and an unreleased blues number called "The Walk," originally recorded by Jimmy McCracklin.

As for the other two rejected mixes from the 1969 sessions, Get Back mix #1 (May 28, 1969) has appeared on bootleg under a number of titles, but most notably on *Get Back with Don't Let Me Down and 9 Other Songs* (bogus "Apple" PCS 7080-LP, 1989, bogus "EMI/Parlophone" CDP 7 480032-CD, 1988), and *Get Back with Let It Be and 11 Other Songs* (bogus "Apple," UNK #, LP, 1988). The song line-up prepared by Johns ran as follows:

1. The One After 909
2. Rocker
3. Save The Last Dance For Me
4. Don't Let Me Down
5. Dig A Pony
6. I've Got A Feeling
7. Get Back
8. For You Blue
9. Teddy Boy
10. Two Of Us
11. Maggie May
12. Dig It
13. Let It Be
14. The Long And Winding Road
15. Get Back (Reprise)

The music contained in Get Back mix #1 (May 28, 1969), was also reportedly leaked to U.S. radio stations in the fall of 1969, and was aired as an alleged "advance promotional disc" entitled *Get Back*. Once again, no promotional copies of the album were ever officially released in this form. The May 28, 1969 Glyn Johns mix was most recently bootlegged in 1992, on the CD *Get Back and 22 Other Songs* (Yellow Dog, YD-014, CD, 1992).

The music found on Get Back mix #2 (January 5, 1970) has apparently never been bootlegged. This may be due to the similarity of its song titles to Get Back mix #1. Get Back mix #2 appears to contain the same mixes as Get Back mix #1, sans the "Teddy Boy" title, but with the songs, "I Me Mine" and "Across The Universe" added.

Kum Back and *Get Back To Toronto* were important early underground releases, significant in that they gave fans their very first opportunity to hear raw unfinished Beatles studio music. The initial excitement in hearing idle studio chatter by the Beatles in their creative playground was electrifying! Historically, the album provided a brief document of the Beatles' second-to-last album project. The listening experience clearly outweighed the mediocre sound quality of the early pressings and hooked many Beatles fans into collecting bootlegs.

The sales estimates of *Kum Back* and *Get Back To Toronto* are difficult to calculate. However, it is likely that these discs and their knock-offs collectively sold between 7,500 and 15,000 copies, based upon interviews with early bootleggers. This marketing success encouraged underground record robbers to continue searching the musical seas for other lost doubloons. *Kum Back* and *Get Back To Toronto's* success spawned a significant number of copy-cat bootlegs containing nearly identical music, but with different album titles and graphics. This would not be the last time that music scholars and collectors would be duped into purchasing the same material more than once. This "name game" was merely another marketing gimmick that bootleg purveyors employed to stretch the maximum profit out of a particularly popular release.

SWEET APPLE TRAX

Probably the most notorious and revealing Beatles' bootleg to surface in the 1970s was the two-volume sets entitled, *Sweet Apple Trax Volume One* (Instant Analysis/CBM WEC-4182, 2LP) and *Sweet Apple Trax Volume Two* (Instant Analysis/CBM WEC-4181, 2LP). Released in 1973, these albums chronicled some of The Beatles' January 1969 *Get Back* rehearsals at London's Twickenham Studios.

Sweet Apple Trax elevated Beatles' bootleg collecting from a mere hobby to a

Sweet Apple Trax bootlegs

serious study of songwriting and musical creativity. The albums revealed for the first time continuous periods of musical creation through unfinished takes, experimental jams, and between-song discussions by the band. These recordings had superior sound quality to past bootlegs, coming from the sync soundtrack of the film reels unused in the *Let It Be* film.

Some of the highlights include, Paul McCartney teaching the song "Let It Be" to the band. He works them in schoolteacher fashion, explaining and singing the bass line riffs to John. "It's that easy, you'll get it," he says. Later he is heard working out harmonies to sing with George and John on this Grammy-nominated classic. Lennon is heard tossing out a satirical cover of "House Of The Rising Sun," made famous by The Animals. The album also features an unreleased, free-form extended Lennon-McCartney ad-lib jam of a song the bootleggers called, "Commonwealth/White Power Promenade." The jam illustrates Lennon's quick wit as he offers a line for Paul to use during the song. "When you get to Commonwealth, you're much to common for me." Paul laughs and quickly works the line into the song. This spontaneous collaboration, on a throwaway song, shows that at a point late in their career, the Fab Four still had fun working together.

Volumes One and Two of *Sweet Apple Trax* were released on Instant Analysis, a subsidiary of the Contra Band Music (CBM) label. CBM obtained the tapes in 1973 from their regular supplier of rare musical material, who was also a mail-order bootleg retailer at the time. The authors refer to him as "Nurk Twin." Mr. Twin purchased a sub-master tape on a seven-inch reel (3.75 ips, Radio Shack tape), which contained approximately eighty-eight minutes of January 1969, rehearsals. The tape was obtained from an ex-Apple Corps, Ltd. employee who sold it to an American collector. Nurk Twin subsequently bought the tape from the collector for $300.

Nurk Twin traded this historic tape to CBM in exchange for approximately three hundred copies of the two album sets to be released. This enabled Mr. Twin to retail the albums through his own mail-order catalog at a substantial profit.

CBM initially pressed 5,000 copies of each volume onto vinyl in Philadelphia, Pennsylvania. Many of the copies were shipped to the more lucrative and less risky European underground market. According to Twin, a well known TV/mail-order record company of the 1970s printed the original album covers for CBM. The total raw cost to produce one of these collectibles was $0.90 in 1973. The albums retailed at $3.00 each.

The *Sweet Apple Trax* albums quickly sold out and thousands more were pressed. Many rival bootleggers at the time produced their own knock-off version of these tapes, some under the same title and some with new and different titles, such as *Hahst Az Son, Get Back Session, Get Back Sessions One And Two* and many, many more.

The best selling Beatles bootleg of the early eighties was *The Beatles Black Album*. This three-record set, designed and produced in southern California, was a compilation of "Get Back" era rehearsals recorded in excellent sounding mono. The album jacket was a clever takeoff of the Beatles' *White Album*. It came packaged with raised lettering on an all black cover, song titles and photos listed on the inside, and even included a full-color collage poster similar to that of the *White Album*, but featuring different photos of the quartet. The *Black Album* copied audio material from previously bootlegged albums (*Sweet Apple Trax Vol. 1 & 2, Twickenham Jams* and *Watching Rainbows*) and was itself bootlegged a number of times. Sales figures for the album reportedly placed U.S. purchases at the 3,000 unit plateau.

Ultimately, the largest collection of Beatles' *Get Back* rehearsal sessions assembled in one place was released by bootleggers in 1987 on an 11-LP box set called *Get Back Journals* (TMOQ, 2R-78, 11-LP, 1987). An upgraded CD version of this box set was released by the West Coast's Vigotone label in the fall of 1993. The Vigotone set contained eight discs. The promotional card on the front of the 35mm film box which held the discs boasted, "Over 9 hours of remastered & chronologically resequenced *Get Back* rehearsals from original source tapes!" Because the boxed set contained hours of unstructured rehearsals and trivial discussions, it was not exactly a pleasure to listen to by the casual fan. However, to the music scholar, it was a gold mine of musical history and information. Though these were not proper studio recordings, the group was heard performing with a more simple, stripped-down sound, without the overdubs and orchestration of previous albums. Here was the world's most popular group writing, reading, arguing, quitting, singing, playing and laughing together. At one point, the group, along with their movie director Michael Lindsey-Hogg, band assistant Mal Evans, Yoko Ono and guest Peter Sellers, pull up chairs inside the dark, cavernous Twickenham sound stage to chat. Lennon decides to act out the part of a silly television moderator. He starts by introducing and interviewing Ringo and poking fun at his (Lennon's) own home:

LENNON: "Now we're going on to a rather different group, ah generation gap, and that's Tumble Starker who's sitting here. Now, what do you think about mock tudor shit-houses in Weybridge and places like that?"
STARR: "Well I don't mind them being in Weybridge, it's just when they try and

put them in London, I think they get in the way of all the traffic."

LENNON: "You're so right. As you said yesterday, 'Neither your ass nor your elbow.' I'll never forget it. (laughs)."

This recorded tome also served as perhaps the best first-hand record of the group's diversity. The group was clearly growing up and apart, with new and separate interests.

For collectors who had not tired of the seemingly endless hours of available *Let It Be* rehearsals, Blue Kangaroo produced a first-class series of CDs in 1992. The *'69 Rehearsals* (BK-6901-03, 3 CD volumes) and Yellow Dog's, *The Complete Rooftop Concert* (YD-015, CD) and *Get Back and 22 Other Songs* (YD-014, CD) all boasted excellent sound quality and hitherto unreleased material. The *Get Back...* disc brought to light John Lennon's version of Paul's first teenage composition, "I Lost My Little Girl" and the humorous "Fancy Me Chances."

"I Lost My Little Girl" was written by a very young Paul in 1956. The Beatles had never formally recorded the song. Perhaps because McCartney had never finished off the simplistic lyrics. The song's principal character (a young teen) relates in the first person, how he "woke up late this morning." His head is "in a whirl" which probably describes a hangover. It is only at this point that the character realizes that, "I'd lost my little girl." However, on this January 1969 version, we hear John Lennon singing lead. It's a very funny send-up of the song as John takes a few "indecent" liberties with Paul's lyrics. At the start of this tape we hear Paul prompting Lennon, reminding him of the song's lyrics. Then John takes off on his own as he sings, "It was only then I realized / it came to me all of a sudden / I'd lost my little girl / I think the police had taken her away due to her inconvenience / something to do about interstate nude..." Just another unreleased example of Lennon and McCartney at play in the studio, reminiscing about a younger more innocent time. The rehearsals from the *Get Back* project served as evidence that the songwriting team of Lennon/McCartney could still work well together, despite all of the outside pressures at this late point in their career.

European black market purveyors reportedly have an additional 30-plus hours of tape from the *Let It Be* film sessions, so collectors and music scholars may see many more Beatles bootlegs from this time period (January 1969) in the future.

FEBRUARY 1969-JULY 1969
THE ABBEY ROAD SESSIONS

February 22, 1969, could be considered the beginning of the end for The Beatles as a recording group. This was the first day that proper recording began for the *Abbey Road* album, which would be their last official group effort.

More than a decade later, in 1979, collectors were allowed to hear the first bootleg of *Abbey Road* outtakes aptly titled by the studio's address, *No. 3 Abbey Road NW8* (Audifon, AR-8-69, LP). This bootleg was greeted with great anticipation by music scholars and collectors, as it represented "new" illicit material sourced from the group's final studio recording sessions. Side one offered listeners alternate or stripped down versions of "Golden Slumbers/Carry That Weight," "Her Majesty," "You Never Give Me Your Money," "Octopus' Garden," "Maxwell's Silver Hammer," "Oh! Darling," and "Something." The songs were notable for some of their "rough" edges which were edited off the commercial release of *Abbey Road*. For example, "You Never Give Me Your Money" and "Something" both featured interesting and previously unheard extended jams tacked on at the end of each song. "Oh! Darling" featured a pre-final take of Paul McCartney's sweet sounding lead vocal *prior* to the screaming, raw blues version presented on the finished album. Finally, "Her Majesty" presented the song's last chord intact, which was cut off the official *Abbey Road*.

In 1991, Yellow Dog Records reissued the *Abbey Road* bootleg song material in upgraded quality on a CD entitled *Unsurpassed Masters 5* (YD-005, CD). Additionally, the disc included an early mix of the song medley found on side two of the *Abbey Road*. Described as "A Huge Medley (Parts 1 and 2)" by the bootleggers, it provides the listener with some alternate vocals, a different song order and an instrumental version of the song, "The End."

The *Abbey Road* session outtakes were significant to fans, scholars and collectors. The songs were yet more "new" archive discoveries which people could use to study the musical progress, style, and taste of the late period Beatles. Taken together with the early 1960s Beatles' rehearsals and the Decca Auditions, these bootlegs represented new pieces to the puzzle documenting the rise and fall of the Beatles as a group. The *Decca* tapes are some of the earliest, embryonic Beatles recordings available, while the *Abbey Road* sessions are the final, most polished recordings made prior to their break up.

THE RAREST BOOTLEG COLLECTIONS

In 1984, a landmark underground album entitled *Live At Abbey Road Studios* (4000 Holes, ARS 2 9083, 2LP) was released as a result of an audio-visual tour of EMI's Abbey Road Studios presented during the summer of 1983. The two-record set was packaged to look like a record from the Mobile Fidelity Sound Lab, displaying session information on a reel-to-reel tape.

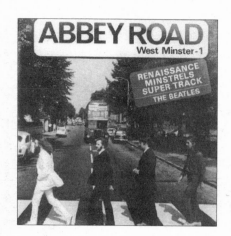

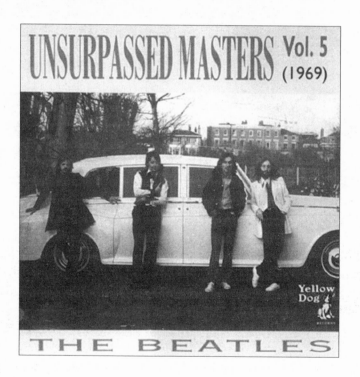

Abbey Road *bootlegs*

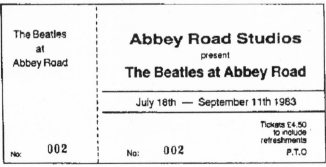

The groundbreaking Live At Abbey Road Studios *album with ticket*

Though security was tight for the studio tour, a couple of enterprising people were able to smuggle in a recorder to tape the show. This bootleg captured the entire studio tour (including outtakes, unreleased songs and narration) and gave many collectors their first opportunity to hear a small portion of what EMI and The Beatles had hidden away in their vaults for years. In fact, this is one of only two times that EMI has ever permitted the public performance of outtakes and alternate takes of The Beatles! The other occasion was for the 1992 film documentary which aired on the Disney Channel (in the U.S.) entitled, "The Making of Sgt. Pepper," which has since been bootlegged as well.

Live At Abbey Road Studios featured recordings of songs that were not presented in their entirety while others combined the music with over-dubbed narration. Highlights of this set included a raging vocal performance by John Lennon on the outtake song "Leave My Kitten Alone." Recorded on August 14, 1964, Lennon's voice is filled with raw energy on this tune, which would have made a great closer for The Beatles' live shows. Equally stunning is George Harrison's solo acoustic take of "While My Guitar Gently Weeps." The hauntingly beautiful performance by Harrison stands in stark contrast to the loud, electric performance of the same song (featuring Eric Clapton on guest lead guitar) officially released on *The Beatles (White Album)*. The extensive bootlegged set was eagerly received by collectors.

Side A	*Side C*
Love Me Do	Norwegian Wood
How Do You Do It	I'm Looking Through You
I Saw Her Standing There	Paperback Writer
Twist And Shout	Rain
	Penny Lane
Side B	Strawberry Fields Forever
The One After 909	
Don't Bother Me	*Side D*
A Hard Day's Night	A Day In The Life
Leave My Kitten Alone	Hello Goodbye
I'm A Loser	Lady Madonna
She's A Woman	Hey Jude
Ticket To Ride	While My Guitar Gently Weeps
Help!	Because

This release was merely the tip of the iceberg for the vast amount of unreleased Beatles' recordings that would start to surface in the middle 1980s.

THE LANDMARK SESSIONS ALBUM

In the mid-eighties, a few decent sounding Beatles bootlegs appeared on the black market containing improved quality recordings of previously bootlegged songs. There were also some bootleg compilations containing a handful of "new" songs collected from a variety of sources. Although these albums contained a few musical discoveries, with full-color professional packaging, they were just the harbingers of what would become the landmark release of 1980s Beatles bootlegs—*Sessions*.

Sometime in 1984, EMI executives asked the late John Barrett (a noted musicologist) to sift through their vaults for the purpose of finding an album's worth of material worthy of becoming a Beatles album of true rarities. This Barrett did. The album was entitled *Sessions* with a planned release in 1985. There is little doubt the album would have achieved platinum record award status had it not been vetoed by the Beatles. At the time, the Beatles and Yoko Ono (Executrix of the Estate of John Lennon) were still embroiled in lawsuits with their record company over royalties, which may have been the cause of the album's release being vetoed. (The official label copy for the aborted *Sessions* is illustrated on the following page).

Test pressings were made and a cover was designed for *Sessions*—however, after the album was scrapped, these pressings were supposed to have been destroyed. The same was thought to be true for the accompanying single sleeve, which was to feature the unreleased rocker, "Leave My Kitten Alone" and an alternate take of the song "Ob-La-Di, Ob-La-Da." They obviously were not destroyed, as bootlegs of the album soon appeared on store shelves, perfect to the last detail. Even the liner notes were copied, stating, "This is the Beatles album that millions of fans have been waiting for…an entirely new collection of previously unreleased originals and some alternate versions of familiar tunes." The first issue of the bootleg was aptly titled *Sessions* (bogus EMI, 064-2402701, LP). Thus, what would have been an instant hit record album for EMI, became instead EMI's greatest non-release—and the bootleggers' greatest success! It should be noted here that in 1992, both the British and American media reported that there might be a *Sessions*-type commercial release coming sometime in the near future. Emphatic denials and rumored release dates were reported with great regularity, yet there has been no such album officially released as of the publication of this book.

The label copy, illustrated here for the first time, indicates Geoff Emerick (who engineered several original Beatles' albums) was assigned the task of remixing the songs on the unfinished *Sessions*. Several of the songs are especially

2?3-24?2?02

A	SDE	1	TYPE	LP/MC	CHANNELS	5	RPM	33		©

TITLE, COMPOSER, AUTHOR, ARRANGER, PERFORMERS

Sessions

	TIME MIN	SEC	CATALOGUE NO	SOURCE MATRIX NO
1. Come And Get It (Paul McCartney)	2	26		
2. Leave My Kitten Alone (Turner/McDougall)	2	54		
3. Not Guilty (Harrison)	3	17		
4. I'm Looking Through You (Lennon/McCartney)	2	52		
5. What's The New Mary Jane? (Lennon/McCartney)	5	59		

THE BEATLES

(p) 1985 Original Sound Recordings made by EMI-Records Ltd.
Original Recordings produced by George Martin
Re-mixes produced by Geoff Emerick

PUBLISHER 1,4,5. Northern Songs-2.MPA Music Ltd.-3.Ganga B.V.

IPM CODE **700** CODE OF ORIGIN

LANGUAGE	English	PERFORM. DETAILS		MUSIC CLASS **430**
RECORD. PLACE		RECORD. DATE		TYPE OF REPERTOIRE
DATE OF TAPE APPROVAL	PRODUCER	BALANCE ENGINEER		☐ LOCAL ☒ GROUP
				☐ LICENSED ☐ THIRD PARTY

CAT NO	064-2402701 7?? 2402701	TRACK ???	PARLOPHONE	(1C) ?7??	(P)

B	SIDE	2	TYPE	LP/MC	CHANNELS	S	RPM	33		©

TITLE, COMPOSER, AUTHOR, ARRANGER, PERFORMERS

Sessions

	TIME MIN	SEC	CATALOGUE NO	SOURCE MATRIX NO
x 1. How Do You Do It? (Mitch Murray)	1	55		
x 2. Besame Mucho (Velasquez/Skylar)	2	33		
3. One After 909 (Lennon/McCartney)	2	53		
4. If You're Got Troubles (Lennon/McCartney)	2	21		
x 5. That Means A Lot (Lennon/McCartney)	2	25		
6. While My Guitar Gently Weeps (Harrison)	3	21		
7. Mailman Blues (A.Price)	1	50		
+ 8. Christmas Time (Is Here Again) (Lennon/McCartney/ Harrison/Starkey)	1	08		

THE BEATLES   ← MONO
(p) 1985 Original Sound Recordings made by EMI-Records Ltd.
except + (p) 1967 Original Sound Recordings by EMI-Records Ltd.
Original Recordings produced by George Martin   Re-mixes produced by Geoff Emerick
PUBLISHER 1.Vic James Music-2.Southern Music-3,4,5,8.Northern Songs-
6.Harrisongs Ltd.-7.ATV Music Ltd.

IPM CODE **700** CODE OF ORIGIN

LANGUAGE	English	PERFORM. DETAILS		MUSIC CLASS **430**
RECORD PLACE		RECORD DATE		TYPE OF REPERTOIRE
DATE OF TAPE APPROVAL	PRODUCER	BALANCE ENGINEER		☐ LOCAL ☒ GROUP
				☐ LICENSED ☐ THIRD PARTY

REMARKS MCS : EMI HOLLAND	GATEFOLD + SPECIAL INNERBAG	MUSIC BOX TITLE SUFS	COPYRIGHT ☐ FREE ☐
		SHEETS	☐ GEMA ☒ BIEM ☒ STEMRA

AVAILABLE FOR REPRODUCTION FOR ALL COUNTRIES	DEPARTMENT A&R Holland	DATE 14-12-1984	NAME AND SIGNATURE Hans van Exter

Label copy for the aborted Sessions

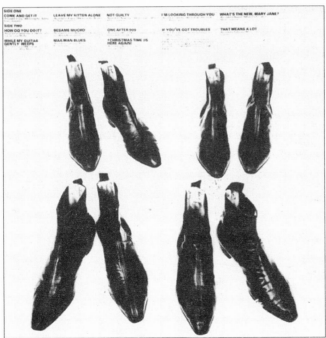

Front and back cover of the landmark Sessions *album*

interesting. The first is "Come And Get It," which was a huge hit for the Apple band Badfinger. On *Sessions*, we are able to hear Paul McCartney's demo of the song, used as a guide to the Badfinger band for arrangement purposes. Paul would produce Badfinger's nearly identical version a week later. Everything from the vocal phrasing, guitar and piano parts, to the drums sounded like a carbon copy of Paul's demo version. It is no wonder that music critics of the time felt that Badfinger was merely a clone of the Beatles.

Another rarity featured Paul again on vocals with the Beatles. "That Means A Lot," recorded in early 1965, was never officially released. However, it featured an amazing "scream" vocal by Paul at the song's climax, when he yells, "Can't you see, yea…ahhhhh!"

There are also a couple of songs on *Sessions* that should never have been released, *even* by the bootleggers. One such case was Ringo's rendition of "If You've Got Troubles." This Lennon/McCartney throwaway features a frustrated Ringo trying to make sense of a poor melody and terrible lyrics. During the song's instrumental break, a flustered Ringo yells out, "Rock on, anybody!"

Another reject that should stay tucked in the studio vaults is John Lennon's "What's The New Mary Jane?" (recorded on August 14, 1968). This piece was an experimental noodling, typical of Lennon and wife Yoko Ono's free-form style of the period. The version on *Sessions* was edited and remixed by EMI to present the song in a more musical framework. Alas, this version is merely an abbreviated version of the much longer (over six minutes) opus featuring John, Yoko and George Harrison singing, talking, screaming, playing and making noises. It stands alone as the worst song recorded and officially credited to The Beatles. In fact, The Beatles as a group purportedly vetoed John's desire to release the song as a Beatles' single. Lennon, at one point, considered releasing the song under the name Plastic Ono Band, but that plan was scrapped as well. All for good reason, as "Mary Jane" was really only a self indulgent musical joke.

Three years after the *Sessions* album of 1985, there emerged yet another *Sessions* (bogus Parlophone/EMI, CDP 7480012, CD)—this time on compact disc. This *Sessions* album has the distinction of being the *first* Beatles bootleg to ever appear on compact disc. And although it shared the title with the original album, not all of the songs included were the same as on the original. Yet it, too, is a collectible release due to its distinction as the first black market Beatles CD.

ULTRA RARE TRAX: A BEATLES UNDERGROUND RENAISSANCE ON COMPACT DISC

The popularity of compact discs had an interesting effect on collectors of rare tape recordings. It brought hundreds of hitherto-unreleased tapes out of the closet and into the black market underground. A rebirth of Beatles bootlegs occurred in late 1988 with the appearance of *Ultra Rare Trax Volume I & II* (The Swingin' Pig, TSP-CD-001, TSP-CD-002, CD). An underground consortium of collectors and entrepreneurs using the name The Swingin' Pig recognized the profitability of their rare tapes, containing superb-quality Beatles outtakes and alternate takes pilfered from the vaults of EMI Records. They pressed them onto a limited run of approximately 3–5,000 compact discs. The first *Ultra Rare* CDs sent shockwaves throughout the legitimate recording industry. Suddenly there were stereo releases of songs from the first four Beatles albums (which had been released as mono CDs by EMI and Capitol Records). Not only that, but the sound quality was even better than the legitimate compact discs!

Ultra Rare Trax: Volumes I & II also featured outtakes and alternate takes of songs such as, "I Saw Her Standing There," "One After 909," "She's A Woman," "I'm Looking Through You," "The Fool On The Hill," "Paperback Writer," "There's A Place," "That Means A Lot," "Day Tripper," "I Am The Walrus," "Norwegian Wood" and many more. It was a stunning collection even at just 30 minutes per disc, filled with mistakes, broken guitar strings, false starts, jokes and jams. Perhaps the musical highlight of the series was the amazing first take of "Can't Buy Me Love." This rejected alternate take features lush background vocal harmonies which were abandoned on the final take. For long-time collectors and fans of the group, listening to alternate versions of familiar songs was like hearing the songs again for the first time.

How these recordings came to fall into the hands of bootleggers still remains shrouded in mystery. The *Ultra Rare* bootlegs appear to have been made directly from tapes dubbed off the master tapes. Since the master tapes of these songs are still locked "safely" in the vault, it is clear that someone on the "inside" had to have assisted in their procurement. Paul McCartney suggested in a 1990 TV interview that engineers or even studio musicians working at the studio could have been involved. There was an attempted robbery in the late eighties at EMI/Abbey Road; however, it was (in McCartney's words) "so disorganized at EMI, the robbers couldn't find anything."

According to noted Beatles' historian, Allen J. Wiener, EMI had, in the past, dismissed a couple of its employees over the years who had access to the unreleased Beatles' master tapes. Thus, the probability that the tape copying was done on the inside cannot be ruled out.

Another explanation for the escape of historical Beatles recordings is that the tape copies could have been made by "runners" for author Mark Lewisohn, who at the time was cataloging EMI's Beatles tapes for his book, *The Complete Beatles Recording Sessions* (Harmony, 1988). As the rumor unfolds, unbeknownst to Lewisohn, the "runners" (assistants given the job of relaying the tapes to and from the vaults so Lewisohn could listen to the tapes) would not immediately return the tapes Lewisohn had finished, to the vaults. Instead, they could have kept back tapes and digitally copied them on portable equipment as time allowed, before returning them to the shelf. It is important to note that this explanation is merely a theory based upon reports from the very people who are involved in the underground music industry, and thus, lack credibility. When asked about this theory in a 1992 interview with historian Allen Wiener, Lewisohn conceded he hadn't thought of this explanation, but did not deny that it was a possibility. As Lewisohn's book preceded the release of *Ultra Rare Trax* by a mere few months, it appears obvious that bootleggers used the book's release as both a smoke-screen and a boost for marketing their CDs. Their ploy also caused some to wrongly accuse Mark Lewisohn of the misdeed.

According to EMI employee Mike Heatley, in a November 1988 interview with *ICE The Monthly CD Newsletter*, he was puzzled as to how The Beatles' tapes had escaped. Said Heatley:

> What we don't know yet is if (the tapes) escaped recently, or if they're something that someone managed to get years ago and just sat on. I've had several people say to me, "There must still be a leak from Abbey Road because this stuff keeps on appearing." Well, if it was only material from Abbey Road that was appearing, then I would say that's probably right. But recently, a lot of material that was recorded well before Abbey Road has, after many years, started turning up. It's almost as if some collector from way, way back has sat on this stuff for years and then allowed it out. For instance, we've been looking for years for any of the old BBC recordings from 1962, and they were never, ever found. And yet three months ago, while in New York, what do I find? A bootleg. I don't know; it just doesn't make any sense.

The sound quality on the *Ultra Rare Trax* series was phenomenal. Many people are of the opinion that the one-inch masters were used and thus, it had to be an "inside job." Heatley told *ICE*, though, "I would dispute that completely…they could've been done on quarter-inch tape many years ago." He also denied stories that CD test pressings sent to the Beatles might have been a

TOP: *The Swingin' Pig's* Ultra Rare Trax *CD bootlegs*
ABOVE: *Vinyl follow-ups, purportedly released by an underground competitor*

source or that Mark Lewisohn had anything to do with the tapes leaking out.

Still others believe that these studio outtakes actually slipped out at two distinct times in the 1980s. The first leak purportedly occurred during the studio compilation project for EMI's aborted Beatles album, *Sessions*. A limited amount of tape dubs were made of certain unreleased Beatles songs reviewed for the project. A person or persons later sold the copies through a middleman, which then made their way into bootlegger's hands.

A second leak is also said to have occurred around 1987, during the production of a radio special on The Beatles. Again, tape copies were made and distributed through an intermidiary to both The Swingin' Pig and Yellow Dog Records. The price was said to be in the $20,000 range for about six hours of tape.

Unconfirmed rumors tell a story that Yellow Dog had not intended to release its tapes, as part of their "good faith" agreement with the previous tape owner. However, once Swingin' Pig broached the market with its "Ultra Rare Trax" series, it effectively forced the hand of Yellow Dog to follow suit with its heralded "Unsurpassed Masters" series. Although the original tapes are said to be back at EMI, the damage had already been done. Many hours of rare music were ultimately released without the permission of either the group or its record label. One fact is certain—the trail of the greatest musical theft in history is now as cold as the one seeking John F. Kennedy's *other* assassins.

In February of 1989, Capitol Records, U.S. distributors of the Beatles catalog, sent a stern "Cease and Desist" letter to retailers suspected of selling these illegal CD recordings. Capitol threatened legal action against retailers who continued to sell *Ultra Rare Trax* and similar recordings. The letter had little deterent impact or effect. Following the release and importation into America of *Ultra Rare Trax: Volumes I & 2*, Volumes 3 through 6 were pressed in the vinyl configuration—purportedly by an underground competitor using The Swingin' Pig name. The Swingin' Pig CD configurations soon followed, but proved a disappointment compared with the first two volumes. Another Euro-bootlegger knocked off released some of the same recordings under the *Back Trax* series name, producing his discs in Korea. American and Japanese record retailers sold these recordings as fast as they could stock them. In light of heightened media attention surrounding theses historic illegal Beatles' recordings, public hunger for these and similar recordings increased dramatically.

The result is that EMI Records UK and The Beatles' Apple Ltd. are now planning a six-CD set for commercial release in 1995 that will contain previously unissued material from the vaults. George Martin, The Beatles' erstwhile producer, is heading up the project which will involve sifting through some 400 hours of Beatles studio tapes as well as their performances on TV, radio, in concert and their home demonstration tapes. The impetus for this momentous release was due to bootleggers. According to Martin, at a 1993 press conference, "I'm rather looking forward to ripping off the bootlegs. They've been stealing from us for a long time; now it's our turn." Martin explained that although The Beatles opposed the release of outtakes in the past, they have "come to terms with it all, and they've said that if there is going to be a definitive version of what we've done, then we ought to have a say in what it is." Of course, all of Martin's suggested inclusions in the chronicle would require approval of the three remaining former Beatles.

A by-product of the *Ultra Rare Trax* phenomenon was that many record companies were again made aware of the economic viability, as well as the public's desire for unreleased songs and alternate takes by their favorite artists. Bootlegs were no longer thick, awful sounding records which could simply be ignored as a nuisance. They were instead, excellent sounding CDs which posed a real economic and artistic threat to commercial artists. Consequently, major blue-chip artists such as Eric Clapton, Bob Dylan, Crosby, Stills & Nash, Elvis Presley, Elton John, the Byrds, the Monkees, David Bowie, Frank Zappa, the Allman Brothers, the Who, Derek and The Dominos, Cream, and Jimi Hendrix soon featured unreleased music on "best of" collections and boxed set retrospectives. Record labels created new divisions responsible for searching through company archives and preparing reissues for compact disc and cassette. After two decades, record companies were finally catching up with the general public's desire for new and rare music by their favorite artists. Giving the public what they wanted had been a justification of rock and roll bootleggers for twenty years. Now finally, the legitimate industry realized a new profit center could be gained from copying the concept developed first by bootleggers.

Frank Zappa, painfully aware that his concerts were taped and often bootlegged, successfully cut into the bootleggers' market by re-releasing some of those bootlegs himself. This series was fittingly called "Beat The Boots" (on Rhino Records) and contained exact copies of the original Zappa bootlegs down to the album cover artwork. Paul McCartney even authorized the release of his 1991 MTV "Unplugged" television performance under the cheeky (yet appropriate) title, *Unplugged: The Official Bootleg*. McCartney's spokesman, Joe Dera, said the idea of releasing the album came about because McCartney knew of the inevitability that the show might be bootlegged. He wanted to beat the bootleggers at their own game and have some fun with it at the same time. Unbeknownst to McCartney, the performance was still bootlegged onto compact disc, containing the complete performance, rather than an edited version which appeared on the commercial release.

UNSURPASSED MASTERS

Following closely on the heels of *Ultra Rare Trax* was a series called *Unsurpassed Masters* on the Yellow Dog label. Picking up where The Swingin' Pig company left off, Yellow Dog began releasing a series of compact discs in 1989, featuring more outtakes of the same superb quality as *Ultra Rare Trax*. While a few of the early Yellow Dog releases duplicated some of the same songs on *Ultra Rare Trax*, subsequent CDs brought to light many new and fascinating outtakes and acetates. One such example, featured the "Peter Sellers Tape" (given to Sellers by Ringo) containing rough, unfinished studio versions of *White Album* songs. One special highlight contained the complete, uncut version of "Sexy Sadie" (a thinly veiled slander of Maharishi Yogi). The unfinished take contained a rare, extended instrumental bridge toward the end of the song. Also in the late 1980s, an Italian company named Bulldog Records began releasing a series of live Beatles concert recordings with the trademark, "It Was More Than 20 Years Ago." This mark was a clever play on words that partially incorporated a nostalgic line from the Beatles' *Sgt. Peppers* album ("It was twenty years ago today…"). It further explained that their live releases were technically "legal," due to their expiration from protection after 20 years under European copyright laws. Beatles concerts were pressed in great numbers by this label (in excellent sound quality) and included the following historic shows: Tokyo, 1966; Paris, 1965; Houston, 1965; Rome, 1965; and San Francisco, 1965. Bulldog had reportedly paid publishing royalties and copyright mechanicals to the songs' authors. However, the recordings were still considered bootlegs when they entered the United States and other countries for distribution.

Other companies benefitting from the more liberal European loop holes in copyright laws were Early Years (*Get Back Sessions,* and *White Album Demos*); Pyramid (*At The BEEB,* live albums from Melbourne, Paris and San Francisco); Living Legend Records (*Live in the USA, Look What We Found, Unreleased Tracks*) and Great Dane Records (more live Beatles' concerts). Even the Far East had a hand in the production of bootlegs in the late eighties where copyright laws were similarly lax or rarely enforced. The NML label was reportedly located in Korea, known mainly for releasing *Back Track Volumes 1-3*.

TOP: *Two of* Yellow Dog's Unsurpassed Masters *CDs*
ABOVE: *A* advertisement for Bulldog Records' live series released in the late '80s

THE BEATLES GARAGE TAPES

Purchased both privately and at a London auction in 1989, the "Alf Bicknell" tapes were bootlegged onto CD in late 1992 by Kremo Music Productions. The disc was imaginatively titled, *The Garage Tapes: For Sale By Auction* (Kremo, SELCD-18, CD). Alf Bicknell had been The Beatles' chauffeur and bodyguard during their world tours of the 1960s. Once the live appearances ended in 1966, Alf moved on, but not before John Lennon gifted him a grab bag of miscellaneous audio tape reels made behind the scenes whenever the group was outside the public eye. Thereafter, the tapes were forgotten, languishing in Alf's garage for some twenty years, before being rediscovered.

The tapes were rumored to include some legendary performances, heretofore unheard by the world. But alas, once music historians had the opportunity to hear them, the legend quickly crumbled. The informal recordings included snippets of John and Paul singing "Over The Rainbow," George composing "Don't Bother Me" in a hotel room in 1963, several attempts by John to prepare a demo of "If I Fell," and finally, John, George, Paul and Gerry Marsden (of Gerry and the Pacemakers) reading from *The Bible* ("The Lord is My Shepherd" and "There Is A Green Hill"). Unfortunately, the music was fragmented, sound quality was poor and the "Bible readings" were only slightly amusing. Only the most die-hard fans and historians could appreciate this disc.

ARTIFACTS

In early 1994, as the three former Beatles announced plans for a reunion and discussed the possibility of finally opening the vaults filled with 400 hours of unreleased material, an Italian Company beat them to the punch. In January of that year, Big Music's *Artifacts—The Definitive Collection Of Beatles Rarities, 1958-1970* hit the streets of the U.S. music underground with a splash. The glossy five-CD set came packaged with a lengthy booklet describing the six hours of unreleased music. The set was described by one critic as "the ultimate bootleg boxed set on The Beatles."

The anthology of songs found in the box are arranged in chronological recording order and placed in historical perspective by accurate liner notes. The set begins with The Beatles' earliest recordings as The Quarry Men and concludes with their final *Abbey Road* sessions. In between, listeners are treated to the most comprehensive and historically significant rehearsals, auditions, demos, alternate takes, outtakes, live performances, Ed Sullivan shows, and BBC broadcasts. Though most of the material had appeared across hundreds of bootlegs in the past, no bootlegger had ever sought to capture the best sounding, and most com-

TOP: Two of the three bootlegs from the NML Back Track *series*
ABOVE: *The* Garage Tapes *bootleg*

Big Music's box set, Artifacts—The Definitive Collection Of Beatles
Rarities, 1958–1970

plete essence of unreleased Beatles recordings into a single box set. One of the most fascinating sessions featured is found on Disc Four which is titled, "Inner Revolution" (1968). The listener is ushered into the hallowed studio to "sit in" with The Beatles as they begin to rehearse what would become the group's biggest selling worldwide single…"Hey Jude." Eavesdropping on this seven-plus minute rehearsal allows the listener to hear the creative communication between partners Lennon and McCartney even while recording this run-through. As Paul starts singing the familiar opening, John works out his rhythm part on acoustic guitar while adding some extraneous grunts and groans. At one point, when Paul sings, "The movement you need is on your shoulder," John joins in with the same lyrics in a firm, yet silly tone. This is John's way of reinforcing Paul's use of these words, which McCartney had originally stuck in for practice purposes only. When Paul told John he would replace the words later, John told him that the words were good and should be kept in the song.

During the "nah, nah, nah" chorus of the song, John and Paul enjoy experimenting with various vocal styles while they play along. At one point, John yells out "Coo, coo ca-jude," a playful reference to the long fade of his song, "I Am The Walrus," which had used the word "joob" instead of "jude." Following the rehearsal, the tape kept rolling as The Beatles did impromptu versions of songs believed to be titled, "Las Vegas Tune," and "St. Louis Blues." The entire rehearsal was filmed for a documentary, and most of it is included on *Artifacts*.

Although The Beatles, Apple and EMI finally agreed to open up the vaults, they would need to dig deeper into the archives to counter the black market success of *Artifacts*. After rave mention in publications such as *The Washington Post*, the CD newsletter *ICE*, and *Goldmine*, the *Artifacts* box set (retailing at $100 each) sold out its first two production runs of several thousand copies. The enormous success of *Artifacts* spawned a 1994 follow-up aptly titled *Artifacts II*, and 1995's *Artifacts III* with yet more unreleased Beatle and solo Beatle gems. It also caused the highly competitive Yellow Dog label to issue its own version. Yellow Dog announced in September of 1994 its plans for an ambitious collection of three 4-CD boxed sets of "rare live, studio, radio, TV and film recordings." These boxes, released around Christmas of 1994, contained a compilation filled with hours of repackaged bootleg Beatles songs, aptly titled, *The Ultimate Collection Volumes 1–3*.

Some twenty-four years have passed since the group broke up. However, one fact was crystal clear from the underground success of *Artifacts*, that the public still craved "rare" material from The Beatles and were willing to pay a small king's ransom for the rare opportunity to hear it. Similar to the mid-'70s, 1995 witnessed a sharp decline in the release of "lost" Beatles gems. The boxed sets of Big Music and Yellow Dog (which mainly repackaged material previously boot-legged) signaled the end of an eight year renaissance for Beatles bootleggers sail-ing the "high CDs." There is still the probability that rare Beatles music may sur-face at future auctions or in private transactions. Only time will tell if the musi-cal well of illicit Beatles material has run dry.

THE LONG AND WINDING ROAD

There has been no decrease in interest in the Beatles or their music in the 1990s. Total worldwide commercial sales of their music has been reported to be near the one-billion unit mark. The three surviving former Beatles continue to make live appearances and release new recordings. They are also working together on a multi-part film series documenting their career as a group. Likewise in the underground, compact discs of the quartet's unreleased works, as well as unpub-lished solo material continue to be released. "Beatlemania" appears to be a social and economically profitable phenomenon, destined to last well into the next cen-tury. Right or wrong, bootlegs of the Fab Four will continue to be an integral ele-ment of both collecting and documenting the Beatles' music history and their message. Subsequent chapters compile the in-depth opinions of The Beatles and The Beatles' bootleggers, in their own words, on the subject of the black market. This is followed by the complete underground discography of the lost Beatles recordings.

Moral issues aside, if it were not for the enterprising individuals who have produced illegal rock and roll bootlegs over the past twenty-plus years, the world would have lost much of the historically valuable material written and performed by The Beatles—perhaps the greatest musical and cultural influence of the twen-tieth century.

4

The Beatles On Bootlegs:
In Their Own Words

It would be a gross understatement to say that The Beatles were four busy lads in the 1960s. From their semi-humble beginnings in Liverpool and all-night performances in Hamburg's seedy nightclubs to three world tours, hundreds of inane press conferences, numerous worldwide radio and television appearances, promotional and feature filmmaking, demo recordings and studio work, it is easy to understand why there is such a wealth of material that has never seen the light of day (at least commercially).

Keeping up with a grueling tour and recording schedule did not leave the group or their staff with time to chronicle, catalogue or collect all of their non-commercial work product (or by-product, as the case may be). Instead, this seemingly endless task has, by default, been passed on to numerous private collectors, archivists and historians worldwide. Many of the unreleased Beatles' recordings have been sold underground in the form of bootleg records, cassettes, compact discs and videos. This chapter explores the collective Beatles' impressions of bootlegs, bootleggers and prospects for officially issuing their previously unreleased material. Their quotes are taken from the many, many press conferences and interviews they have given over the years.

BEATLES AS COLLECTORS

Soon after the breakup of The Beatles, John Lennon and Ringo Starr started collecting bootleg recordings of their unreleased work. John Lennon seemed to concentrate his efforts on bootlegs while Ringo Starr expanded his collecting to include not just unreleased recordings, but also films, publications, photographs and assorted memorabilia. Ringo might be the world's most expert Beatles' historian and collector.

Paul McCartney and George Harrison, however, are less enthusiastic—at least publicly—in their appreciation of collecting Beatles recordings, though recently, there are some signs that this is changing. Paul's "people" keep a close eye on the Beatles-related rock and roll auctions which are conducted semi-annually by Sotheby's, Christie's and other auction houses. If anything of personal historic interest draws McCartney's attention, he'll snatch it up (it's hard to outbid someone worth over $600,000,000.) McCartney is especially drawn to the earliest recordings and performances— such as an early live Cavern Club concert tape and the shellac record, "That'll Be The Day," made in 1958 by the pre-Beatles group, The Quarry Men.

Back in September of 1974, John Lennon enthusiastically told the press, "I collect the memorabilia—why not, it's history man, history! The things I really want are the bootlegs; some of them are even better than the final products that we released—like the *Beatles in Sweden* bootleg." The performance by The Beatles in Sweden in 1963, is considered one of the best live concerts to have survived over the years.

While making a guest appearance as a disc jockey on KHJ-FM in Los Angeles on September 27, 1974, Lennon again showed his proud expertise of Beatles bootlegs. When a caller asked him to confirm if The Beatles had ever recorded a song called "Have You Heard The Word?," John explained, "No, no…uh I think they got that mixed up with 'The Word'…the Beatles' song '(The) Word' on *Rubber Soul*, 'cause I know there's a bootleg on it, but there's no such song. It sounds like us. It's a good imitation." The bootleg album that this song appeared on was called *Have You Heard The Word* (CBM, 3624, LP). The song was actually written by Steve Kipner and Steve Groves and featured a Beatles sound-alike ensem-

ble. According to Beatles historian Allen J. Wiener, this song was such a good imitation of Lennon, that his widow Yoko Ono mistakenly registered the song title for copyright protection on September 20, 1985.

In 1971, John Lennon responded to questions of whether there existed a lot of Beatles material that had not yet been released. Lennon's response was at first tentative, but slowly he started to expound on a number of recordings which

Used by permission of Barb Tylor

have subsequently surfaced:

> Well I don't...I can't think what it is. The only tapes I know of are *Hollywood Bowl*, *Shea Stadium*, and somebody that did something on us in Italy. But it's all the same songs over and over anyway. There were no other German tapes that Polydor didn't release...The only stuff that could be...would be some auditions we did for Decca around in '61 or '62, something like that.

In a 1988 interview, Yoko Ono attempted to explain her late husband's fascination with collecting bootleg recordings:

> Now when John [said] he doesn't mind it and all that, I think it was a totally different situation, because while the bootleg was going on, he could make his live records. With my thing it's all right, because I'm going on making new music, so it doesn't bother me so much. That's how it was when John was alive; probably it didn't bother him so much because he [could] keep on making new music. John had a laugh when he felt that his music was so popular that anything of his was bootlegged. He knew that given a choice between his current music and bootlegs, people are going to buy his albums.

Yoko is certainly correct in describing John's enthusiasm and fascination with being bootlegged. In fact, just two days before he died, John Lennon told interviewer Andy Peebles of the BBC, "...I buy all the pirate records, file them away and...keep them. Yeah, stuff from Sweden, things like that where there was good live shows done." It has also been reported that Lennon used to regularly purchase Beatles' bootlegs in New York City record stores and would exchange tapes of unreleased Beatles material with a fellow New York Beatles archivist.

To her credit, Ms. Ono deserves praise for the many posthumous releases of John Lennon's work that she has chosen to share with his fans. In the years since Lennon's passing, Ono released the following works: *Milk And Honey* LP; *Menlove Avenue* LP; *Live In New York City* LP and video; *Imagine*, the LP concept video; *Imagine: John Lennon* the film, LP and video; *Lennon*, the 4 CD box set; *The John Lennon Video Collection* and the long-running series on Westwood One Radio Network called "The Lost Lennon Tapes," which aired countless hours of previously unheard Lennon demos, outtakes, and interviews. While most of the "Lost Lennon" material has also been bootlegged, there are reports of a pending multi-CD box set which will collect the best of "The Lost Lennon Tapes" and more, for commercial release.

In November of 1990, Ringo Starr was asked by reporter Jeffrey Ressner whether John Lennon's love of bootlegs and trading tapes with fellow collectors was responsible for many tapes leaking out to the bootleggers. In a moment of witty sarcasm, Ringo responded, "You'll have to ask John about that."

During the same interview, Ringo explained his own interest in bootlegs in a more serious light:

> I'm as interested as anyone else really. I mean, I get tapes from all over the world by people, you know—they're just bootlegs. I know I don't have copies of them. Someone has stolen the tape from EMI or, you know, from Capitol or from somewhere in the world and they send me the tape.

When asked whether he has kept up over the years with the multitude of bootleg releases, Ringo flatly responds, "No, there's too many bootlegs." However, Ringo Starr is indeed a collector. "I've never had a bootlegged CD, but I have bootleg albums," he stated recently. "I used to live in Amsterdam, and that's the capital of bootlegged material over there."

Paul McCartney, during his 1989–1990 world tour, told a press conference filled with reporters that he did not collect Beatles bootlegs. Instead (tongue in cheek) he told them, "I bootleg other people's concerts, but shhh, don't tell anyone."

Paul and George have downplayed the existence of large volumes of unreleased material. This may be due to a misunderstanding of the type, variety and quantity of recorded material that has been bootlegged (demos, outtakes, alternate takes, live shows, etc.). Most of their responses to questions from the media seem geared specifically toward the handful of completed outtake songs that never made their way onto commercial Beatles albums. According to EMI company session notes, there are indeed very few completed outtakes from The Beatles' many sessions. However, there are hundreds of hours of alternate takes, chatter, arguments, jokes and avant garde "noise" tapes sitting in the vaults. At a 1989 press conference, Paul explained, "We were very tidy with most of our material, which we erased or got rid of, so there isn't much in the way of outtakes. There's not much of it, but you probably could make a rarities album." Although there were few songs left off of The Beatles' albums, the bootleg CD series, *Unsurpassed Masters* and *Ultra Rare Trax* have already given collectors several hours of alternate versions (takes) of familiar songs, as well as a number of unreleased tracks.

In the fall of 1990, Paul McCartney specifically addressed the "Ultra Rare Trax" bootleg series, and how the tapes may have leaked out:

> This comes from all the outtakes and all the…Well, the thing is, we were never really very careful. I mean, we went down to EMI to record and when the recording was done, we went home. You know, we didn't watch where they put the tape. So all you needed was one engineer to let a friend in one night, or even take a little copy for himself. You'd be surprised how kind of available that stuff is. You've just got to know where the file is, and get in one evening. It's funny, some guys broke into EMI once to try and get some tapes, but they couldn't find it. They couldn't find all our (Beatles) stuff. It was like amongst all this crazy stuff…We'd have little demo tapes just to check on whether the mix was the mix we wanted you know. And it falls by the wayside. You move house or something…and a box goes. I think that is where it all comes from.

George Harrison has never professed his love, at least publicly, for collecting the bootleg recordings. When asked by *Musician* magazine about a bootleg called *The Silver Wilburys* (which features Harrison, Bob Dylan, John Fogerty, Taj Mahal and Jessie Ed Davis jamming in an L.A. night club) George responded, "Some people have got a nerve." Despite his apparent dislike of these recordings, George spoke openly of a few gems he has tucked away from his Beatles days:

> We've got the real versions of the ones that have been bootlegged, and we've got plans to put all of that out. And the BBC has a lot of tapes. I just realized that I've got a really good bootleg tape—demos we made at my

PAUL MCCARTNEY:

"**I** bootleg other people's concerts, but shhh, don't tell anyone."

Paul & Linda, 1989 L.A. press conference—Belmo photo

RINGO STARR:

"**P**ersonally, I would like to put out all the bootlegs, all the outtakes that we didn't want out, but are out. Beatles bootlegs by us!"

Ringo, 1992 Cincinnati, OH—Belmo photo

The Beatles on bootlegs: In their own words

house on an Ampex four-track during *The White Album*. Mainly there's different versions of stuff, and stuff that people know of as bootlegs from our club days."

It appears, therefore, that of the four Beatles, Lennon and Starr turned out to be the two bootleg collectors. Although McCartney and Harrison have not been as enthusiastic about their archives, one has to wonder if they are not "closet" collectors of unreleased Beatles recordings.

BOOTLEG PHILOSOPHY

For the past 20 or more years, The Beatles have been aware that their every waking moment was being recorded in print, on tape and bootlegged thousands of times. How do they feel then, about this overkill of documentation and those who profit by it? On a few rare occasions, The Beatles have commented on their opinion concerning the people who have profited by the theft of their music.

During his 1989–1990 world tour, Paul McCartney admitted that he was a "bootlegger" of other people's concerts. When asked if this position was consistent with his personnel prohibiting others from taping or photographing his shows, McCartney responded, "Yeah. Some guy accosted me on the street the other day and said, 'Your company just sued me for bootlegging. And I just saw you say you like bootlegs.' And I said, yeah, (but) you got caught." One has to wonder if a security guard will someday have the thankless job of throwing Paul out of a rock concert for attempting to tape it.

Ringo Starr clearly favors the release of alternates and outtake tracks. In 1990, Ringo was shown a copy of *Belmo's Beatleg News*, an international journal that regularly updates, reviews and documents the newest black market Beatles recordings. The continued long-term interest in underground recordings and journals discussing unreleased music of The Beatles came as no surprise to Starr. However, he did have an opinion concerning how and by whom the bootlegs should be released. Ringo rendered this view:

> You know people are interested. I mean I used to get uptight. I always felt that what we put out was what we thought was the best. And then you know the bootlegs came out and there were enormous sales on them. So you know with our agreements I put, you know, my two cents in, that I want to put out The Beatles bootlegs by The Beatles. You know, instead of someone else putting it out, we should do it.

Ringo is clearly aware of the volume of unreleased material being distributed by such purveyors, as well as the potential loss of revenue. Starr's philosophy is to beat the bootleggers at their own game. This view, shared by other recording artists such as Frank Zappa, Bob Dylan, The Allman Brothers and Badfinger, has already been put in motion.

In a letter written in September 1980, author Jim Berkenstadt formally requested John Lennon and Yoko Ono's philosophy on Beatle bootlegging. At the time, the author never realized that this would be his one and only communication with the late Mr. Lennon, albeit through his assistant. Their formal response, postmarked September 29, 1980, was penned by Helen Seaman who was a personal assistant to the Lennons at the time. It was written when John and Yoko were busily finishing up sessions on the *Double Fantasy* album. The letter is reproduced here in its entirety. Of course, the translation of this correspondence to the author's question on bootlegging was a very diplomatic "no comment."

It is of course the responsibility of The Beatles' lawyers and Apple Corps Ltd. to prosecute people who manufacture and distribute illicit recordings and unlicensed memorabilia. Naturally, readers should already know the position taken by The Beatles' legal staff with respect to bootleggers. However, for those who are still not sure, one has only to review the public remarks of longtime Beatles' attorney Leonard Marks. "With The Beatles there is always some outstanding litigation against, you know…bootleggers, counterfeiters, companies stealing their videos, etc. We try to be selectively aggressive and get the most bang for our buck in protecting The Beatles' name, likenesses, and catalogs." The moral here…bootleggers beware!

BEATLES ROUGH DRAFTS AND PICASSO'S SKETCHES
Although several music historians have done an enviable job of documenting The Beatles' creative process, the clamor by fans, collectors and historians to *hear* this body of rough drafts continues unabated. Indeed, some of this material has already been bootlegged onto the aforementioned CD series, *Ultra Rare Trax* and *Unsurpassed Masters*.

In October of 1982, author Jim Berkenstadt wrote an article for *Goldmine* magazine explaining how the release of Beatles' "rough drafts" would provide a rare insight into the evolutionary process of both The Beatles' artistic creativity, and of rock and roll music in the 1960s. In support of this argument, the author equated The Beatles' musical "rough drafts" to those of famed artist Pablo Picasso:

> As it is currently considered valid for major universities to study slides of
> Pablo Picasso's rough drafts of *Battle of Guernica*, then we must certainly

LENNONO
STUDIO ONE
1 WEST 72ND STREET
NEW YORK, NEW YORK 10023

John and Yoko regret that, owing to pressure of work,
they have had to make it a rule not to read unsolic-
ited manuscripts or lyrics, listen to tapes, answer
questionnaires, contribute to anthologies or sym-
posiums, or reply to questions on student's theses,
etc.

They receive so many of these and similar requests
that they are sorry to say that it has become impossible
to deal with them all and, at the same time, fulfill
their own writing committments.

Sincerely,

Helen Seaman
HS:is   Assistant to
                              John and Yoko

Lennon-Ono assistant Helen Seaman's "no comment" letter

place equal importance on the "rough drafts" of The Beatles...Granted, Americans can choose from several highly polished Beatles albums in the stores, but the commercial aspect of The Beatles is merely a fragment of the complete picture of these artists. Students, historians and fans alike must be given an opportunity to delve into the "rough drafts" of The Beatles' music.

According to former Beatles press agent Tony Barrow, "The recording studio was their laboratory; they left the tape machines running all the time." As the years between the end of The Beatles and the present grow longer, the interest in studying The Beatles' unfinished work product continues to garner interest.

Paul McCartney has on several occasions admitted that he sometimes listens to bootleg Beatles music, but he has been ambivalent about releasing recordings of alternate takes containing mistakes. "If someone comes to me and says, 'Look, we've got this very charismatic little album of outtakes...' and I like it, I don't have a problem with that." He explained further to *New York Times* Reporter Allan Kozinn in 1990:

> I do like to hear some of the bootlegs where we're setting up things...I often have arguments with other people. I say Picasso's art is all great. And they say well, this Blue period; and I say if he was great, his shit was great too. His (Picasso's) sketches, of course. I was just being a little vernacular there, calling sketches shit. I do agree with that. In fact, I side with that argument. In our case (Beatles) I do think it's fine as a study thing—they did this. But the thing is, we traditionally tried to release the very best of our work.

When asked in a 1990 television interview about the pressure to have The Beatles' record company release all of its unreleased archives, McCartney was careful to articulate his disapproval.

> Well the difficult question is like, (release) "every bit of what?" You mean all the takes we didn't like? That's what people seem to want. It's a bit funny for us, you know. You work, you do like nine takes of a thing and we say "no"..."Take number nine, great! We finally got it right." And now they want to release takes one to eight? It doesn't make much sense to me. I mean I think you should say for the rabid collector, okay, maybe *you've* got to have it all. But I personally wouldn't be that interested in it...All of the other stuff between the takes I love. Obviously I don't really like hearing bum takes of stuff because I'm looking at it professionally and thinking, oh that was when I goofed, that was when I played the wrong note. I'm not

particularly interested in that. But I can see how other people are. I mean, I used to like that in other people's records.

McCartney further points out the potential problem with future generations of Beatles fans. "If you start making the alternate takes available, in 10 years people may not know which was the finished take and which wasn't. I'd rather avoid the confusion."

Commercial label releases of previously unreleased material, however, go to great lengths to point out the differences. Currently, such albums offer historical booklets, extensive liner notes and design album titles which clearly help music listeners tell the difference between an artist's initially released catalog and the rare previously unreleased works. There are many examples: Titles such as *Bob Dylan: The Bootleg Series Vol. 1-3*; Frank Zappa's 10 CD boxed set, *Beat The Boots*; and even McCartney's own live album taken from a performance on MTV entitled, *Unplugged: The Official Bootleg*.

Ringo Starr has carefully considered the historical import of releasing the rough draft versions of their songs:

> Personally, I would like to put out all the bootlegs, all the outtakes that we didn't want out, but are out. Beatles bootlegs by us! We always felt that what came out is what we wanted out. That was the musician in us. We weren't really interested in the avid fan who wants anything. I think we're moving more along those lines now, because some of the "take 2" would really be interesting.

But what about bootleg recordings that might not promote the group or artist in a favorable light? Or worse yet, that are taken out of context by the general public? One example of this has already surfaced with The Beatles. In 1986, a London tabloid accused Paul McCartney of racist leanings after hearing bootleg Beatles outtakes from the *Get Back* sessions that allegedly featured him singing in a non-flattering manner about Pakistanis. The song entitled, "No Pakistanis," (a very early incarnation of the song "Get Back") appears on the infamous bootleg record, *Sweet Apple Trax* (Instant Analysis, WEC-4182, 2LP, 1973).

Reproduced below is a portion of the lyrics to the unpublished Beatles' tune entitled "No Pakistanis" that a London tabloid based its accusations on from the January 1969 Beatles' rehearsal session:

"NO PAKISTANIS"
(Paul singing): Don't dig no Pakistanis takin' all the peoples' jobs...
Get back, get back, get back to where you once belong,

> Get back, get back, get back to where you once belong...
> Didi-a-do-ran was a Pakistani living in another ohhhhh,
> All the folks around don't dig no Pakistani takin' all the peoples' jobs...

McCartney's defense to the accusations of racial prejudice was that the lyrics actually "talked out against overcrowding for Pakistanis. The [paper] wishes to see it as a racist remark. But I'll tell you, if there was any group that was not racist, it was The Beatles. I mean all our favorite people were always black. I think the line said 'too many people, living in a council flat'." The lyrics illustrated above do not contain the line about "too many people, living in a council flat." That particular lyric *did* surface in a subsequent run-through, as the song began to take the shape of the final tune later published under the title "Get Back."

In fact, McCartney's interpretation of the "No Pakistanis" lyric is correct. Perhaps the best historical evidence to support his version of the song's meaning is found in a recorded conversation at a later *Get Back* rehearsal. This particular dialogue from 1969 surfaced on the 1993 bootleg titled *The Get Back Journals* (Vigatone, Vigo-107, 8CD).

During this practice session, Paul has already dropped the Pakistani lyrics. After rehearsing for some fifteen minutes, George Harrison inquires of Paul if there are only two lyrical verses. Harrison has obviously noticed the word changes to the song. Paul explains, "You see, it (the song) started out as a protest song" against British policies toward Pakistanis immigration. He offers, "I liked the word 'Pakistani'." But in the end, Paul drops the political lyrics in favor of a humorous transsexual theme, adopting the now familiar "Sweet Loretta Martin" verse.

Indeed, if McCartney were racist, he would not have been likely to permit a black person (keyboardist, Billy Preston) to participate on sessions for the *Let It Be* and *Abbey Road* albums. Not only was Preston the *only* session player ever credited on a Beatles album, but he and Doris Troy (a black woman) were both signed to solo contracts with The Beatles' Apple record label. Later in his solo career, McCartney would further demonstrate his interest in racial harmony by releasing the hit song "Ebony and Ivory" with Stevie Wonder. For those who have not heard the song, it was written in an effort to enlighten people of all races to the possibility of living together in peace and harmony.

In every public instance, The Beatles always demonstrated support for minority artists, for instance, citing their particular influence on the group at press conferences. However, a review of another bootleg outtake reveals at least one song whose lyrics might suggest a different point of view. Reproduced below are a portion of lyrics to another unpublished song performed by The Beatles entitled, "Negro In Reserve," which has been bootlegged:

NEGRO IN RESERVE
(John singing): Behind you, there's a hole in the hard case,
There's a hole in the hard case,
at a hole in the hard case…
And we always got a Negro in reserve.
…always got a Negro in reserve.

As for the song "Negro In Reserve," one can only wonder what this lyric is all about. Created spontaneously, the song is mostly gibberish, sung in the style of an old southern black sharecropper. But in the hands of a tabloid journalist, it could easily be misconstrued in a negative fashion.

The two songs clearly point out the issue and importance of an artist's control over his "rough drafts." Careful consideration of lyrical and musical contents must be made by artists before certain outtakes are released to the public. Bootlegged rehearsals of songs in their primitive state are often edited by bootleggers and can be taken out of context. This can often lead to the potential harm of an artist's reputation. In the case of The Beatles, a valid concern exists in preserving a balance of the original music history and group perspective along with the generally positive reputation developed by the artists. Thus, the decisions on all post-breakup Beatles releases are carefully weighed by the group's surviving members and Yoko Ono.

FUTURE RELEASES FROM THE BEATLES

Now that the legal battles waged between The Beatles and their record companies are over, some unreleased recordings may finally see the commercial light of day. This section explores the specific songs and groups of recordings that The Beatles have personally mentioned as candidates for release. However, fans should not get their hopes up for an avalanche of previously unreleased Beatles recordings. Rupert Perry, managing director of EMI, has told the press, "There's been a lot of speculation. People think there are plans to come out with all sorts of unreleased things. That's not the case." Keeping this in mind, we turn to the Fab Four for their comments on recordings they might like to see released.

One of the rarest and oldest recordings of The Quarry Men is a 45 rpm record of John, Paul, George and the other members singing, "That'll Be The Day" and "In Spite Of All The Danger." Paul McCartney is now the sole owner of this one-of-a-kind record, which was the first disc ever made by the nucleus of The Beatles. At a 1990 press conference, McCartney was asked about the prospects of releasing this rare recording to the public and how the recording came about in the first place. He provided the following background:

> Yeah…um we have transferred it. I'm not sure if it's actually transferred to CD yet because we did it a few years ago, to digital. But it is transferred to you know [a] fairly good modern medium kind of thing. Yeah, I'm happy to release it. It's really a question of like when and how to do those kinds of things. I really just got hold of it because it was the very first recording we did with The Quarry Men kind of thing. You know, we went down to a little studio in Liverpool and did this thing. And we each paid a pound each. So, it was like about five pounds to make the record, you know. And that's going back a little while of course. Anyway, we said, 'Okay, you can keep it for a week, I'll keep it for a week, he can keep it for a week' and so on and so forth. And we lent it to this fellow who is on the record, this guy who'd joined us, really for a couple of dates, who was a Liverpool friend of ours. And he kept it for 23 years you know. So, when it finally surfaced, he said 'Well I paid my pound' (laughs). Anyway, when it finally surfaced, I kind of bought it off him. And said, 'Look you know, I'd like to have this just so as we keep it safe.' So, I've run off a few copies of it. Just um…for friends and that. And I've got the old original just um, you know, kind of in good condition and stuff. And maybe one of these days, it would be nice…I mean I'd love people to hear it 'cause its a fairly ropey record. But it is the first little thing we ever did. And um, you know, there's this kind of magic to it.

There's no doubt among collectors and music historians that this release would indeed be "magical." A small portion of the song, "That'll Be The Day" was released in the United States on September 21, 1987, as part of a video documentary called *The Real Buddy Holly Story*. These two songs would surely highlight an album of outtakes by The Beatles. (An edited version of "That'll Be The Day" does appear on a volume of the bootleg record series, "Lost Lennon Tapes" and on The Beatles' bootleg box set *Artifacts*.)

Though he has not endorsed their release, George Harrison has occasionally made reference to some interesting gems sitting in the vaults. In 1987, George enthusiastically discussed them with *Musician* magazine: "Like there was a song I did with John and Yoko called, 'What's The New Mary Jane?' There are some things which were just our routining the song, or one of us singing the song that they just happened to tape before we learned the song. I know there's a version of 'While My Guitar Gently Weeps' with just me and acoustic guitar." This version has been released underground as part of the tapes that were to have made up the aborted EMI Beatles album *Sessions*, and "What's The New Mary Jane?" has been bootlegged many times.

In 1965, The Beatles decided to record a rare instrumental entitled "12 Bar Original," which was a standard twelve-bar blues arrangement. It is noteworthy for its length (over six minutes), its lack of vocals, and that it prominently features producer George Martin on organ. The recording is fascinating in that it differs greatly in sound and genre from the other work of The Beatles during this time period. It reflects the group's little known interest in the burgeoning British blues scene of the day that featured guitarists like Eric Clapton, Jeff Beck and Jimmy Page.

At the record release party for the live CD, *Ringo Starr And His All Starr Band* (Rykodisc, RCD-10190, CD, 1990), Ringo shed new light on this composition's authorship as he spoke to noted Beatles' journalist Peter Palmiere. "We all wrote the track and I have an acetate of one of the versions." The "12 Bar Original" is yet another good candidate for an official album of Beatles outtakes. It has already been released underground on the *Ultra Rare Trax* and *Unsurpassed Masters* series.

Perhaps the greatest wealth of rare live-in-the-studio Beatles recordings rests in the vaults of the BBC radio archives. In the 1980s, the BBC began broadcasting some radio specials that featured many rare Beatles performances and songs that were never commercially released by the group.

On December 6, 1980, while doing an interview to promote the release of his *Double Fantasy* album, John Lennon spoke with great enthusiasm and nostalgia about these recordings:

> I heard some of the tracks…Somebody must have pirated them…Bernie?
> …in America you know. I've heard Saturday Club. And we did a lot of
> tracks that were never recorded on record…for Saturday Club, a lot of stuff
> we'd been doing at the Cavern or Hamburg and that. Well there is some
> good stuff in there and we were well-recorded too! "Three Cool Cats"…I
> think we did. I think I picked up a pirate record of it, but I'm not sure
> because I buy all the pirate records.

Moving forward to the 1990s, there has been a good deal of conjecture regarding the eventual release of "lost" Beatles' performances. When asked about a timetable for the release of rare Beatles music, Ringo was pragmatic and forthcoming in his explanation:

There's no timetable for stuff that's never been out, you know…It's the decisions we have to make now. Okay, we made the decision it would be nice to have it out. And we have to make a decision. Do we do it weekly? Should we do it—you know there are a thousand combinations. So you know all those decisions we have to sit down and talk about.

To date, no one has been able to secure an extensive interview with any of the former Beatles to investigate the issues related to bootlegs in any great depth. The "sound bite" quotes provided in this chapter are meant to give the reader a generalized portrait of The Beatles' impressions and opinions on the issue of Beatles bootlegs. Their thoughts on collecting and releasing unreleased material are as diverse as their individual talents. Will we someday hear the musical gems long stored in the vaults of EMI Records? Will the release of such potential projects sink the bootlegger's ship of profits? Only time will tell. As long as hundreds of hours of live concerts, studio alternates, outtakes, demos, radio and TV appearances remain unreleased, black marketeers will continue to fill the void of collectors worldwide.

As the legend of The Beatles continues to grow, so will the interest in studying their unreleased works. One thing is certain: as long as unreleased material remains "in the can," fans, collectors and historians will continue the pressure to "squeeze" the works out. It will be necessary for the surviving Beatles, or their former producer George Martin, to listen to hours of material and cull out the most historical and highest quality works. Many crucial and historical musical decisions will need to be made during this process.

Perhaps Paul McCartney best summarizes the reason why people continue to study and collect The Beatles' music, both released and unreleased. As he explained to *New York Times* reporter and Beatles expert, Alan Kozinn:

> If you were that good as The Beatles were, and if you were that interesting, as the combination of our four talents were—Lennon, McCartney, Harrison, Starkey—and if you made up the chemistry, as we did, you've got to expect to be picked over. People wanted to know why she (Greta Garbo) wants to be alone, just because she made a bunch of good films. Charlie Chaplin will always be the cheeky tramp. When you do that well, you've got to live with the consequences of it…But you sort of have to accept it as it's squeezed out of the tube. It just comes out like that.

Inside Interviews With The Beatles' Bootleggers

In an effort to present both sides of the moral issues related to the black market sales of Beatles recordings never intended for release, the authors present interviews with three confirmed insiders who have had differing degrees of involvement in the world of bootlegs. The work of these three persons spanned essentially three different decades. Their opinions and the statements of fact they assert herein, are their own. They do not represent the author's perspective, but rather are presented to afford a rare opportunity to hear the "other side" from the underbelly of the record industry. Their memories and stories, though perhaps not always accurate, are both informative and at times amusing.

AN INTERVIEW WITH BEATLE BOOTLEGGER MR. NURK TWIN (1972–1982)

AUTHORS (A): Just a general question to lead off. How did you first get involved in the bootleg music scene?

NURK TWIN (NT): Let's see. I didn't buy my first bootleg until right after the Bangladesh Concert. We were in Atlanta...my wife and I, and we walked into a record store down there and it opened up a whole new world.

A: What year was that?

NT: It was 1971.

A: What was the bootleg you saw, do you remember?

NT: Yes, it was the first concert for Bangladesh on CBM (Contra Band Music). It was the worst piece of trash I'd ever bought (laughs). But I bought a bunch of stuff that day. That is what prompted me that day. I got some good stuff that day though. I picked up...oh let's see...the *James Taylor*—Rubber Dubber, *Back In '64 At The Hollywood Bowl* (Beatles) on Pinetree Records, a very rare one. I got a second or third issue printing of *Kum Back* (Beatles). Not the original one.

A: So that was your first exposure in that you...

NT: Well I had read about it before that.

A: Would that have been in *Rolling Stone* magazine for example?

NT: Well yeah. Because you know, they were reviewing bootleg records. They reviewed the Rubber Dubber releases as they came out. Also *Live 'R Than You'll Ever Be*, the Stones' Oakland show. They got a lot of press coverage for that release. But I was never able to find that one.

A: Looking back to the late 1960s and early 1970s, how and from what sources did these illicit tapes come from? Could you give me some examples?

NT: I would read *Rolling Stone* and see advertisements in the back for the rare recordings. Trade Mark of Quality (TMOQ) was advertising there. The label with the "pig" logo. I think Recycled Records in Berkeley and several places...all California. They were advertising for their catalogs. I picked up on it and as a result of that, oh six-to-nine months later I got in touch with some of these people about their wholesaling to me.

A: And that was so that you could sell the bootlegs as a retailer?

NT: Originally, that wasn't the idea. The idea was to feed my hobby. But it quickly moved on beyond that.

A: Because that helped to more than support the hobby didn't it?

NT: Oh absolutely. I mean there were a limited amount of titles out back then. In 1971, the stuff was retailing at about $3. The cost to dealers was from $.90 to $1.25, depending on whether it was on colored wax or not.

A: Do you think that the break-up of the Beatles, and the fact that they would not be releasing any more material, contributed to the growth of bootlegging in the 1970s?

NT: The timing I guess was good. Oh yes, the *Kum Back* bootleg was reviewed in *Rolling Stone*. I think it was actually written up in *Stereo Review* at the time too, if I'm not mistaken.

A: Do you think factors such as reviews in magazines that were read by the youth of the day contributed significantly to the growth?

NT: Yes, I'd say so. And one other thing was, right after they (The Beatles) broke up, within a year the (TV and radio) specials started coming out. That's when some of this special material started being unearthed. So naturally, people took advantage of that. We are talking about the really early pieces that appeared like, *Last Live Show*, which they called "Shea Stadium," but it wasn't. It was really the "Ed Sullivan Show." A lot of mislabeling and misleading information surfaced.

A: Now at some point, you got involved with two of history's most prominent underground record labels right?

NT: Well several. I pretty much knew everybody.

A: Did you mainly work with CBM and TMOQ?

NT: Well no. Actually TMOQ. I also worked with Kornyphone (The Amazing Kornyphone Record Label a.k.a. TAKRL). I used to deal a lot with them. There were several people involved with that. I dealt with all of them at TAKRL. But that was somewhat later, about 1975 or so. Early on I worked with CBM, that's when he was based in Virginia. Virginia Beach…Norfolk I guess.

A: Where was TMOQ based?

NT: They were in Burbank, California.

A: As for CBM, there has been some controversy among collectors, that there were two different groups. One was called Contra Band Music and another was called CBM. Weren't they one and the same?

NT: Exactly. They were one and the same. Of course, he also had off-shoot labels like King Kong and Instant Analysis, when he went to a new pressing plant.

A: What were these people like to work with? Were you a formal employee of theirs or an independent?

NT: No, no, no. When I got into this, I was just real interested in the music. When I ran my first ad in October of 1972 in *Rolling Stone*, I got a lot of requests for a catalog that I did not yet have (laughs). I mean there were only a handful of titles at that point. The big titles at that point were *Yellow Matter Custard* (The Beatles), *Neil Young Live at the L.A. Music Center*, an all-time classic...*Live 'R Than You'll Ever Be*, and the various configurations of the *Get Back Sessions* (The Beatles).

A: The Japanese consider CBM to be one of the worst companies of all bootleggers. They felt the record material was bad, poor-quality vinyl was used, and because of a low cutting level there was a lot of noise.

NT: I actually think the Brooklyn and Bronx bootlegs (fake Shalom label and blank label) are the worst stuff ever. I think that's worse than anything CBM ever did. He had the real thick records with bubbles in them. Just a total disregard for quality. He didn't care. The guy wasn't a music fan. If it was Grateful Dead or Beatles, he put it out.

A: Did you ever hear of the Melvin label? It seems that in the 1970s they only released Beatles bootlegs.

NT: Oh yeah. They were just big fans and comedians. You know they had their funny titles like *Beatles vs. Don Ho*. It was great stuff (laughs). That was just a labor of love for them. I doubt they ever made any money. Funny stuff though. I haven't bumped into any of those guys in quite some time. They're still around. I think most of them are involved in the legitimate business. They are in radio and...They were Melvin in the late 1970s primarily.

A: What do you know about the Tobe Milo label?

NT: He's been out of it for a long time. I saw him a few years ago at a Beatlefest. He still collects. That was just a little fluky thing he did for a while. Almost as a gag you know. He put out of few titles and had numbered limited editions. I remember when the Beatles' bootleg *Casualties* came out. Up to that time, it had a good reproduction of one of the butcher cover shots. And it came out in a blank label. I got the first 100 of them and did a numbered edition of them as the first 100. I sold them at quite a premium!

A: He seemed to take pride in the production of each release?

NT: Yes. He has been out of it for years. He only had that handful of a few titles himself. Like *Sam Houston* (Beatles) and *Brung To Ewe By* (Beatles). All cool stuff you know.

A: I must admit that I was fooled into thinking that *Casualties* was a real promo when it first came out.

NT: That was well done. I can't remember who did that album or *Collector's Items* (Beatles). But I'm sure they came out of California.

NT: Let's see, where was I?

A: I was asking you what these people were like to deal with? Were they also fans and collectors or were they just out to make a profit?

NT: Both. I mean, most of them were young people in college just like I was at the time. CBM for instance…he was in law school at the time. I won't mention his name. He was in law school at the time when I sent off for his list, which he advertised in the back of the *Stone*. Of course, that was back in the days when a one inch ad or a seventeen word classified was $85, as opposed to $600 now.

A: So the cost of doing business back in the 1970s was certainly cheaper?

NT: Oh yeah. But, I requested his wholesale list. He called me up. I went to see him. Before you knew it, I was supplying him with rare material. I sent him tons of stuff.

A: And how were you locating material to supply to him?

NT: Well, through my ad, people would write in and when I finally did get my list out, I said if you have material out there let me know about it. And that was about the time when the BBC radio series was starting to air in the States.

A: About what year do you believe that was?

NT: Uh, that was in '72.

A: Beatles at the BBC? Or just in general, BBC cuts?

NT: Well no, the first. As I recall, there was a whole series of BBC "In Concerts."…that's where that early Led Zeppelin came from. And then Pink Floyd in 1972. You know, they were all great quality. They came right off of BBC Transcription discs. That was about the same time that the King Biscuit Flower Hour started.

A: And of course, "In Concert" and "King Biscuit" started to air great quality live shows on U.S. radio of the most popular artists of the day…

NT: And of course, they would immediately show up on bootlegs the next week! (laughs).

A: …on record?

NT: That's right.

A: How did CBM, TMOQ, TAKRL and others select which artists and which concerts or studio tapes they were planning to release? Was there any type of system to the releases?

NT: Well they mainly put out the "supergroup" recordings. I mean the Beatles, (the Rolling) Stones, and (Bob) Dylan were the big three. (Led) Zeppelin soon followed. In late 1972 and early 1973, that is when more audience tapes started being made. Prior to that time, it was primarily studio outtakes and BBC material.

A: Weren't tape recorders still quite large at the time? How were people smuggling them into the live shows?

NT: Well, the audience tapes were done on you know, archaic by today's standards, little home portable tape recorders. By 1972, cassettes were in. I was taping shows myself with cassette. Some of the early people I traded with would send me these little five inch reels of shows.

A: And so some of these tapes made on both cassette and reels became bootleg albums?

NT: Oh yeah.

A: What would you say is the most famous show you taped back in the early 1970s?

NT: Oh that I personally taped?

A: Yes.

NT: Oh gee, I don't know. I taped about everything. Much of it never made it on to vinyl. I mean a few things did. *Bob Dylan at Charlotte, January 1974*. I made a pretty decent tape of that. That ended up hitting the record stands. It wasn't one of the better ones though. There were some tapers out there back then that knew what they were doing compared to me (laughs).

A: So you were learning as you did it?

NT: I just wanted the stuff. I mean when Dylan hit the road in '74, he did I think forty-two shows. I had forty-one and a half of them on tape you know. This is by the end of the tour.

A: How many others beside yourself in the early-to-mid 1970s were supplying tapes directly to CBM, TMOQ and the other major bootleggers?

NT: I was the only person supplying tapes to CBM. Of course, this was at the same time that the radio shows started coming out with the live shows. So if you were in a market that carried the show, the bootleggers could tape it themselves. You know a lot of the stuff came out of L.A., so Kornyphone people and Godzilla, TMOQ and all those people, they all knew each other.

A: Was The Amazing Kornyphone Record Label (TAKRL) also located in L.A.?

NT: Yes.

A: Was TAKRL owned and operated by different personnel than TMOQ?

NT: Yes, but they knew each other. There was a whole network of them out there. I mean the old timers at that time were the Rubber Dubber people. They started the TMOQ company to the best of my...the way I have been able to piece the puzzle together. Because even way back then, all we ever had were first names to go on. I didn't know any last names of anybody until about the middle 1970s. By that time, the old timers were out of the picture and new Kornyphone people came along and they put out loads of stuff. They were quite prolific (laughs).

A: Do you recall how you were compensated when you would supply a tape to CBM or TMOQ for example?

NT: They would pay me in discs.

A: In other words copies of the records that they had made from your tape?

NT: Right.

A: And you would in turn sell those records through your mail order catalog?

NT: Right.

A: How about the live album of the *Beatles at Hollywood Bowl?* Any idea how that recording leaked out?

NT: That was interesting because that was one of the first pieces I ever bought. Of course, it was great quality at the time. I found out it was made off an acetate of the combination of the '64 and '65 performances. Through the grapevine I was able to buy that actual acetate many years later at a Beatlefest convention.

A: The rumor on that one is that it had "walked out" of Capitol Records' front door.

NT: Well the acetate did and the guy I got the piece from was an engineer or engineer's helper at Capitol. He was walking around with it at Beatlefest. And I gave him three hundred dollars for the thing. Much to my surprise, when I got home to play the thing, it had the skips that are on the original pressing. So I knew what it was. That was pretty intriguing you know. Now, so I got it back and I sold it about a year or two later for about $1500 you know, as a collection piece. Then the guy I sold it to called me up and wanted me to buy it back. I got it back somehow on a trade or something. I then resold it and the person I resold it to, resold it. Now some collector has it for $10,000 (laughs).

A: Jumping ahead for a minute, the highlight of the late 1980s and the early 1990s in terms of bootleg releases of rare Beatles material, was The Swinging Pig issues of *Ultra Rare Trax*. And also Yellow Dog Records' release of the *Unsurpassed Masters* series containing studio alternates and outtakes of The Beatles. Any idea how this excellent sounding material leaked out after so many years?

NT: Well I've heard rumors, one of which I totally do not believe, but has circulated around. When (Mark) Lewisohn was doing his book, he was privy to these tapes. I'm not saying he let them out because I *know* he didn't.

A: Discounting that rumor, do you have any idea? Do you think it was maybe an engineer or someone on the inside?

NT: Well you know, in the last three or four years, so much material has come out. And I'm not just talking about tapes. I'm talking about documents, important artifacts that have found their way into the hands of collectors, including record awards and other old stuff. So there has got to be a connection there. I think there is probably one source who we'll never actually know. I've been out of the whole bootleg underground for so long, I really don't have any idea. Every once in a while I see one of those old characters around. I don't ask any questions.

A: Back to the 1970s when you were active. *Sweet Apple Trax* is perhaps the most famous of all Beatles bootlegs. Its hard to imagine one that caused more excitement among collectors and music scholars. Maybe it was the times, or maybe it was the first really good sounding studio recordings of The Beatles containing their January 1969 film rehearsals. Can you give us the background on how you came about obtaining the tapes and how you got involved with that one?

NT: Yes. One of my customers wrote me about it and called me on the phone. He said he had this tape. I said that I'd like to hear it. And he brought it up from Florida. We did the deal for it. I called up CBM and said, 'I've got something *hot* here. What do you think? It's eighty-eight minutes.' I didn't get a master (tape) by any stretch. When he brought it to me, it was on Radio Shack tape at 3 & 3/4 inches.

A: And obviously the Beatles did not use Radio Shack tape in 1969. Anyway, what year did you purchase the tape?

NT: I think that was around 1974.

A: Did the tape come from an ex-Apple Records employee?

NT: Well the fellow I got it from, got it from an Apple person.

A: And who was the fellow you purchased the tape from?

NT: He was just a collector. I had gotten lots of tapes from this guy and everything I had gotten from him was *really* good! And this tape was no exception.

A: What did the tape cost you?

NT: Uh, I can't quite remember.

A: Was it in the two or three hundred dollar range?

NT: Yes…five hundred bucks maybe. And I think I gave it to CBM and he gave me probably two hundred and fifty sets of the four-record deal. Of the original release.

A: The original was a four-record set?

NT: The original was two, two-record sets. It was called *Sweet Apple Trax Volume I* and *Volume II*. And it was released on that sepia-tone color. Two color thin pack.

A: That album came out on Contra Band Music then?

NT: Uh, it was on Instant Analysis. But that was (owned by) CBM.

A: Did CBM use a logo that featured a drawing of a pirate with a dagger?

NT: Yeah, that was one of them.

A: And then Instant Analysis I think used a mad scientist cartoon character right?

NT: Right. Then CBM also used the King Kong logo.

A: The Gorilla?

NT: Yes. When they (CBM) started doing the stuff on Instant Analysis, the pressings got better and they began using the dyna-groove system, which was better wax, because if you are familiar with the early CBM product, they were really lousy pressings.

A: So did they press *Sweet Apple Trax* in Philadelphia?

NT: Well it's always been my understanding that all that (CBM) stuff was done at a plant in Philadelphia. To confirm that…years later, I got a call from a New York guy that had a store and he was offered a truck load of CBM material. And he took what he wanted and I drove up to Virginia and bought the rest of the stuff. Thousands of pieces. It ended up being about one-hundred fifty-count boxes of what I ended up with. It was all CBM material and it all had come from Philly originally. The stuff came with clotheslines full of labels not yet put onto discs. And blank jackets and inserts. I mean just stacks and stacks of stuff. A legitimate record dealer in Virginia had bought out this warehouse and pressing plant. Just a little post script. They had gotten lots of legitimate stuff as well, including acetates—I mean thirty-five gallon drums full of metal stampers, mothers, acetates, labels, original Sun Records labels. He got stuff from years and years past. By the time I got to the stuff, all that was left were the boots. He got a real goldmine!

A: It certainly sounds like it. Now, in terms of production costs of *Sweet Apple Trax*, what did it cost for production of each album?

NT: I don't know what it would have cost him (CBM) to put it out. When he was wholesaling the pieces out, that one was the first one where he charged a premium just because of the nature of the material. It was the first of the new frontier pieces.

A: How many sets were in the first pressing?

NT: It is my understanding that they went to Europe before they even shipped here.

A: It has to be one of the biggest selling Beatles bootlegs of all time.

NT: It certainly is one of the most re-bootlegged ones as well. The guy in New York put out the double-gatefold color cover version. A lot of people think that's the original, but it's not.

A: The one on the Newsound Record label?

NT: Ah yes. The cover is nice and everything, but it is inferior to Instant Analysis. That guy used a terrible pressing plant as well in Brooklyn or Bronx. He had the worst stuff by far.

A: Did he master his copy from the Instant Analysis vinyl?

NT: Yes. That's how he got it. They just knocked each other off constantly.

A: Did that bother rival companies? The back and forth knocking off of each other's product?

NT: You know, I mean, that's expected.

A: Was there any editing done to the tape you provided to CBM?

NT: I don't know if there was or not. I can't remember. I know that a lot of the stuff I gave to CBM always came out on another label later. Especially The Beatles stuff. Beatles and Dylan were primarily the big two back then.

A: Didn't you also have something to do with a few other Beatle bootleg titles like *Have You Heard The Word, L.S. Bumblebee* and *Maryjane*?

NT: Right.

A: Do any interesting stories come to mind about those releases?

NT: Well I was given the tapes, or I bought the tapes from somebody in Jersey I believe, someone who had advertised that he had weird material. When I gave the tapes to CBM, he put them out just the way I gave them to him. That's why they have no relation. Some of the songs have nothing to do with anything else on the record—kind of reckless in the way they were assembled.

A: One of those bootlegs contained the song "Peace of Mind." People have historically argued over whether or not that is a Beatles song. What is your theory on whether or not there is Beatles involvement in that song?

NT: It beats me. That's one that really kind of bothered me.

A: It seems that a lot of bootleg titles from the 1970s seemed to carry the same catalog number. Why did that happen?

NT: I don't know. Well Wizardo…you know, he was also somehow associated with Kornyphone (The Amazing Kornyphone Record Label). I think he grew out of TMOQ. Like I said, all those guys were very interrelated…There is one piece they actually put out and they had their faces on the cover itself! (laughs) Kind of a gag. They called it the B. Tuff Band (spells it). Wizardo was right there smiling on the cover. It is a very rare piece though.

A: What was the music inside?

NT: I don't think I ever listened to it. He was a frustrated musician.

A: Let's talk about what you know about the manufacturing process, once the tapes were procured by bootleggers. Typically, did these bootleggers have their own vinyl presses or did they farm this work out?

NT: No, they farmed them out. I mean if you had the money, you could get anything pressed.

A: Did the record pressing plants in the 1970s care whether the recordings were licensed or not?

NT: No. Not at all. Not until the middle 1970s did that start to play into things, because when (Paul) McCartney did the Wings Over America tour, that triple (bootleg) set on red, white and blue vinyl really sent some shock waves through the bootleg industry because the legitimate record industry recognized it. And that's when Kornyphone/Wizardo started getting shook. They got calls from their (record pressing) plant saying, 'don't come around for a while.'

A: That set you are referring to, *Wings From The Wings*, sold pretty well didn't it?

NT: Oh, it was…man it was a killer! I remember a Beatles convention in Boston. That piece had just come out. And for some unknown reason, I encouraged the maker of that piece, who was Kornyphone, to come on out to Boston. He did, to market them. It kind of cut my throat because I had a hundred of them there. And he had a van full of them! (laughs) He of course cut a better deal than I could.

A: Back in the middle 1970s at these conventions and festivals, bootlegs were allowed to be sold at the tables right on the main floor correct?

NT: Yes. At the early Beatle conventions as well. I did the first ever Beatlefest at the Commodore in New York in September of '74. I was the only person there that was exclusively selling bootlegs. It was like Christmas in September! (laughs) Of course, nowadays, you cannot find boots on a convention floor.

A: Do you recall what you earned at that particular convention selling bootlegs?

NT: I think I took in four or five grand, which was a lot of money for 1974. Especially at $3.50 per pop. $4.25 for doubles.

A: What was the unit cost to press long-play records back in the early 1970s?

NT: Probably about fifty cents each. A lot of these guys would just have the plant press up the thing. They'd do the inserts and the shrink-wrap, if it was to be shrink-wrapped themselves.

A: So the bootleggers determined the artwork, the graphics, if any, on the label or the outside cover?

NT: Yeah. Back then there was very little artwork.

A: Was there any type of quality control involved in the manufacturing process?

NT: No.

A: The insert sheets must have been quite inexpensive because most of them were merely photocopied weren't they?

NT: Exactly. Or it was two-color printing.

A: So the finished raw cost of the album was only about sixty cents?

NT: If that much. I doubt if it was even that much.

A: So then the wholesale price back then was about ninety cents each, right? And the retail price was about three or three-fifty for a single disc?

NT: Yes. I think my first catalog was about $3.10 for (album) singles.

A: On another subject, you stated previously that rival bootleggers all tended to know each other well...

NT: ...Well, let me qualify that. The East Coast guys knew the East Coast guys. They shared pressing plants. And all the West Coast people knew each other.

A: If one bootlegger obtained a good tape, would the competitor attempt to copy it off the vinyl and re-release it?

NT: Yes.

A: Did they all assume that this was part of the business?

NT: Oh sure.

A: Did anyone ever take these knock-offs personally?

NT: Not that I know of. I mean sometimes they weren't knocking each other off. When BBC Led Zeppelin came out, which was a killer, a biggie, I supplied the original tape for that piece on CBM and before long, it was out on TMOQ. But they (TMOQ) got an original tape themselves. Their tape was actually better than what I had originally supplied. The same thing (occurred) with the BBC (Pink) *Floyd's of London*. These shows were available to other people.

A: When you were supplying tapes to these companies, did you get involved at all in creating titles for the albums?

NT: Yes, well *Floyd's of London* was one of the one's I came up with.

A: In the production of these albums, with inserts, I've noticed over the years that there are quite often in-jokes, clues, or an inside nod to the people involved.

NT: Oh yeah. Sometimes in the run-off (wax) where the matrix number is located, there would be little messages. One was "Ha Ha, catch me if you can." There were several of them.

A: So in some cases, bootleggers were actively taunting the authorities or perhaps teasing?

NT: Yes. Especially Wizardo. That was just in his character. He was a nutty guy. He was pretty cool.

A: In 1975 and 1976, when pressing plants started to receive pressure from the record companies and the RIAA to stop pressing bootlegs, what did bootleggers do to combat this?

NT: They paid more money to get it done.

A: So the pressing plants continued to cooperate with them?

NT: Oh yeah. There was a plant out in L.A. that was doing RCA and CBS (record company) contract work. Some of the big CBS titles had just come out and the pressing plant couldn't handle it all, so they'd farm it out to other plants. And on several occasions, when something like that was going on, I think around 1978 when *Darkness On The Edge Of Town* came out, there was a big advance order for that. It couldn't be handled by just the main plant, so they farmed it to another plant in L.A. I remember getting a call from Wizardo and Kornyphone, saying "the plant just called us up. We had to get all our stampers and stuff out because CBS was moving in" (laughs). At about that same time, there was a "Colombo" episode on (TV), that dealt with record piracy. And they did the shoot of the pressing plant, in this particular pressing plant, where the bootlegs were (actually) made (laughs). And there again, my people...my friends out there, got called saying "you've got to come get all this stuff outta here (laughs). ABC's coming in here to shoot a TV show." So we were all excited about the "Colombo" episode which ended up being totally ridiculous. It had nothing to do with reality.

A: Over the years, many bootlegs have appeared with titles which basically misled consumers as to the origin of the tape. For example, *Live At Whiskey Flats* purported to be the Beatles in an Atlanta show, but was not in fact. What was the reason behind this misinformation?

NT: Well, originally I don't think it was deliberate. Whoever did the first pressings of those things...when they were knocked-off, they just retained the same name and the legend grew, you know.

A: But what about the first person to press them. Were they just mistaken as to the source?

NT: Uh pretty much. I mean the guy that did *Last Live Show* (Beatles) in New York, I just don't think he knew what that was. Finally after all these years, the Beatles Atlanta show has shown up. Or snippets of it. I don't think its going to be coming out. There's a tape from a journalist from Sweden or someplace who's in Atlanta and he's talking over the tape. But I think there's three complete songs and snippets of several others plus his Swedish voice-overs. It's not really circulating among collectors. I've been offered the tape as memorabilia. But it's out of my realm now.

A: There has been some discussion that later in the 1970s, bootlegs were mistitled so that if the authorities were actively cracking down, by listing incorrect information, it would be harder to trace back the recording to its source. Do you have any information to substantiate this practice?

NT: Oh I don't know. I don't buy that. I'd say, more often than not, bootleggers didn't know the correct source of the recordings they were pressing.

A: Why was the same material often repressed under a different title? Wasn't this just another way to stretch every possible dollar out of the tape?

NT: Oh yeah! Competition among the thieves in the den there, you know (laughs).

A: Were the big three bootleg companies of the 1970s CBM, TMOQ and Wizardo?

NT: Well the mid-'70s anyway. Things changed. I mean most of these people just drifted away from it around '77. A lot of things were more sophisticated. People were getting in trouble and then moving on to another line of work.

A: Although you are no longer involved in the underground record industry, who do you see as the artists whose titles are the biggest sellers today on compact disc?

NT: I guess all The Beatles stuff is bigger than anything else, I would think. R.E.M. has got a huge catalog. I just saw all that new stuff when I was in New York. I think R.E.M. has had ten new titles in the last six months. You know, in the late 1970s the Springsteen phenomenon happened. And that's when I sold…Bruce (Springsteen) outsold The Beatles on bootlegs. About when *Born To Run* came out, he was still pretty much a cult figure. When *Darkness On The Edge Of Town* came out, there was just a flurry of things. Of course he's still wildly popular in the boot circuit. As soon as he hits the road there will be more state-of-the-art material coming out.

A: Back into the 1970s, with TMOQ and CBM. Did the logos these companies used, such as the pig with the cigar and the pirate with the knife in his teeth, have any special significance?

NT: Well the pirate thing of course is obvious. The pig thing…Stout may have actually done that pig design, but I'm not sure. He is a pretty well-known artist. And he did a lot of the covers for a lot of the TMOQ releases. Stout has also done other *legitimate* album covers way back when too. He has a cult following. You should have seen the original cover for *Radio London*—*The Who* and the Stones' *All Meat Music*. All fantastic stuff.

A: What was the system of bootleg distribution in the 1970s? Were promo copies utilized?

NT: No promo copies. Record shows started popping up. And these records would show up at conventions and head shops and used record stores. It was a haphazard network, but the material got out there! I never really followed the entire trail, but a lot just went overseas. They made a lot of money over there. I mean, I know so much stuff went over to Japan back then.

A: Has the distribution system become more sophisticated into the 1980s and now in the 1990s?

NT: I think so. I don't really follow it anymore.

A: There seems to be a lot more advertising in several record collector magazines today...

NT: Oh yeah. It's surprising to me there hasn't been a crackdown again. There really hasn't been one in several years. They must not be looking at record collector magazines lately. It's blatant as hell.

A: In the 1970s, *Rolling Stone* magazine would occasionally write record reviews of bootlegs. Do you think this was a benefit to bootleg sales?

NT: Well it certainly didn't hurt.

A: Don't you think that in some respects *Rolling Stone* was philosophically aligned with the underground record industry?

NT: Yeah, I guess in the middle 1970s they were! It would depend on who wrote the article. I used to sell to a couple of writers who wrote for *Rolling Stone*. A couple of them actually came to see me and interview me. They were just totally intrigued with this whole thing you know.

A: When TMOQ and CBM released each title, did they do much in the way of documenting their own record release? In other words, did they record the title, the number of discs pressed, the catalog number, the release dates, the number of discs sold for each title?

NT: I really don't know. It was out of my scope or relationship.

A: Well how about you as a retailer. Did you keep track of what you sold?

NT: No. I didn't keep track of what I sold. I sold a load of *Sweet Apple Trax.* I was strictly retail. I had a couple stores here and there that I sold to. I was into selling to the collectors. If you have seen any of my old, old catalogs, I was a stickler for detail. I had sound quality ratings, all the tracks, the source. It was like the *Hot Wacks* book became for collectors. I would carry all pressings, because some of the collectors would want all three or four pressings of the same disc. I had people who collected all the different color inserts (laughs).

A: How many copies were pressed per title run in the 1970s?

NT: There again, I really just don't know. I'd put out a new list three or four times per year and maybe a supplement a few times per year with the latest Floyd or Zeppelin or whatever. You know, I'd sell a few hundred of a title over a period of time. That was nothing compared to what was going on throughout the U.S. and abroad.

A: Were any of these underground companies paying taxes on this income?

NT: I don't know. CBM was paying mechanicals (royalties) in 1972 according to the '72 Copyright Law. There was like a standard two-cent royalty rate per song. And they (CBM) were sending money off to Capitol or whoever. The law changed again in 1976 I think, because I knew people that were selling the famous truck stop 8-tracks. That type of thing. Those were actually counterfeits. But they were paying royalties on this stuff. But the record companies, more often than not, refused to cash the checks. That was one of the reasons that there were crackdowns on bootleggers in the late 1970s, because according to the law, bootlegs were considered the same as counterfeiting. Two totally different things, but under the law…it was the same thing.

A: Whereas a counterfeit takes a successful album, by a successful group and merely copies it, a bootlegger takes something a group really never has any intention of releasing…

NT: Right.

A: Which bootleg titles, if you can recall, were the biggest bombs that did not sell well?

NT: Uh, Seals and Crofts never sold too well (laughs).

A: How about Barry Manilow? Has he ever been bootlegged?

NT: I never saw one! (hysterical laughter.) There was a marketplace for *most* everybody. Some pieces were put out purely as a…you know, whoever made it. They just liked the artist and just wanted the piece out, whether it sold a lot or not.

A: In the past, and at present, the most popular Beatles bootleggers seem to enjoy changing their names every couple of years. Can you explain the rationale for this? Is this just to stay one step ahead of the law?

NT: I guess that's part of it. And I guess the other thing is, actual change of ownership did occur.

A: It seems like the family trees of, for example, TMOQ and CBM are fairly complex. Do you think anyone ever kept track of these name changes within the companies or did they haphazardly go from one name to the next?

NT: Probably not. Again, it was all haphazard.

A: What happened to you in 1982 that changed the way you had been doing business?

NT: Well by that time, I was hardly selling any vinyl at all. I had a massive list of cassettes. Mostly live shows. At the time, I think I had like 175 Springsteen titles on my list. And so CBS was pretty much behind my bust, although Beatles titles were mentioned as well.

A: Were you indicted by the authorities?

NT: Yes.

A: What was your penalty or sentence if any?

NT: They took a lot of stuff. I had a forty thousand dollar fine.

A: Was that the end of your days in the bootlegging profession?

NT: Uh yeah, definitely.

A: What are some of your former bootleg colleagues doing today?

NT: Well, the original CBM guy, to the best of my knowledge, is a copyright attorney (laughs). Kornyphone, as far as I know, is in real estate in Los Angeles, doing very well. I haven't a clue as to what happened to any of the TMOQ people—1982 is the last time I saw any of those folks. They were caravaning around following the Stones on tour.

A: How would you say the underground music industry has changed from the 1970s to the 1990s?

NT: Certainly quality control exists now. Nothing bad comes out (today). If anything comes out, it sounds good.

A: Is that because music collector's expectations have been raised over the years by the very good sounding releases?

NT: Yes.

A: Are the profit margins significantly different with the compact discs sold underground today?

NT: It is hard to tell, because most of them are pressed overseas now. They probably get them pressed up pretty cheap. I've been involved in some legitimate CD releases in recent years, so I know what a legitimate CD costs to manufacture. Of course, it depends on the quality of the artwork you add. But as far as just getting a piece done, you can get a finished product in a box with a color insert for about five bucks.

A: Of course, while legitimate CDs retail for about fifteen dollars, most of the bootleg CDs sell for twenty-five or thirty dollars.

NT: That's pretty much the standard today. Wholesale on a lot of that stuff is…when it comes over here, is in the ten dollar range. When you get into the New York market, you can add about thirty to forty percent to get to retail. But then again it just depends.

A: Why did vinyl bootlegs vanish?

NT: When I got out of it in 1982, I didn't want to know anything more about it. I just let that whole part of my past go away. There was like a void there of several years where I did not know anything about what was going on. I do know, that when Springsteen hit the road for the *Born In The USA* tour, that was really the last hurrah for massive quantities of bootleg vinyl. The market was so flooded then that of course, the red flag's got to go up.

A: The vinyl bootlegs seemed to improve in quality as the underground music industry moved from the 1970s to the 1980s. Both the quality of the vinyl pressed and also the higher quality record covers.

NT: ...Yeah, they were getting into the nice artwork and all those things.

A: What caused the changes in improved quality?

NT: Well, one guy does it and I guess the next guy has got to do it. Most of that good stuff was originating in Europe. So people over here had to do the same thing. Or felt they had to do the same thing.

A: So a lot of the good quality material from Europe gave U.S. bootleggers the initiative to improve on the quality of the releases?

NT: Yeah.

A: With the recent development of legitimate record companies releasing box sets, containing outtakes and rarities, do you foresee this move as the end of bootlegging?

NT: No. I don't think so. I mean it's been going on this whole century! It started with opera. Back at the start of the century.

A: What about the fact that legitimate companies can never release enough material to satisfy the consumers of a particular artist?

NT: Right. Especially for the major artists.

A: The Beatles broke up over twenty years ago. There have been well over a thousand different bootleg titles containing their unreleased works...

NT: ...A thousand? I didn't know that.

A: Given the magnitude of underground releases, do you think there is any Beatles material left out there?

NT: Yep (laughs). The twenty minute version of "Helter Skelter" is out there. There is a lot of live stuff out there. They have still to see the light of day, but next to all these *Unsurpassed Masters*, I mean, so what? It just doesn't get any better than that you know. A lot of the stuff I'm aware of is just more live material, which I particularly like myself. You know, if they put out a CD of every show from the Beatles' 1965 tour, they'd (bootleggers) all suffer. Because, you know, the shows were all the same. McCartney said what he said (at each performance), right on cue.

A: And still does at his recent shows!

NT: There was no spontaneity to their shows after they came to the States. McCartney has always been stiff on stage. He's a professional and everything, but he is very stiff up there...even now.

A: Do you have a favorite bootleg?

NT: That's a tie. There's a lot of them. A lot of the stuff that has come out in the past couple years has really knocked me out. Like the *Unsurpassed Masters* Beatles material.

A: Whatever happened to a planned album of the Beatles live at Carnegie Hall?

NT: There's a mystery right there. I think that was assigned a (catalogue) number and a Capitol pressing number and everything. That just has to be lost, that is all I think. With the contacts I had, if it was still in the vaults, we would have heard it by now (laughs). I just think something happened to that particular one.

A: Are you implying that record company studio vault security is not 100% tight, even in this day and age?

NT: No. That is exactly what I'm implying!

A: Looking back on it philosophically, does it bother you at all that the artists involved in the releases that came from your tapes, might not have wanted some of these things to be released to the public?

NT: Well I mean, we looked at this whole thing as music for the people. We didn't see it as competing with commercial product at all. And I still don't. I don't have any apologies about that part of the thing.

A: What about the argument that record companies have to incur the initial risk of discovering and signing talent, and recording, promoting and distributing legitimate artists? Then the bootleggers come in and take the easy ride releasing pieces only from the best bands?

NT: Oh I don't think that is a good argument. Of course, things have changed and gotten much more sophisticated since I was involved in this thing. I can see today where there is concern with the CDs, but the material still co-exists and they've got better things to do than run around popping these people.

A: I'd like to thank you for taking the time to educate us on what you knew about the underground record industry.

NT: My pleasure.

AN INTERVIEW WITH BOOTLEG GRAPHIC ARTIST, RETAILER AND CONCERT TAPER, LORD BUDDHA (1975–1977)

AUTHOR (A): How did you first get involved in bootleg recordings back in the 1970s?

LORD BUDDHA (LB): I started off basically as a fan. A little while after bootlegging first came out, I'd gone…they were carried in a lot of record stores back then including a very large record store chain out here. They'd carry a lot of bootlegs. As a matter of fact, the owner of this chain is reputed to have put out one of the first Crosby, Stills & Nash bootlegs. There was a live double album from the Forum. Anyway, there was one record store and they had a Hendrix bootleg that came out on a label called Immaculate Conception. And I bought it. It turned out basically just to be a pirate off the *Woodstock* album and very poorly done. And I thought, I'm never going to buy another bootleg.

A: So what motivated you to change your mind?

LB: Well it was maybe two years after that, at a swap meet. There was a stand out there that sold the bootleg albums and they had one of The Beatles, *At The Hollywood Bowl*. And I thought, even if it sounds wretched, I've got to take a chance. I bought it and it turned out to be fabulous! That was such a delightful surprise, that I was pretty much hooked. And after a while, I got to like that sound…those cavernous-sounding recordings are some of my favorites. So from there, I started buying them and I started selling them simply as a means of being able to get them at wholesale (price) and get first crack at them. I got to know the fellow that was selling them at that swap meet. We ran into him in line at a Captain Beefheart concert. He started wholesaling to us. He later went off to college and sold us his business at the swap meet. It turned out to be, you know, kind of a nice way of supporting yourself through college.

A: It seems like quite a few people involved in bootlegging started out that way.

LB: Yes. And that spun off into my partnership with a woman, who afterwards, opened up a record store that I managed.

A: So then you had access to lots of records of all kinds.

LB: Almost the next natural step in that scenario is to make them (bootlegs) yourself. It wasn't that hard to do. It seemed like the fun, natural thing to do. I was still living at home as well. Stuff would be arriving at our home from East Coast distributors by UPS and my mom would be signing for it. We never thought about it being criminal at all, because at the time (prior to 1976) the Copyright Law didn't cover bootlegs. The understanding we had then, was that there was no criminal law covering this, only civil law. If an artist ever wanted to sue us, they could, but the general feeling of artists back then was that bootlegging was cool!

A: That's right, they felt it was a badge of honor back then.

LB: John Lennon collected them, Keith Richards did, Charlie Watts and many other artists did as well.

A: Besides selling bootlegs, weren't you also involved in taping shows and doing graphic artwork on bootlegs as well?

LB: Yes. A friend of mine got a tape recorder and we just started taping shows. I think the first one we did was George Harrison. On the '74 tour, he did a show in Long Beach. And we taped that and did the cover art for it.

A: What was the title of that album?

LB: It's been such a while, I'm going to look it up in *Hot Wacks* here if I can find it…I just found it. We called the album, *Let's Hear One For Lord Buddha*. And I think the label was called Herby Howard or something like that. We wound up doing a couple of things like that, and they all wound up being weird and funny for some reason or another. That one there, I misspelled Lord Buddha because they were in such a rush to get this album out. One of the guys from this company was this easy going drug-head. The other guy looked like some kind of guy who couldn't make it in the mafia. He looked like he'd much rather be a thug. He came down, and again I'm still living at home, and this guy sat on my bed waiting for me to finish up the artwork. The album's called *Let's Hear One For Lord Buddha*, which is what George (Harrison) would shout out at his concerts in his hoarse voice. And I misspelled Buddha because I was in such a hurry to get this guy out of the house!

A: So was this hand-drawn artwork?

LB: It was a couple of photos which my friend had taken at the show, the actual concert. It also has a minor distinction, somewhere during the taping of it. This was a sit-down-on-the-floor type show. Several rows ahead of us, some kids were standing up. In the middle of the taping, I yelled, 'Get down you slugs' (laughs). Later at the record store one person said to me, 'that's your voice isn't it?' He thought I was yelling it at George (Harrison)!

A: What other projects do you recall working on?

LB: A couple of other things. I did the album art for a *Ten Years After* bootleg, which I think they came up with the tape themselves (Herby Howard). We also did the artwork for a Jim Croce bootleg, which I think is one of the poorest-selling bootlegs of all time. And just because these guys were so thick…what we did was to give them a photo of Carlos Santana…

A: …And they put that photo on the Jim Croce album?

LB: Yeah, and they said, 'Wow great photo of him!' (laughs).

A: When you created the artwork on a particular bootleg, would you use a pseudonym as credit for your work?

LB: No. Probably the only people who used to take credit was the Kornyphone (TAKRL) guy. He used at least half-a-dozen pseudonyms.

A: Do you recall some of those names?

LB: There was Dr. Art Gnouvo, spelled g-n-o-u-v-o or something. Dr. Terence Telly Phone and he had a couple of other names as well.

A: You also worked with the folks at Vicki Vinyl.

LB: Yes.

A: Can you tell me more about the Vicki Vinyl label? What was its first release, if you remember?

LB: I can't even remember what the first one was. But there was a period of time where it just seemed like everyone we knew just started making their own little records. Like we knew these school teachers who were big Springsteen fans, who put out the first Springsteen bootleg. This was right before the big *Time* and *Newsweek* rush started on him. These people were really what I would call the second generation bootleggers, of which Vicki was one of the biggest on the West Coast. At least the FBI thought so.

A: I assume you had contact with the FBI in the 1970s. What were they like to deal with?

LB: There were some real careerists in the FBI who made a lot of big cupy-points and got promotions after busting these kids. But the average FBI guy, and I talked to a couple, were relatively embarrassed by this thing because they had spent a long time becoming FBI agents, and it wasn't so that they could chase kids who were making these cute little toy records. They were merely trying to satisfy the commercial recording industry.

A: So the only reason they were even looking into bootlegging was due to the pressure brought to bear by the industry and their association, the Recording Industry Association of America (RIAA)?

LB: Yes that's what I was told. Basically, the record companies have these large lobbying powers in Washington. They also had pretty intensive power as well where they could do a benefit for a politician. They made some strong affiliations in the Capitol for favorable legislation that way. So a lot of undue pressure was applied on bootleggers. So while all these other heinous crimes were going on in this country, the FBI was spending their time running around chasing these kids.

A: Were you involved in taping any other Beatles-related bootlegs?

LB: I had some involvement in the triple record Paul McCartney live box set. It was called *Wings From The Wings*. It also came out in various forms cheaply.

Originally, it came out in three different colors of vinyl: red, white and blue. That was from his '76 tour. It was funny. A lot of these records were pressed in the same pressing plant that had done a lot of colored vinyl in the sixties—you may remember, like the old Fantasy record label. They used the old fashioned biscuits. And they had some wise-guy, little oriental man, who looked like he should have been working in a tramp steamer. He just said, 'It's bi-centennial…three records…why not make the three red, white and blue?' So they did that and it became a real good seller.

It is also, from what we hear, the release that scared the record industry into putting out the official McCartney album as a triple set. When Capitol originally made an announcement about their release, they announced it as a two-record set. And they had a real hoopla over our triple album because unfortunately, the bootleg and commercial record industries were both centered in the same two cities, L.A. and New York. And the major source of disseminating bootlegs into the L.A. area was a record swap meet in the Capitol Records parking lot! And I think it really shocked some of the executives who would come in to do some work on the weekends. They would walk through the parking lot and see all these Paul McCartney triple album sets (laughs). So that started one of the FBI "heats" at that time.

A: Changing the subject for a minute. Can you describe the apparent rivalry among second generation West Coast bootleg manufacturers? What was it like at the time?

LB: Most of these people were more or less friends. Because it was sort of a certain comradery where you're doing something unique. There was also no enjoyment in getting ripped off by the other guy. To some people, there was this honor and integrity among bootleggers. To the other people, it was like a game. They took pleasure in scamming the other guy and getting the material out at the same time, stealing their discs.

There is one bootlegger, Wizardo. He had one bootleg with the group Gentle Giant, where at the end of side two, there is like a two-minute phone conversation. He had recorded one of the other bootleggers. He just put on this tape of this bootlegger ranting and complaining about yet another bootlegger. "This guy's shit, he rips everybody off, no one can stand him…" They don't identify the guy he is talking about, but everybody else in the business assumed he was talking about *them* (laughs). And it caused a lot of ill-will for awhile.

A: Do you recall whether the Wizardo label ever had a business relationship with

TAKRL?

LB: They were really tough competitors, but for some reason I think every once in a while, he would supply them with a tape. Because every so often, on a Kornyphone record you would see them thanking W. Z. Ardo. But also, just as often they (TAKRL) would do that to piss him (Wizardo) off. Maybe if they were putting out a particularly bad sounding tape they'd thank him on it (laughs).

A: How did the "Saint Valentine's Day Massacre" come about?

LB: One label, Trade Mark of Quality (TMOQ), had recorded a show of Bob Dylan live with The Band in '74, and was putting out a box set on it. Again, I think we taped it at the (L.A.) Forum and it was a complete concert. It was I think the first deluxe box set to come out as a bootleg. Beautiful, glossy, full color cover with a photo of Dylan. Maybe because the box itself was not ready yet, these records themselves were sitting at the pressing plant. They weren't out on the street. This other bootlegger at the Kornyphone (TAKRL) label slipped in there and was able to grab two of the discs and just copied his own masters off of those and had a two-record version of the set before this other guy's (TMOQ) had hit the street.

A: When you would tape shows or do the artwork for record covers, how were you compensated?

LB: I wasn't basically. Maybe I'd get a copy or two of the album.

A: Were you ever caught attempting to smuggle a tape recorder into a show?

LB: Inside the shows, hardly ever. It almost seemed like some agreed thing. If you could get it through the door, they'd leave you alone. At the time in the late '70s, I do not believe it was illegal to tape the show. What was illegal, was to reproduce it for profit. But trying to explain this in the middle of a live concert to some big beefy bouncer is a little difficult. My favorite one was when a woman friend of mine and I were recording an Elton John concert. Tape decks back then tended to be real large. Like the size of a small coffee table.

A: How did she get that into the show?

LB: She would wear a long dress and kind of put a sling on this thing and carry it between her legs. Which generally worked. But on this particular occasion, at

Dodger Stadium, her battery compartment came open. And she was walking up the ramp at the Stadium and these big D cells are flopping from between her legs (laughs) and rolling down the ramp behind her. And I'm picking them up behind her. And that was pretty enjoyable.

There were other wonderful bootleg moments when people would get their recorder inside and then realize they had forgotten their microphone or their tape. Of course, at a certain point a lot of bootlegs started to come out from the many radio broadcasts like the "King Biscuit Flower Hour." All were taped right off the radio.

A: Do you recall any of the bootleggers you associated with preparing promotional copies of their records and sending them out to magazines, in order to have them reviewed?

LB: We never sent any to *Rolling Stone*. After some years, *Rolling Stone* turned antagonistic toward us. By the time we went through that big Bruce Springsteen lawsuit, they got downright scary.

A: Many artists in the early 1970s thought it was very cool to be bootlegged. Were you aware of your associates ever sending a copy of their latest bootleg to an artist?

LB: There's not too much I can think of. The closest example I can think of…again, I knew the person who put out the first Springsteen bootleg…and in 1975, I was able to get Springsteen a copy of that. On his West Coast tour, he played the Roxy. About a week later, he was playing up in Santa Barbara. I drove up with a bunch of friends and saw the show. Then afterwards, I brought a copy of this record up to some folks who were going to get to talk to him. And we hung around long enough afterward backstage to be able to give him this album. I think we called it *The Jersey Devil*. He was delighted. He was standing next to his bass player, Gary Talon. He said, 'Hey look at this, we've been bootlegged. We finally made it!' They were going through the album trying to figure out who's on what song and where it was taken from. It was like they had finally made the big time. They had made the cover of *Time* and *Newsweek* and now they were on a bootleg (laughs).

A: How do you respond to the viewpoint that the artist involved in the bootlegs that you helped release never wanted these particular performances released to the public?

LB: Well, I don't know. I can see some justification for that. You know, if I wrote a book that I decided I didn't like, and threw it in the trash and then it came out…So I can see both sides of the issue nowadays, which is something I didn't so much, back then. But I think in a lot of respects, particularly given the nature of the music industry, I think bootlegs are very humanizing. You know, in an industry which is becoming more and more concerned with the notion of portraying musicians as "gods." The little imperfections on bootlegs show that these people do have flaws and do make mistakes. And also, I think it lets people in on the creative process a little bit. For example, hearing how the lyrics originally started on a bootleg before the artist finally comes up with something good. You know, George Harrison would come up with some god-awful solos before he would come up with some good stuff. I like it (bootlegs) because it takes the mythology out of it. It makes it seem like anyone can do it. And to me, the greatest thing that happened to music in the last twenty years was to remind people of the greatness that can be inside anybody. Instead, the process has turned it into merely some party music. I think in some small way, bootlegs helped to bring it all down to earth a little bit. Along with being exciting.

You know, a lot of the best music happens live. Those little moments that don't happen in the studio. And the artist doesn't always have the big apparatus there to capture it. It's just fun stuff. It is a form of history. There are Columbia record executives, who at the same time they are going after bootleggers, would say, "Thank god somebody had the foresight to record these Charlie Parker shows." The record industry has always treated its artists as a type of disposable commodity. They used to just burn them (artists) out and throw them away. They didn't care what they had on tape. John Entwistle of The Who said that he didn't realize how much stuff they had done until he looked at all the bootlegs that were out there. So they definitely serve a purpose.

A: Was it around 1978 or so when you retired from bootlegging?

LB: Yes, we were pretty well encouraged to do so by the FBI, CBS Records and other authorities after they caught us bootlegging Springsteen. CBS had the third largest law firm in Los Angeles County, experts in copyright law, and we had a Chula Vista divorce lawyer.

A: So I gather you did not win your defense against the record company?

LB: No. Vicki Vinyl was fined something like $1.5 million dollars. I was fined something like $10,000. The real problem was that we were each assessed one-half of CBS' reasonable court costs. They spent I think $135,000. The judge determined that $105,000 of that was reasonable.

A: Time to file bankruptcy wasn't it?

LB: Which I did indeed. I had about $400 to my name at the time. The best thing is that CBS was such a huge corporation. When my attorney sent them the notice of bankruptcy, they couldn't figure out what the hell it was for. Generally when they receive this kind of notice from a private citizen, they assume you are defaulting on the Record Club. I got this form letter from the CBS Record Club saying that they had no record of me and wanting to know why I felt I owed them some $60-odd thousand dollars (laughs).

A: One last question. What do you perceive are the central changes that you've observed in the way the underground music industry worked in the 1970s compared to the compact disc bootleggers of today?

LB: It's much more the kind of business *now* that I think the commercial record industry used to paint it to be. I think it (bootleg industry) does seem more interested in money now. It used to be that if people didn't like an artist, they sure as hell wouldn't put a bootleg out by them. There's all sorts of artists that did not get bootlegged in the 1970s because the bootleggers couldn't stand them. It wasn't affected at all by the market place. Whereas now, whatever's hot, whether it's U2 or the Cure or whatever, is what gets bootlegged. It's much more of a money business now. I don't know what kind of volume they sell in. If it's 5,000 per run or something…you know CDs cost much less to make than a record did. It used to be that bootlegs (records) would sell for less than a commercial record. Whereas now, the bootleg CDs sell for double the price of a regular CD and very often three times more.

A: Thanks for your recollections.

LB: Sure thing.

AN INTERVIEW WITH ITALIAN BOOTLEGGER RINALDO TAGLIABUE, OWNER OF GREAT DANE RECORDS, MILAN, ITALY (1989-PRESENT)*

AUTHORS (A): Firstly, how do you answer the charge that the artists involved in your releases never wanted these particular performances released and sold to the general public? As the performers, don't they have the right to control what is released of their work?

TAGLIABUE (T): Actually, none of the artists involved in Great Dane's productions express any negative opinions regarding our releases. If they did, we'd expect their opinion to be negative, mainly because all these artists have exclusive contracts with major record companies and they might get in trouble if they express any approval.

These items are legal not only in Italy, but in most European countries. But it's not correct to say they're available to the general public; you won't find Great Dane product in most record stores. Our customers are very special; they are collectors. In most cases they possess impressive quantities of regular records. But some of them search for more, and Great Dane provides this need.

Live recordings have always been sought after by collectors, from classic to lyric, from jazz to rock. During the years they've simply moved from magnetic tape to vinyl and now compact discs, but the story's still the same. We don't think the artist should have the right to control what already belongs to the public. Live performances and radio broadcasts are played to the public and from our point of view, the performance doesn't belong to the artist anymore. On the other hand, studio material is the author's property and must be under his control. That's why Great Dane publishes live concerts only.

A: How do you respond to the charge that a label like CBS takes the initial risk in signing—and then spends perhaps millions of dollars over the years promoting—an artist like (Bruce) Springsteen, and a label such as Great Dane comes along and takes a "free ride?"

T: The answer is very simple: it's a matter of numbers. To huge companies like CBS, "taking the risk to sign an artist" means nothing in terms of pure cost; it's a drop in the sea. Of course Great Dane takes a "free ride" publishing records from artists like Springsteen, The Rolling Stones and Led Zeppelin, but the record companies have the ability to publish those things and put Great Dane out of (business) at once. They simply don't do it because this will generate a pure loss for the companies and no real extra profit for the artists.

So Great Dane has good reason to exist because we publish things that otherwise will never be available—or available among very few people with bad quality. A CD reproduces music with no quality loss and this is a big thing for the collector. In some cases, we get tapes that even record companies don't have, and that's amazing. Many collectors cooperate with us, suggesting releases and helping us find original masters to a concert.

A: Is it true that you put aside royalty money for the artists involved? What about for the respective record labels, and the songwriters? Shouldn't Eddie Cochran's estate be compensated if "Summertime Blues" helps sell your *Tales From The Who* CD (on which the group performs it live)?

T: As a legitimate record company, we pay all royalties due to songwriters, publishers and performers. The first two royalties are collected by the S.I.A.E. (Italian Company of Authors and Publishers), and the amount due is automatically based on the length of each song. And we keep on a special account the amount due to the artist, and the (amount) of this "fair" royalty is determined in some Italian law regulations. So Eddie Cochran's (estate) received royalties from Great Dane.

A: Have you been contacted by any representative of the artists (label, manager, publisher, etc.) about "ceasing and desisting?"

T: We haven't been directly contacted by any label, but we know there's big interest from record companies about our activity. We received a visit by a writer from the A.F.I. (Association of Italian Phonographers) magazine, and he wrote a nice article about us.

I don't know if the record labels (apply any pressure) to CD factories, but I'm guessing they do. We expect (any given) record plant to refuse our production order, but there are now so many independent plants in Italy and Europe that this would not create a real problem for us.

A: How do the copyright laws work in Italy that make your releases legal there, but seemingly almost nowhere else?

T: It would be surely boring giving you in detail how the Italian law works, and why we reach the opinion that what we do is legitimate. I just want to let your readers know that we spent a lot of time studying before beginning this activity, so we have full knowledge about what we are doing.

A: Why is it that American collectors end up paying so much—twenty to forty dollars apiece—for your CDs? How much do you get per disc when you whole-sale them out to a European distributor?

T: Americans pay so much because we don't sell to any U.S. distributor. So they enter the U.S. through other ways, most of the time with "bootleg" records, which have higher (margins) and therefore, so are the final prices. In Italy, Great Dane products are sold at the same price as official releases, and sometimes lower. It's hard to say what our profit is since Great Dane has no employees; the owners do everything on their own.

A: How do you go about selecting which artists and titles you release? Why haven't you made any CDs of artists from the '80s, like U2, R.E.M. or Prince?

T: Since Great Dane consists of a group of collectors, we select artists using our "heart." More seriously, though, we select our production considering three things: popularity of the artist, quality of available tapes and the sales potential. There's nothing original in this, except for the fact that we consider Europe as our market. We've decided to publish concerts at least ten years old because there might be some restrictions in the Italian regulations. In some cases you can pub-lish more recent music, but we've decided against doing it for right now.

A: How many of each release do you manufacture, and why are the quantities so small?

T: We press quantities in proportion to sales potential, with a lower limit of 1,000 and an upper limit—right now—of 4,000. Our goal is to meet the demand, and if it grows, we'll increase our pressings. We don't want to make big quantities of any title; we prefer to sell out one selection and publish another CD by the same artist. At the bottom line, we want to make our discs collectable; for this reason, we will never push sales. We prefer to be pulled by the customers.

A: What titles do you foresee releasing in the near future?

T: Great Dane has exciting programs for (the) 1990s. We will continue publish-ing Springsteen in order to cover all his tours. We'll put out some Led Zeppelin, Pink Floyd and Genesis. We're collecting music also for some Beatles and Dylan releases, and very soon an exciting U2 CD. At the same time we have plans for some "minor" releases from Ry Cooder, King Crimson and ZZ Top.

Black Market Beatles

We want to receive the cooperation of any collector, and are open to any suggestion. Making a new release is one of the most exciting things in this business.

*Reprinted by permission of the *ICE* newsletter.

The Beatles' Underground Discography

HOW TO USE THE BEATLES' UNDERGROUND DISCOGRAPHY

A discography is an organized guide to sound recordings. You are holding the world's largest discography ever assembled on The Beatles' underground or bootleg recordings. Contained within the more than 1,600 titles are hundreds (perhaps thousands) of hours of unreleased Beatles concerts, demos, rehearsals, outtakes, alternate takes, TV/radio appearances and more! The discography covers Beatles bootlegs released during the period 1969–1994.

This discography contains Beatles bootlegs originating from around the world. The albums hail from Taiwan to America, from England to Germany, from Italy to Japan, from Australia to Korea, from Luxembourg to Brazil…and all points in between! No stone has been left unturned in this historical exploration to categorize every known Beatles bootleg ever manufactured or distributed on vinyl, compact disc, or cassette. The authors have sought to verify the actual existence of each entry by utilizing at least two different factual sources (e.g., the actual disc or a photograph of the album, etc.). It is important to note, however, the authors do not manufacture, distribute or exchange the recordings listed in this book, nor do they know how to locate such recordings. This is a discography, not a sales catalog. The authors are merely music historians dedicated to cataloging this body of illicit sound recordings. The majority of the titles listed in the discography are no longer in print and would be extremely difficult to locate.

What you will *not* find in this discography, is the following information:
• Beatles interviews and press conferences containing little or no music.
• Beatles performances sold or traded underground on any visual format (e.g. laser disc, VHS video, Beta video, etc.)

• Pirate discs. These are unauthorized reproductions of commercially released recordings. There are some cases where a "grey area" exception exists as to whether or not a disc listed should be included as a bootleg. In such a case, other objective factors were used to make a determination (e.g., who the manufacturer is, how the disc was distributed, etc.)

• Counterfeit discs. These are unauthorized, exact reproductions of commercially released recordings, including the album cover artwork and label graphics.

The arrangement of this discography is alphabetical by album title. The word "the," when preceding an album title, is not used in alphabetizing. In some cases, album titles had to be abbreviated or even shortened in order to preserve the ability to sort this listing into other manageable formats. An example is the bootleg title, *When It Says Beatles, Beatles, Beatles On The Label, Label, Label, You Will Like It, Like It, Like It On Your Turntable, Turntable, Turntable.*

When reviewing this discography, the reader should keep in mind the incredible lack of quality control that existed in the underground music industry in the 1970s and 1980s. A company's catalog number was often determined arbitrarily or assigned by the particular record plant when pressed. This is unlike a commercial label (record company) which usually numbers its catalog of artists' releases in a sequential system. In the underground, it was not uncommon for different album titles to contain the same catalog numbers, just as identical recordings were often given different album titles. The lack of record keeping makes the entire process quite difficult to catalog. However, the authors have endeavored to organize this discography into an easy-to-read format, to facilitate reference, collecting and historical data analysis.

HOW TO READ THE COLUMNS

Every column organizes a different category of data about the particular bootleg recording. From left to right, the five columns appear in the discography as follows:

ALBUM TITLE	LABEL	CATALOG #	FORMAT	YEAR
1	2	3	4	5

1. ALBUM TITLE

This is the name that the bootlegger has chosen to call the particular release. Caveat Emptor! The title given by underground record purveyors does not always accurately reflect the recordings found inside. In some cases, the titles have been shortened for space considerations.

2. LABEL

The label indicates the name which the bootlegger has chosen to represent their company for this particular release. The reader should note that the label names and logos printed herein are reproduced for historical, reference and collector purposes. A number of bootleggers have, on many occasions, chosen to use legally registered commercial trade mark label names for their releases, as a subterfuge. Make no mistake, there are *no* commercial label releases listed in this discography. The discography lists a significant number of bootleg titles under recognizable commercial company names, including, without limitation, the following: Capitol, EMI, Parlophone, Apple, NEMS, Decca, Swan, Odeon, Vee Jay, Beeb Transcription, BBC and others. The reader should not confuse the bootlegs here which illegally use commercial names with actual record companies or their fine products. There is no connection between them whatsoever. All label names which herein use commercial names should be read with the precedent word "bogus." For example, "bogus" Capitol Records.

As for European companies which believe their releases listed herein are *not* bootlegs, *they are*, once smuggled into the U.S.A. Since a large quantity of compact discs manufactured in Europe are clearly intended for U.S. exploitation and distribution, the authors consider these European discs to be bootlegs based upon U.S. Copyright laws. Examples of these companies which are producing previously unreleased Beatles recordings without the permission of the artist or their label are Yellow Dog, The Swingin' Pig, The Early Years and Living Legend Records.

Whenever the term "UNK" appears in this or other columns, it indicates that the information either does not exist or that it was unavailable at the time of publication.

3. CATALOG

The bootleg manufacturer's identifying number for a release. The number can usually be found in one of three places on a vinyl album: the cover, the record label, or etched in the runoff wax of the record. On a compact disc, the catalog number is usually located on the disc and on the spine or back cover of the jewel box insert sheet. On some entries in this category, the symbol "UNK" may appear in the catalog number column. This indicates that the information either does not exist or that it was unavailable at the time of publication. The symbol "UNREL" may also appear on occasion. This stands for unreleased. On a few rare occasions, bootleggers manufactured certain titles for release and then pulled them from circulation before release.

4. FORMAT

This category describes the medium in which the sound recordings have been fixed in a tangible form by the manufacturer. In other words, the recording appears on a vinyl record, compact disc or some other format. This column will also provide other helpful identification of the release to the reader. The complete key to abbreviations for this category is listed below:

LP – vinyl long-playing album (33 & 1/3 rpm)

12" – the diameter of the LP

PD – picture disc record or compact disc

CV – colored vinyl record

CD – compact disc

EP – extended play vinyl record or compact disc

7" – the diameter of a vinyl record with 1, 2 or more songs

45 – a 7" vinyl record (usually running at 45 rpm)

2LP – a number placed in front of LP, CD, etc.—indicates the release is a multi-unit set

BX – a multi-unit set packaged in a box

CASS – cassette

FLX – a plastic flexi-disc record

ST – stereo

MO – monaural

CD5" – a compact disc single or EP

CD3" – a compact disc single or EP

5. YEAR

This category indicates the year in which the bootlegged release is *believed* to be first distributed. In some cases, it is difficult to determine the specific year of an underground release. In those select cases, the *decade* of release is provided. On a few lines in this category, the symbol "UNK" may appear. This indicates that the information was unavailable at the time of publication. The symbol "UNREL" may also appear in this column. On a few occasions, bootleggers manufactured certain titles for release and then pulled them (or had them involuntarily pulled) from circulation before release.

A discography, sorted by bootleg record manufacturer, can be found in the appendix of this book. This listing only includes the most prolific or most important manufacturers of Beatles bootlegs over the past twenty-plus years.

The authors welcome any updates, corrections or additions to the discography that readers may forward to the attention of the publisher.

ALBUM TITLE	LABEL	CATALOG #	FORMAT	YEAR
14 UNRELEASED EARLY BEATLE CUTS	DITTOLINO DISCS	D-1	LP-12"	1971
1962 LIVE RECORDINGS	BAKTABAK	STAB 2001-15	15-45-7"	1988
1963-1969 (20 NEVER PUBLISHED SONGS)	FAB FOUR RARITIES	FFR-9116	CD	1991
1964 & 1965 ED SULLIVAN SHOWS, THE	MELVIN	MR-14-M	LP-12"	1980
1967	ADAM VIII LTD.	CD 49-019	CD	1991
1967 AKA SGT. PEPPER	PARLOPHONE	PCS-1967	LP-12"	1988
1968 DEMOS, THE	HOWDY	555-04	CD	1991
1968 DEMOS 1, THE	VIGOTONE	VIGO-100	CD-BX	1993
1983 ABBEY ROAD SHOW	BSC	92BSC-4001	CD	1992
1ST REC. HOUR OF LET IT BE SESSIONS	YELLOW DOG	YDB-104	CD	1994
20 NEVER PUBLISHED SONGS	TMOQ	73030	LP-12"	1973
20 NEVER PUBLISHED SONGS	NO LABEL	633-XU	LP-12"	1973
20 NEVER PUBLISHED SONGS	FAB FOUR RARITIES	FFR-9116	CD	1991
20 NEVER PUBLISHED SONGS	CBM	WEC-3030	LP-12"	1972
20 X 4	RUTHLESS RHYMES LTD	JPGR-1177	LP-12"	1977
20 X 4	REMIME/AUDIFON	JPGR/REM 204	LP-12"	1979
21	MELVIN	MM02	LP-12"	1975
2ND REC. HOUR OF LET IT BE SESSIONS	YELLOW DOG	YDB-204	CD	1994
300,000 BEATLE FANS CAN'T BE WRONG	LIVING LEGEND	LLRCD-031	CD	1989
300,000 BEATLE FANS CAN'T BE WRONG	NO LABEL	B1 + B2	2LP-12"	1989
3RD REC. HOUR OF LET IT BE SESSIONS	YELLOW DOG	YDB-304	CD	1994
4 EVER	BEAT RIFF	MNS-54006	LP-12"-PD	1985
4 EVER	BEAT RIFF	NO #	LP-12"	1985
69 REHEARSALS	BLUE KANGAROO	BK-01,02,03	3CD-BX	1992
69 REHEARSALS VOL. 1	BLUE KANGAROO	BK-6901	CD	1992
69 REHEARSALS VOL. 2	BLUE KANGAROO	BK-6902	CD	1992
69 REHEARSALS VOL. 3	BLUE KANGAROO	BK-6903	CD	1992
A HARD DAYS NIGHT/LONG TALL SALLY	BEAT	BE-12-141	45-7"-CV	1977
A HARD DAY'S NIGHT SPECIAL	MIDO ENTERPRISE	ZS-9101	CD	1991
A NIGHTMARE IS ALSO A DREAM	BELGIUM	B3+B4	2LP-12"	1987
A PARLOPHONE REHEARSAL SESSION	ADAM VIII LTD.	CD 49-011	CD	1991
A SLICE OF SWINGIN' PIG VOL. 1	THE SWINGIN' PIG	TSP-PRO-001	CD	1989
A SLICE OF SWINGIN' PIG VOL. 2	THE SWINGIN' PIG	TSP-PRO-002	CD	1989
A STUDIO RECORDING	CATSO	NO #	LP-12"	'70s
A WORLD LEGEND	NO LABEL	UNK	LP-12"	1981
ABBEY ROAD	TOSHIBA	CP-35-3016	CD	1990
ABBEY ROAD	BRAZIL	BTA-003/004	2LP-12"	1985
ABBEY ROAD NW 3	APPLE	PCS-7124	LP-12"	1979
ABBEY ROAD NW 3	BOX TOP	NO #	LP-12"	1986
ABBEY ROAD NW8 + WATCHING RAINBOWS	NO LABEL	POS-7124/5	2LP-12"	1979
ABBEY ROAD OUTTAKES	BOW BELL	NK-001	CD	1993
ABBEY ROAD REVISITED	WIZARDO	WRMB-353	LP-12"	1976
ABBEY ROAD REVISITED	WIZARDO	WRMB-353	LP-12"-CV	1976
ABBEY ROAD REVISITED	CBM	WEC-3907	LP-12"	1973
ABBEY ROAD SESSIONS	BLACK DISC	ZPP-1083	LP-12"-PD	1981
ABBEY ROAD SHOW 1983	NML	ARS-83-2	CD	1990
ABBEY ROAD SPECIAL	MIDO ENTERPRISE	ZS-9109	CD	1991
ABBEY ROAD TALKS	NEBULOUS	ALT-SW-383	LP-12"	1982
ABBEY ROAD UNDER CONSTRUCTION	MELVIN	MM-19-UNREL	LP-12"	1981
ABBEY ROAD WEST-MINSTER 1	BLACK DISC	2441	LP-12"	1981
ABBEY ROAD '83	UNK	UNK	CD	1993
ABC MANCHESTER 1964	WIZARDO	WRMB-361	LP-12"	1976
ABOUT SGT. PEPPER	APPLE	BFR-001	45-7"	1987
ACETATES	YELLOW DOG	YD-009	CD	1991
ACROSS THE UNIVERSE	TOBE MILO	5Q-3VC4946	45-7"-EP	1978

ALBUM TITLE	LABEL	CATALOG #	FORMAT	YEAR
ADRIANO THEATRE - ROME, 1965	BEAT	02-202	LP-12"-CV	'80s
AIN'T SHE SWEET/ NOBODY'S CHILD	ATCO	45-6308	45-7"	1978
AIR TIME (JOHNNY & THE MOONDOGS)	WARWICK	M-16051	LP-12"	1982
AIRTIME	SUBWAY	MX-4729	LP-12"	1982
ALF BIKNELL'S GARAGE TAPE	VARIO	VARIO-18	CD	1992
ALIVE AT LAST IN ATLANTA	WALRUS	TVC-1001	LP-12"	1972
ALIVE AT LAST IN ATLANTA	TMOQ	71007	LP-12"	1972
ALIVE AT LAST IN ATLANTA	LXXXIV	SERIES #43	LP-12"-CV	'70s
ALIVE IN LONDON '64	HIGHWAY HIGH FI	HHCER-111	LP-12"	1974
ALL THINGS MUST PASS (PT. 1: ELECTRIC)	YELLOW DOG	YD-016	CD	1992
ALL TOO MUCH	SCORPIO	93-BE-21273	CD	1993
ALL YOU NEED IS LOVE	JAP	UNK	2LP-12"	1990
ALL YOU NEED IS THIS	LIVING LEGEND	LLRCD-034	CD	1989
ALMOST GROWN	KING	MLK-002	LP-12"	1983
ALPHA OMEGA VOL. 1	AUDIO TAPE	ATRBH-3583	4LP-12"	1973
ALPHA OMEGA VOL. 2	AUDIO TAPE	ATRBH-3584	4LP-12"	1973
AN OFFWHITE X-MAS	BEATLEG	12188	CASS.	1988
ANN/OH! DARLING	ESP	E-1000	45-7"	'70s
ANTHOLOGY	TEICHIKU	50CP-227/8	CD	1990
ANTHOLOGY	TEICHIKU	TECP-50177/8	CD	1990
APPLE SLICES	BEAT	L-005	LP-12"	1977
AROUND THE BEATLES	TOBE MILO	10Q9/10	LP-12"	UNREL
AROUND THE BEATLES	WIZARDO	WRMB-349	LP-12"	1976
ARRIVANO I "CAPELLONI"	CLEAN SOUND	CS-1008	LP-12"	1985
ARRIVE WITHOUT AGING	VIGATONE	VT-6869	CD	1993
ARRIVE WITHOUT TRAVELING	VIGATONE	VT-LP69	LP-12"	1992
ARTIFACTS	BIG MUSIC (KTS)	4018-4022	5CD-BX	1993
ARTIFACTS II	BIG MUSIC (KTS)	BM-008	5CD-BX	1994
AS NATURE INTENDED	VIGATONE	VT-122	CD	1994
AS SWEET AS YOU ARE	CBM	WEC-3316	LP-12"	1973
AS SWEET AS YOU ARE	WIZARDO	116-208	LP-12"	1976
AS SWEET AS YOU ARE	WIZARDO	208	LP-12"	1976
AS SWEET AS YOU ARE	NO LABEL	D-1	LP-12"	1970
AS SWEET AS YOU ARE	DITTOLINO DISCS	D-1	LP-12"	1970
AS WELL AS ABBEY ROAD	ALTERNATIVE	0071	LP-12"	'70s
AT HOME AND ON THE BOARDWALK	MALCOM	1/2	CD	1993
AT SHEA STADIUM	RUTHLESS RHYMES LTD	1180	LP-12"	1978
AT THE ALAMO	TUNA	214	LP-12"	'70s
AT THE ALAMO	TUNA	214	LP-12"	1980
AT THE BEEB	EMI/PARLOPHONE	CDP-7-48002-2	CD	1987
AT THE BEEB VOL. 1	PYRAMID	RFT-CD-005	CD	1989
AT THE BEEB VOL. 1	BEEB TRANSCRIPTION	2171/S	LP-12"	1988
AT THE BEEB VOL. 10	BEEB TRANSCRIPTION	2181/S	LP-12"	1988
AT THE BEEB VOL. 10	PYRAMID	RFT-CD-024	CD	1990
AT THE BEEB VOL. 11	PYRAMID	RFT-CD-025	CD	1990
AT THE BEEB VOL. 11	BEEB TRANSCRIPTION	2182/S	LP-12"	1988
AT THE BEEB VOL. 12	BEEB TRANSCRIPTION	2183/S	LP-12"	1988
AT THE BEEB VOL. 12	PYRAMID	RFT-CD-032	CD	1990
AT THE BEEB VOL. 13	PYRAMID	RFT-CD-033	CD	1990
AT THE BEEB VOL. 13	BEEB TRANSCRIPTION	2185/S	LP-12"	1988
AT THE BEEB VOL. 2	BEEB TRANSCRIPTION	2173/S	LP-12"	1988
AT THE BEEB VOL. 2	PYRAMID	RFT-CD-006	CD	1989
AT THE BEEB VOL. 3	PYRAMID	RFT-CD-007	CD	1989
AT THE BEEB VOL. 3	BEEB TRANSCRIPTION	2174/S	LP-12"	1988
AT THE BEEB VOL. 4	PYRAMID	RFT-CD-018	CD	1989

ALBUM TITLE	LABEL	CATALOG #	FORMAT	YEAR
AT THE BEEB VOL. 4	BEEB TRANSCRIPTION	2175/S	LP-12"-CV	1991
AT THE BEEB VOL. 4	BEEB TRANSCRIPTION	2175/S	LP-12"	1988
AT THE BEEB VOL. 5	BEEB TRANSCRIPTION	2176/S	LP-12"-CV	1991
AT THE BEEB VOL. 5	BEEB TRANSCRIPTION	2176/S	LP-12"	1988
AT THE BEEB VOL. 5	PYRAMID	RFT-CD-014	CD	1989
AT THE BEEB VOL. 6	BEEB TRANSCRIPTION	2177/S	LP-12"	1988
AT THE BEEB VOL. 6	BEEB TRANSCRIPTION	2177/S	LP-12"-CV	1991
AT THE BEEB VOL. 6	PYRAMID	RFT-CD-015	CD	1989
AT THE BEEB VOL. 7	BEEB TRANSCRIPTION	2178/S	LP-12"	1988
AT THE BEEB VOL. 7	PYRAMID	RFT-CD-019	CD	1989
AT THE BEEB VOL. 8	BEEB TRANSCRIPTION	2179/S	LP-12"	1988
AT THE BEEB VOL. 8	PYRAMID	RFT-CD-016	CD	1989
AT THE BEEB VOL. 9	PYRAMID	RFT-CD-017	CD	1989
AT THE BEEB VOL. 9	BEEB TRANSCRIPTION	2180/S	LP-12"	1988
AT THE BEEB '62–'65	CONTINUING SAGA	RSR-252	2LP-12"	1988
AT THE CAVERN CLUB	CBM	WEC-3906	LP-12"	1973
AT THE HOLLYWOOD BOWL	TMOQ	S-208	LP-12"-CV	1974
AT THE HOLLYWOOD BOWL	TMOQ	S-208	LP-12"	1975
AT THE RAREST	INTERNATIONAL JOKER	SM-3591	LP-12"	1973
AT THE ROYAL VARIETY PERFORMANCE	NO LABEL	UK-2826	LP-12"	1984
ATLANTA WHISKEY FLATS	BOX TOP	NO #	LP-12"	1986
AUSTRALIA 1964	BULLDOG/CROCODILE	BGCD-156	CD	1990
AUSTRALIAN TOUR 1964	ANF	ANF-7011	CD	1989
AWAY WITH WORDS	NO LABEL	340-702876	3LP-12"	1976
AWAY WITH WORDS	WIZARDO	WRMB-505	3LP-12"BX	1976
A/B SINGLE ACETATE	WIZARDO	WRMB-315	LP-12"	1975
BACK IN 1964 AT THE HOLLYWOOD BOWL	(JAP) LEMON-REISSUE	UNK	CD	1992
BACK IN THE SADDLE - 8TH AMENDMENT	TAKRL	ZAP-7872	LP-12"	1977
BACK IN '64 AT THE HOLLYWOOD BOWL	LEMON	CSR-143	LP-12"	'70s
BACK IN '64 AT THE HOLLYWOOD BOWL	CBM	4178	LP-12"	1973
BACK IN '64 AT THE HOLLYWOOD BOWL	NO LABEL	CSR-143	LP-12"	1977
BACK IN '64 AT THE HOLLYWOOD BOWL	SHALOM	4178/4162	LP-12"	1974
BACK IN '64 AT THE HOLLYWOOD BOWL	BERKELEY	N-2077	LP-12"	1976
BACK IN '64 AT THE HOLLYWOOD BOWL	INSTANT ANALYSIS	1032	LP-12"	1975
BACK TRACK FOUR	CLASSICAL	CL-004	CD	1994
BACK TRACK PART THREE	NML	BT-6369-2	CD	1989
BACK TRACK PART TWO	MNL	BT63682	CD	1989
BACK UPON US ALL	TAKRL	#1969	LP-12"	1977
BACK UPON US ALL - 4TH AMENDMENT	TAKRL	ZAP-7864	LP-12"	1977
BACKTRACK	MNL	BT62672	CD	1988
BACKTRACK PART THREE	NO LABEL	NO #	CD	1988
BACKTRACK PART TWO	NML	BT-6368-1	CD	1988
BACKTRAX SESSIONS	KING KONG	3922	LP-12"	1988
BACKTRAX SESSIONS	KING KONG	WEC-3922	LP-12"	1988
BALLAD BEATLES	OVERSEAS	30CP-159	CD	1991
BANZAI	GREAT DANE	GDR-9006	2CD	1990
BANZAI	GREAT DANE	GDR-9006	2CD-BX	1990
BATTLE	TMOQ	RP-24	LP-12"	'70s
BATTLE	CBM	N-2027	LP-12"	1973
BBC 1962–1966	RADIO TRANSCRIPTION	CBB-20	3LP-12"	1985
BBC BEATLES: COMPLETE CATALOG	PANDA	UNK	7CD	1993
BBC STUDIO SESSION NEXT VOLUME	ANF	ANF-7520	CD	1989
BBC STUDIO SESSION VOL. 1	ANF	ANF-7501	CD	1989
BBC STUDIO SESSION VOL. 10	ANF	ANF-7518	CD	1989
BBC STUDIO SESSION VOL. 11	ANF	ANF-7519	CD	1989

ALBUM TITLE	LABEL	CATALOG #	FORMAT	YEAR
BBC STUDIO SESSION VOL. 2	ANF	ANF-7502	CD	1989
BBC STUDIO SESSION VOL. 3	ANF	ANF-7503	CD	1988
BBC STUDIO SESSION VOL. 4	ANF	ANF-7504	CD	1989
BBC STUDIO SESSION VOL. 5	ANF	ANF-7505	CD	1989
BBC STUDIO SESSION VOL. 6	ANF	ANF-7506	CD	1989
BBC STUDIO SESSION VOL. 7	ANF	ANF-7507	CD	1989
BBC STUDIO SESSION VOL. 8	ANF	ANF-7508	CD	1989
BBC STUDIO SESSION VOL. 9	ANF	ANF-7509	CD	1989
BBC '62–'65	CLEAN SOUND	CS-820	2LP-12"	1985
BEATLE VERSIONS	UNK	PPCD-1317	CD	1992
BEATLE VERSIONS	CARLS	4TX-010	CD	1991
BEATLE VERS. OF SOLO B. SONGS & MORE	POLYPHONE	PH1317	CD	1991
BEATLEG XMAS-1987	BEATLEG	842W-23	CASS	1987
BEATLEG XMAS-1989	BEATLEG	WS 01-A/B	EP-7"-CV	1989
BEATLEGGED LIVE	CRABAPPLE	001	LP-12"	1971
BEATLEMANIA	NO LABEL	335 A/B	LP-12"	'70s
BEATLEMANIA 1963–1969	ZAKATECAS	ST-57633XU	LP-12"	'70s
BEATLES	BRS	BRS-71162	LP-12"	1989
BEATLES	MODERN JAZZ	EFG-1200	LP-12"	1979
BEATLES, THE	BRS	BRSCD-73159	CD	1989
BEATLES, THE	BEACON	508	EP-7"	1978
BEATLES, THE	BOX TOP	RI-73030	LP-12"	1986
BEATLES, THE	TMOQ	73030	LP-12"	1973
BEATLES, THE	NO LABEL	ATRBH-3583	LP-12"	1973
BEATLES, THE	LXXXIV	SERIES #55	LP-12"-CV	'70s
BEATLES, THE	APPLE	EP-1	2-7"-CV	1990
BEATLES, THE	NO LABEL	ATRBH-1-8	4LP-12"	1973
BEATLES, THE ANIMALS SKY PILOT, THE	MTR	MTR-317	EP-7"	'70s
BEATLES, THE (BLACK ALBUM)	EVA	TWK-0169	3LP-12"	1981
BEATLES, THE (BLACK ALBUM)	NO LABEL	TWK-0169	5LP-12"	1981
BEATLES, THE (BLACK ALBUM)	RUTHLESS RHYMES LTD	TWK 0169/L4344	3LP-12"	1981
BEATLES, THE (BLACK ALBUM)	NO LABEL	TWK0169/L4344	5LP-12"	1982
BEATLES 1960–1962	TEICHIKU	38CP-134	CD	1990
BEATLES 1962 LIVE RECORDINGS	BAKTABAK	CTAB-5001	CD	1990
BEATLES 1964	BEAT RIFF	MNS-54009	LP-12"	1985
BEATLES AMONG THE BULBS, THE	BEATLES UNLIMITED	BU1-1984	LP-12"	1984
BEATLES AND THE ROLLING STONES LIVE	JOKER	SM3591/B	LP-12"	1973
BEATLES AS NATURE INTENDED, THE	EMI/PARLOPHONE	PCS-7080	LP-12"	1988
BEATLES AT SHEA	TMOQ	UNK	LP-12"	'70s
BEATLES AT SHEA STADIUM	IDLE MIND	1180	LP-12"	1976
BEATLES AT THE BEEB	EMI	CD-P7-48002-2	CD	1988
BEATLES AT THE BEEB	LONDON WAVELENGTH	UNK	3LP-12"	1982
BEATLES AT THE BEEB 1/2	BEEB TRANSCRIPTION	2171/2173/S	2LP-12"	1988
BEATLES AT THE BEEB 3/4	BEEB TRANSCRIPTION	2174/2175/S	2LP-12"	1988
BEATLES AT THE BEEB 5/6	BEEB TRANSCRIPTION	2176/2177/S	2LP-12"	1988
BEATLES AT THE BEEB WITH PETE BEST	DREXEL	BEEB-6263	LP-12"	1988
BEATLES AT THE BEEB-TV	PANDA	BBCBCD-1454	CD	1994
BEATLES AT THE HOLLYWOOD BOWL, THE	PARLOPHONE	5C062-06377	LP-12"	'80s
BEATLES BBC, THE	DREAM	DR-36282	LP-12"	1982
BEATLES BEST	LIVE HOUSE SENSATION	JAP	CD	1989
BEATLES BROADCASTS	CIRCUIT	LK-4450	LP-12"-PD	1985
BEATLES BROADCASTS	CIRCUIT	LK-4450	LP-12"	1985
BEATLES BROADCASTS COLLECTION	NO LABEL	BBC 1-4	2LP-12	1982
BEATLES BUDOKAN 1966	SAVAGE	L-4342	LP-12"-CV	1985
BEATLES CHRISTMAS ALBUM, THE	RUTHLESS RHYMES LTD	BCC-1/2	LP-12"	1979

ALBUM TITLE	LABEL	CATALOG #	FORMAT	YEAR
BEATLES CHRISTMAS ALBUM, THE	APPLE	SBC-100	LP-12"	1987
BEATLES CHRISTMAS ALBUM, THE	ZAP	7857	LP-12"	1976
BEATLES CHRISTMAS COLLECTION, THE	ULTRA SOUND CORP.	CX-96295	6PD-7"-BX	1991
BEATLES COLLECTOR'S BOX	UNK	UNK	6CD	1991
BEATLES COMPLETE XMAS COLL. 63–69, THE	TMOQ	BCC-104	LP-12"	1973
BEATLES COMPLETE X-MAS...'63–66, THE	YELLOW DOG	YD-031	CD	1992
BEATLES CONQUER AMERICA	LIVING LEGEND	LLRCD-007	CD	1988
BEATLES CONQUER AMERICA	NEMS	SHU-6465	2LP-12"	1985
BEATLES DOCUMENT 1	DOCUMENT	DR-027	CD	1989
BEATLES DOCUMENT 2	DOCUMENT	DR-028	CD	1989
BEATLES DOCUMENT 3	DOCUMENT	DR-029	CD	1989
BEATLES DOCUMENT 4	DOCUMENT	DR-030	CD	1989
BEATLES DOCUMENT 5	DOCUMENT	DR-031	CD	1989
BEATLES DOCUMENT 6	DOCUMENT	DR-032	CD	1989
BEATLES DOCUMENT 7	DOCUMENT	DR-033	CD	1989
BEATLES FOR AUCTION	APPLE	SAPCOR-32	LP-12"	1987
BEATLES FOREVER MORE	NO LABEL	IRT 614/615	5LP-12"	1978
BEATLES FOREVER MORE	NO LABEL	ASS-6508/315	5LP-12"	1978
BEATLES FOREVER MORE	NO LABEL	APO-6506	5LP-12"	1978
BEATLES IN ABBEY ROAD	BFR	PRO-003	2LP-12"	1983
BEATLES IN ATLANTA WHISKEY FLAT	BOX TOP	NO #	LP-12"-CV	1986
BEATLES IN ATLANTA WHISKEY FLAT	TMOQ	71007	LP-12"	1972
BEATLES IN ATLANTA WHISKEY FLAT	CBM	1001	LP-12"-CV	1973
BEATLES IN AUSTRALIA	DOCUMENT	DR-1806	EP-10"-PD	1989
BEATLES IN ITALY	PARLOPHONE	PMCQ-31506	LP-12"-PD	1980
BEATLES IN PERSON AT SAM HOUSTON	TOBE MILO	XMILO-10Q3/4	LP-12"	1978
BEATLES INTRODUCE NEW SONGS, THE	CAPITOL	PRO-2720	45-7"	'70s
BEATLES INVADE EUROPE	STARLIGHT/BIRD BRAIN	BBR-008	LP-12"	1987
BEATLES INVADE EUROPE	INSTANT ANALYSIS	BBR-008	LP-12"	1987
BEATLES LIVE	NO LABEL	BE-1001	LP-12"	1970
BEATLES LIVE AT ABBEY ROAD STUDIOS	4000 HOLES	ARS 2-9083	2LP-12"	1984
BEATLES LIVE AT ABC MANCHESTER	WIZARDO	WRMB-361	LP-12"	1976
BEATLES LIVE AT TEATRO ADRIAN, ROME	CLEAN SOUND	CS-1008	LP-12"	1985
BEATLES LIVE IN BUDOKAN	BLACK DISC	S-3	2LP-12"	1981
BEATLES LIVE IN HOUSTON	TOBE MILO	XMILO-5Q-1/2	EP-7"	1978
BEATLES LIVE IN JAPAN	DOCUMENT	DR-002	CD	1988
BEATLES LIVE IN MILAN 6/24/65, THE	THAT'S LIVE	WN-7005	LP-12"	'80s
BEATLES LIVE IN SEATTLE 1964, THE	TOBE MILO	10Q7/8	LP-12"	UNREL
BEATLES LIVE-JAPAN, THE	TRIO	NO #	LP-12"-CV	'80s
BEATLES LTD. - VINTAGE SONGS	UNK	KE-1001	CD-BX	1992
BEATLES MACH SHAU	SAVAGE	SC-12620	LP-12"	1985
BEATLES OLDIES	UNK	UNK	CD	1991
BEATLES ON STAGE IN JAPAN	PIG'S EYE	NO. 1	LP-12"	1976
BEATLES ON THE BBC VOL. 1 & 2	UNK	R390188/89	2CD	1991
BEATLES ORDER LUNCH, THE	MELVIN	MM-17-UNREL	LP-12"	1982
BEATLES PROMO AND REGARDS, THE	BEATLES MUSEUM	NO #	EP-7"	1991
BEATLES SET, THE	BRS	BRS-137301	3LP-12"	1989
BEATLES SHOW	BEAT-L	006	45-7"	1979
BEATLES SPECIAL COLLECTION, THE	MIDO ENTERPRISE	ZS-9101-9109	9CD-BX	1991
BEATLES STORY, THE	WAVELENGTH	CN1568-S	13LP-12"	1981
BEATLES STORY, THE	AUTH. BBC PROD.	BS-1000-12	13LP-12"	1973
BEATLES STORY, THE	NEMS	NE-6301	EP-7"	1982
BEATLES STUDIO OUTTAKES	TOBE MILO	4Q-11/12	EP-10"	1979
BEATLES TOUR: THE GREAT TAKE OVER	WIZARDO	502	LP-12"	1976
BEATLES VOL. 1	TV PRODUCTS	ATRBH-101-4	4LP-12"	1973

ALBUM TITLE	LABEL	CATALOG #	FORMAT	YEAR
BEATLES VOL. 2	TV PRODUCTS	ATRBH-P9-16	4LP-12"	1973
BEATLES VOL. 2	NO LABEL	TV-8468	4LP-12"	1973
BEATLES VOL. I	NO LABEL	TV-8467	4LP-12"	1973
BEATLES VS CHUCK BERRY	ORIGINAL ROCK	1000	LP-12"	'70s
BEATLES VS. CARL PERKINS	ORIGINAL ROCK	1003	LP-12"	'70s
BEATLES VS. DON HO	UNK	TDS-6331	LP-12"	'80s
BEATLES VS. DON HO	UNK	TDS-6331-RI	LP-12"	1991
BEATLES VS. DON HO, THE	MELVIN	MM08	LP-12"	1979
BEATLES VS. THE THIRD REICH	VE	DX-62	LP-12"	1987
BEATLES VS. THE WORLD VOL. 1	UNK	UNK	LP	'70s
BEATLES WHITE CAN	TEICHIKU	UNK	2CD	1990
BEATLES & R. STONES AT THEIR RAREST	NO LABEL	F-3591	LP-12"	1973
BEATLES '66	SMILIN' EARS	SE-7704	LP-12"	1977
BEATLES '66	TOBE MILO	4Q-7-10	2EP-7"	1977
BEATLES '66	SMILIN' EARS	SE-7704	EP-7"	1977
BEATLES '66	TOBE MILO	4Q7-10VC46234	2EP-7"	1977
BEATLES - BUDOKAN 1966 - MIAMI, THE	HIGH QUALITY	HQ-10	CD	1994
BEATLESMANIA	BLACK PANTHER	BP-CD-025	CD	'80s
BEATLES!, THE	GAMMA ALPHA	WEC-3609	2LP-12"	1974
BEATLES!, THE	CBM	WEC-3609	LP-12"	1974
BEATLES- CHRISTMAS ALBUM	NO LABEL	3323	CD	1990
BEATLES- CHRISTMAS ALBUM	NO LABEL	3323-PD	CD-PD	1990
BEATLES-A HARD DAYS NIGHT, THE	UNIVERSE	UN-4014	CD	1991
BEATLES-MANIA	ANF	ANF-BP-024	CD	1989
BEATLES-MICHELLE, THE	UNIVERSE	UN-4016	CD	1991
BEATLES-PLEASE PLEASE ME, THE	UNIVERSE	UN-4017	CD	1991
BEATLES-ROLL OVER BEETHOVEN, THE	UNIVERSE	UN-4015	CD	1991
BEATLES/STONES LIVE	JOKER	3591	2LP-12"	1973
BEATLES: GET BACK/AT THE BEEB/SESSIONS	UNK	UNK	3CD	'80s
BEAUTIFUL DREAMER	DREAM	NEM-61842	LP-12"	1982
BEFORE THEIR TIME	SHALOM	4749	LP-12"	1974
BEHIND CLOSED DOORS	MOON CHILD	JYC-0051	2LP-12"	1982
BESAME MUCHO/TO KNOW HIM	DECCAGONE	PRO-1106	45-7"-CV	1976
BEST BOX SET	TEICHIKU	TECP-48342/3	CD	1990
BEST COLLECTION	JAP	UNK	CD-PD	1990
BEST HITS 25	TEICHIKU	TECP-25242	CD	1990
BEST I (1962–1964)	TASK FORCE	T-1818	CD	1990
BEST II (1964–1966)	TASK FORCE	T-1819	CD	1990
BEST OF MELVIN, THE	MELVIN	MM-21-UNREL	LP-12"	1982
BEST OF THE BEATLES & JETHRO TULL	CBM	WEC-2A/B	LP-12"	1973
BEST OF TOBE MILO PRODUCTIONS	TOBE MILO	10Q-1/2	LP-10"	1978
BITS AND PIECES	FAB FOUR RARITIES	FFR-91111	CD	1991
BLACK AND WHITE ALBUM	ADAM VIII LTD.	CD 49-018	CD	1991
BLACK & WHITE MINSTREL SHOW	STASH	STASH-638	2LP-12"	1988
BOTH SIDES	MIW	8	LP-12"	1985
BOTTOM OF THE APPLE TAPES	WIZARDO	WRMB-404	LP-12"	1976
BRITISH COLUMBIA '64	WIZARDO	WRMB-340	LP-12"	1976
BRITISH COLUMBIA '64	WIZARDO	WRMB-340	2LP-12"	1976
BROAD ROAD	APPLE	SAPCOR-40	LP-12"	1987
BROADCASTS	CIRCUIT	LK-4450	LP-12"	1980
BROADCASTS	CIRCUIT	LK-4450	LP-12"-PD	1980
BROADCASTS	BOX TOP	GN-70083	LP-12"-CV	1986
BRUNG TO EWE BY	TOBE MILO	4Q5/6VC4589	EP-7"	1977
BUDO KAN HALL	CBM	JAPAN-1900	LP-12"	1975
BUDOKAN	BOX TOP	NO #	LP-12"	1986

ALBUM TITLE	LABEL	CATALOG #	FORMAT	YEAR
BUG CRUSHER 'LIVE'	TMOQ	TMQ-71076	LP-12"	1976
BUMBLE WORDS- SUPER STUDIO SERIES 3	INSTANT ANALYSIS	3624/3626	LP-12"	1975
BURIED TREASURES	WONDERLAND	WL-49001	2LP-12"	'70s
BY ROYAL COMMAND	DECCAGONE	PRO-1108	EP-7"-CV	1976
BY ROYAL COMMAND	VEWY KWEEN WECORDS	PRO-1108	EP-7"-CV	1976
BYE BYE BYE SUPER TRACKS 1	NO LABEL	9469	LP-12"-PD	'70s
BYE BYE BYE SUPER TRACKS 1	CBM	WEC-3922	LP-12"	1974
BYE BYE LOVE	STARLIGHT/TIGER BEAT	TBR/LP3	LP-12"	1988
B. DYLAN @ THE AISLE OF WRIGHT/BEATLES	RAINBOW PROD.	MY-1/2	LP-12"	1970
CANDLESTICK PARK	BEATLIVE	NO #	LP-12"-PD	1984
CANDLESTICK PARK	BEATLIVE	BR001	LP-12"	1984
CANDLESTICK PARK	MASTERDISC	MDCD-007	CD	1994
CANDLESTICK PARK	BULLDOG	BGCD-0016-PD	CD-PD	1990
CANDLESTICK PARK/MELBOURNE	BEATLIVE	GR 20001	LP-12"	1984
CAROL/LEND ME YOUR COMB	MERSEY BEAT	VPMF-5544	45-7"	1981
CASUALTIES	UNK	UNK	CD	1992
CASUALTIES	CAPITOL	SEAX-11950	LP-12"-PD	1980
CASUALTIES	CAPITOL	SPRO-9469	LP-12"	1980
CASUALTIES/COLLECTOR'S ITEMS	NO LABEL	SX11950/SO9462	2LP-12"	'80s
CASUALTIES/COLLECTOR'S ITEMS	NO LABEL	SPRO-9462	2LP-12"	'80s
CAUGHT OFF GUARD	AN AFTERMATH	AM-4	LP-12"	1975
CAVERN CLUB	CBM	WEC-3906	LP-12"	1974
CAVERN CLUB 1963, THE	FALCON	BS-09	EP-7"	1991
CAVERN CLUB REHEARSALS	EARLY YEARS	02-CD-033	CD	1990
CAVERN CLUB TAPES, CIRCA 1962	NML	CT62-2	CD	1990
CAVERN DAYS	SHALOM	3906/7A	LP-12"	1973
CELLULOID ROCK	YELLOW DOG	YD-006	CD	1991
CHALLENGER I (LIVE & UNRELEASED)	VULTURE	VT-011/123	3CD-PD	1990
CHRISTMAS ALBUM	EARLY YEARS	CD-3323	CD-PD	1988
CHRISTMAS ALBUM	NML	NO #	CD	1990
CHRISTMAS ALBUM	EARLY YEARS	02-CD-3323	CD	1990
CHRISTMAS ALBUM, THE	APPLE	SBC-100	LP-12"	1987
CHRISTMAS ALBUM - SECOND AMENDMENT	ZAP	7857	LP-12"	1976
CHRISTMAS FAN CLUB 1965/66	DOCUMENT	XMAS-882	45-7"	1988
CHRISTMAS GREETINGS 1963/64	XMAS	XMAS-1	EP-7"-PD	1989
CHRISTMAS GREETINGS 1965/66	XMAS	XMAS-2	EP-7"-PD	1989
CHRISTMAS GREETINGS 1967/68	XMAS	XMAS-3	EP-7"-PD	1989
CHRISTMAS MESSAGES	IMACULATE CONCEPTION	CBMR-12	LP-12"	'70s
CINELOGUE I (LET IT BE)	CBM	TB-4020	2LP-12"	1973
CINELOGUE II (YELLOW SUBMARINE)	CBM	YSA-1/450-4	2LP-12"	1973
CINELOGUE III (A HARD DAY'S NIGHT)	INSTANT ANALYSIS	HD-1024	2LP-12"	1975
CINELOGUE IV (HELP!)	INSTANT ANALYSIS	1026	2LP-12"	1975
CINELOGUE V (MAGICAL MYSTERY TOUR)	INSTANT ANALYSIS	MM-1028	2LP-12"	1975
CINELOGUE VI	CBM	TB-635	2LP-12"	1975
CINELOGUE VI	KING KONG	TB-4022	2LP-12"	1975
CINELOGUE VI	KING KONG	TB-4022	2LP-12"	1975
CINELOGUE VI	CBM	WEC-3665	2LP-12"	1975
CINELOGUE: MAGICAL MYSTERY TOUR	KING KONG	634	2LP-12"	1974
CIRCUIT SONGS	BOX TOP	TWK-2262	LP-12"	1986
CLASSICS	TEICHIKU	30CP-292	CD	1990
CLASSIFIED DOCUMENT	STARLIGHT/BIRD BRAIN	BBR-014	LP-12"	1987
CLASSIFIED DOCUMENT	INSTANT ANALYSIS	BBR-014	LP-12"	1987
CLASSIFIED DOCUMENT VOL. 2	STARLIGHT/TIGER BEAT	TBLP-1	LP-12"	1988
CLASSIFIED DOCUMENT VOL. 3	STARLIGHT/TIGER BEAT	TBR/LP4	LP-12"	1988
CODENAME RUSSIA	CORE LTD	BL888-3	LP-12"	1987

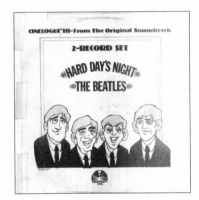

ALBUM TITLE	LABEL	CATALOG #	FORMAT	YEAR
CODENAME RUSSIA	CORE LTD	8869	LP-12"	1988
COLLECTION	TEICHIKU	32CP-442	CD	1990
COLLECTORS ITEMS	CAPITOL	SPRO-9462	LP-12"	1985
COLLECTORS ITEMS	CAPITOL	SPRO-9463	LP-12"	1985
COLLECTOR'S ITEMS	UNK	UNK	CD	1992
COLLECTOR'S ITEMS (VERS. 2)	STRAWBERRY	SPRO-9463	LP-12"-CV	1988
COME AND GET IT	BLUES INN	WS-0418	45-7"	1985
COME ON AND SING	WILBUR	W2-85	LP-12"-PD	1985
COMMONWEALTH	SHOGUN	13112	2LP-CV	1987
COMPLETE APPLE TRAX VOL. 1	ADAM VIII LTD.	CD 49-022	CD	1991
COMPLETE APPLE TRAX VOL. 2	ADAM VIII LTD.	CD 49-023	CD	1991
COMPLETE APPLE TRAX VOL. 3	ADAM VIII LTD.	CD 49-024	CD	1991
COMPLETE APPLE TRAX VOL. 4	ADAM VIII LTD.	CD 49-025	CD	1991
COMPLETE APPLE TRAX VOL. 5	ADAM VIII LTD.	CD 49-026	CD	1991
COMPLETE APPLE TRAX VOL. 6	ADAM VIII LTD.	CD 49-027	CD	1991
COMPLETE BBC CATALOGUE 1 REMASTERED	HABA	HABA-001	CD	1992
COMPLETE BBC CATALOGUE 2 REMASTERED	HABA	HABA-002	CD	1992
COMPLETE BBC CATALOGUE 3 REMASTERED	HABA	HABA-003	CD	1992
COMPLETE BBC CATALOGUE 4 REMASTERED	HABA	HABA-004	CD	1992
COMPLETE BBC CATALOGUE 5 REMASTERED	HABA	HABA-005	CD	1992
COMPLETE BBC CATALOGUE 6 REMASTERED	HABA	HABA-006	CD	1992
COMPLETE BBC CATALOGUE 7 REMASTERED	HABA	HABA-007	CD	1992
COMPLETE BBC CATALOGUE 8 REMASTERED	HABA	HABA-008	CD	1992
COMPLETE BBC CATALOGUE 9 REMASTERED	HABA	HABA-009	CD	1992
COMPLETE BBC SESSIONS, THE	GREAT DANE	GDR-9326/9	9CD-BX	1993
COMPLETE CHRISTMAS COLLECTION 1963–69	CBM	WEC-3316	LP-12"	1973
COMPLETE CHRISTMAS COLLECTION 63–69	TMOQ	71015	LP-12"	1972
COMPLETE CHRISTMAS COLLECTION 63–69	CBM	2 C1/01	LP-12"	1973
COMPLETE CHRISTMAS COLLECTION 63–69	ZAP	1065	LP-12"	1976
COMPLETE CHRISTMAS COLLECTION 63–69	LXXXIV	SERIES #58	LP-12"	'70s
COMPLETE CHRISTMAS COLLECTION 63–69	WIZARDO	WRMB-400	LP-12"	1976
COMPLETE HOUSTON CONCERT, THE	GREAT DANE	GDR-9304/AB	2CD-BX	1993
COMPLETE ITALY & PARIS	ITA	ITA/3688	LP-12"	1988
COMPLETE LET IT BE SESSIONS	WIZARDO	WRMB-315	2LP-12"	1975
COMPLETE ROOFTOP CONCERT, THE	YELLOW DOG	YD-015	CD	1992
COMPLETE SOUNDTRACK TO HELP!	WIZARDO	WRMB-317	2LP-12"	1975
COMPLETE UNCUT SOUNDTRACK TO A.H.D.N.	WIZARDO	WRMB-303	2LP-12"	1975
CONFIDENTIAL DOCUMENT	INSTANT ANALYSIS	BBR-014	LP-12"	1988
CONFIDENTIAL DOCUMENT	STARLIGHT/BIRD BRAIN	BBR-014	LP-12"	1987
CONTROL ROOM MONITOR MIXES, THE	YELLOW DOG	YD-032	CD	1993
CRAZY SHOWS	WORLD PRODUCTIONS	WPOCM-001	CD	1988
CRAZY SHOWS	WORLD PRODUCTIONS	WPOCM-001	LP-12"	1988
CRYING, WAITING, HOPING	WORLD PRODUCTIONS	WPOCM-010	CD	1989
CRYING WAITING/TILL THERE WAS YOU	DECCAGONE	PRO-1105	45-7"-CV	1976
DAWN OF OUR INNOCENCE	MARC	OG-596	LP-12"	1976
DAWN OF OUR INNOCENCE	BEAT	BE-1001	LP-12"	1977
DAWN OF THE ORIGINAL SILVER BEATLES	ROYAL	LH-21477	LP-12"	1977
DAWN OF THE SILVER BEATLES	PAC	VOL-2333	LP-12"	1981
DAY AFTER & DAY BEFORE!	ADO	OG-606	LP-12"	1977
DAY IN THE LIFE, A/GET BACK	BEAT-L	003	45-7"	1979
DAY TRIPPER JAM	KING KONG	NO #	LP-12"	'70s
DE BIETELS TUSSEN DE BOLLEN	BEATLES UNLIMITED	BU1-1984-B19C1	LP-12"	1984
DE BIETELS TUSSEN DE BOLLEN	UNK	UNK	CD	1992
DEC 63	ODD-FOUR	ODD-4A/5B	LP-12"	1979
DECCA AUDITION OUTTAKES	CBM	WEC-3640/41	2LP-12"	1974

ALBUM TITLE	LABEL	CATALOG #	FORMAT	YEAR
DECCA AUDITION TAPES	BERKELEY	B-102	LP-12"	1975
DECCA SESSIONS: 1/1/62	CHARLY	TOPCD-523	CD	1988
DECCA TAPES, THE	BOX TOP	NO #	LP-12"	1986
DECCA TAPES, THE	POD/CIRCUIT	LK-4438	LP-12"-PD	1979
DECCA TAPES, THE	CIRCUIT	NO #	LP-12"-CV	1979
DECCA TAPES, THE	CIRCUIT	LK4438-1	LP-12"	1979
DECCAGONE SESSIONS	SMILIN' EARS	SE-7701	LP-12"	1977
DECCAGONE SINGLES	SEE IDIV. TITLES	————	————	———
DECCAGONES, THE	NO LABEL	CX-369 A/B	LP-12"	'70s
DENMARK & NETHERLAND JUNE 1964	WHY NOT	WNR-3002CD	CD	1988
DIG IT!	CONDOR	303-5117	CD	1989
DIG IT!	NEMS	FAB-1234	LP-12"	1987
DIRECTLY FROM SANTA CLAUS	SANTA CLAUS	SC007	LP-12"-PD	1984
DISTRICT OF COLUMBIA	CBM	WEC-3571	LP-12"	1972
DISTRICT OF COLUMBIA	CBM	WEC-3795	LP-12"	1973
DO IT NOW	WIZARDO	WRMB-381	LP-12"	1976
DOCUMENTS, VOL. 1	DOCUMENT	DRCD-027	CD	1990
DOCUMENTS, VOL. 1	OH BOY	1-9129	CD	1991
DOCUMENTS, VOL. 2	OH BOY	1-9130	CD	1991
DOCUMENTS, VOL. 2	DOCUMENT	DRCD-028	CD	1990
DOCUMENTS, VOL. 3	OH BOY	1-9131	CD	1991
DOCUMENTS, VOL. 3	DOCUMENT	DRCD-029	CD	1990
DOCUMENTS, VOL. 4	OH BOY	1-9132	CD	1991
DOCUMENTS, VOL. 4	DOCUMENT	DRCD-030	CD	1990
DOCUMENTS, VOL. 5	DOCUMENT	DRCD-031	CD	1990
DOCUMENTS, VOL. 5	OH BOY	1-9133	CD	1991
DOCUMENTS, VOL. 6	DOCUMENT	DRCD-032	CD	1990
DOCUMENTS, VOL. 6	OH BOY	1-9134	CD	1991
DOLL'S HOUSE	MAIDENHEAD	MHR-JET-909-1	2LP-12"	1985
DON'T PASS ME BY	CBM	WEC-RI-3316	2LP-12"	1975
DON'T PASS ME BY	CBM/COMET	WEC-RI-3316	2LP-12"	1975
DREAM IS OVER VOL. 1, THE	NO LABEL	JPM-1081	LP-12"	'70s
DREAM IS OVER VOL. 2, THE	NO LABEL	JPM-280102	LP-12"	'70s
DR. PEPPER	APPLE	SAPCOR-36	LP-12"	1987
DR. ROBERT	WIZARDO	WRMB-378	LP-12"-CV	1976
DR. ROBERT	WIZARDO	WRMB-378	LP-12"	1976
DR. ROBERT	OLD GLORY	NO #	LP-12"	'70s
DYLAN/BEATLES/STONES	IRC	741-AK/B-1	LP-12"	'70s
DYLAN/BEATLES/STONES	NO LABEL	V-4089-92	2LP-12"	'70s
EARLY BEATLES LIVE	NO LABEL	BE-1001	LP-12"	1970
EARLY YEARS, 1962, DECCA TAPES, THE	YELLOW DOG	YDB-101	CD	1994
ECHOES OF A DREAM/ 20 X 4	NO LABEL	IRT-614/TBF-615	2LP-12"	1978
ED SULLIVAN SHOW, THE	BEAT	CD-011-2	2CD	1994
ED SULLIVAN SHOWS	STRAWBERRY	NO #	LP-12"-CV	1988
ED SULLIVAN SHOWS	TOASTED	NO #	LP-12"	1988
ED SULLIVAN SHOWS, THE	TOASTED	MR-14-MRR	LP-12"-CV	1990
ED' SULLIVAN SHOW CBS TV STUDIO	STEAM	ZAP-0514	LP-12"	1980
ED' SULLIVAN SHOW CBS-TV STUDIO	STEAM	ZAP-0514	LP-12"-PD	1980
ED' SULLIVAN SHOW CBS-TV STUDIOS	PACIFIC	MK-514	LP-12"	1980
ED'S REALLY BIG BEATLE BLASTS	MELVIN	MM05	LP-12"-CV	1978
EIGHT ARMS TO HOLD YOU	ROCK SOLID	RSR 7003/4	2LP-12"	1987
EIGHT ARMS TO HOLD YOU	ROCK SOLID	RS 12/13	2CD	1991
EIGHT ARMS TO HOLD YOU	SODD	009	LP-12"	1976
EIGHT ARMS TO HOLD YOU	KIMBER	2009/BEAT 1	2LP-12"	1980
ELVIS MEETS...THE BEATLES	BEST SELLER	BSR ES-LP-50	LP-12"	'70s

ALBUM TITLE	LABEL	CATALOG #	FORMAT	YEAR
ELVIS VS BEATLES	SUPERSTAR	ND-10	LP-12"	'70s
EMI OUTAKES	PHONYGRAF	JPGRL-1115	LP-12"	1975
EMI OUTTAKES	MUSHROOM	MR-1371	LP-12"	1976
EMI OUTTAKES	NO LABEL	1371	LP-12"	1976
EMI OUTTAKES	TAKRL	1374	LP-12"	1975
EMI OUTTAKES, THE	HIGHWAY HIGH FI	HHCER-115	LP-12"	1974
EUPHORIA IN AUSTRALIA	DOCUMENT	DRCD-018	CD	1988
EUPHORIA IN AUSTRALIA	DOCUMENT	DR-018	LP-12"	1989
EXTENDED SESSIONS	ROCK SOLID	RSR 7007-8	2LP-CV	1987
EXTENDED SESSIONS	ROCK SOLID	RSR 7007-8	2LP-12"	1987
FAB FOUR	M.A.K.	S-1/2	LP-12"	'70s
FAB FOUR RARITIES	FAB FOUR RARITIES	FFR-9114/5	2EP-7"	1990
FAB RAVER SHOW	TMOQ	2	LP-12"	1974
FABS ON THE RADIO	GEAR	079	EP	1980
FAN CLUB RELEASE 1963/64	XMAS	88/1	LP-12"-PD	1988
FAN CLUB RELEASE 1965/66	XMAS	88/2	LP-12"-PD	1988
FAN CLUB RELEASE 1967/68	XMAS	88/3	LP-12"-PD	1988
FILE UNDER	SHALOM	UNK	LP-12"	1976
FILE UNDER I/II	BOX TOP	GN-70075/77	2LP-12"	1986
FILE UNDER: BEATLES	GNAT	GN-7005-21311	LP-12"	1992
FILE UNDER: THE BEATLES	GNAT	GN-70075-1	LP-12"	1984
FILE UNDER: THE BEATLES VOL. 2	BOX TOP	GN-70077	LP-12"-CV	1986
FIRST CRAZY STRETCH	STASH	STASH-639	2LP-12"	1988
FIRST MOVEMENT	AUDIO FIDELITY	PXS-339-P	LP-12"-PD	1983
FIRST UNITED STATES PERFORMANCE	WIZARDO	WRMB-360	LP-12"	1976
FIRST UNITED STATES PERFORMANCE	ROMAN	WRMB-360	LP-12"	1976
FIRST UNITED STATES PERFORMANCE	RUTHLESS RHYMES LTD	WRMB-360	LP-12"	1978
FIRST UNITED STATES PERFORMANCE	KING KONG	1070	LP-12"	1973
FIRST U.S. CONCERT	WHITE KNIGHT	WK-20	LP-12"	1978
FIRST U.S. SHOW	MODERN JAZZ	EFG-1200	LP-12"	1979
FIRST U.S. SHOW	ODD-FOUR	ODD-4	LP-12"	1979
FIRST 'N LAST - TRADE SECRETS	ATL	CD-6593	CD	1993
FIVE NIGHTS IN A JUDO ARENA	BLACK GOLD CONCERTS	BG 52043	LP-12"	1976
FIVE NIGHTS IN A JUDO ARENA	DE WEINTRAUB	DW 426	LP-12"	1975
FIVE NIGHTS IN A JUDO ARENA	THE SWINGIN' PIG	TSP-011	CD	1989
FIVE NIGHTS IN A JUDO ARENA	THE SWINGIN' PIG	TSP-011	LP-12"	1989
FIVE NIGHTS/SPICY BEATLES SONGS	FYG	7403	2LP-12"	'70s
FOR BEATLES EYES ONLY	FAN BUYS MARKETING	WBC-0002	LP-12"	1973
FOR BEATLES EYES ONLY	FAN BUYS MARKETING	WBC-0003	LP-12"	1973
FOR THE LAST TIME	STRAWBERRY	NO #	LP-12"-CV	1988
FOR THE LAST TIME	AN AFTERMATH	AM-10	LP-12"	1975
FOREST HILLS TENNIS STADIUM	KING KONG	FH-1058/4228	LP-12"	1973
FOREST HILLS TENNIS STADIUM	INSTANT ANALYSIS	FH-1058	LP-12"	1975
FOREST HILLS/LONDON	SHALOM	4228/3687	LP-12"	1976
FORETASTE	NO LABEL	SGT-19670	LP-12"-CV	1987
FOUR BY FOUR	STARLIGHT/TIGER BEAT	TBR/URT 3/4	2-7"-CV	1988
FOUR BY FOUR	STARLIGHT/TIGER BEAT	TBR/URT 1/2	2-7"-CV	1988
FOUR BY THE BEATLES	BBC TRANSCRIPTION	L1453/STC6663	EP-7"	1979
FOUR BY THE BEATLES	AUDIFON	GEP-8882	EP-7"	1979
FOUR SIDES	HONEYSUCKLE PROD	ENG-4002	2LP-12"	1982
FOUR SIDES OF THE CIRCLE	BIG JOLLY	BJR-700	2LP-12"	1981
FOUR YOUNG NOVICES	WIZARDO	WRMB-361	LP-12"	1976
FRESH BEATLES	EARLY YEARS	02-CD-3322	CD	1990
FROM A WHISPER TO A SHOUT	NO LABEL	DISCO ONE	LP-12"	'80s
FROM LIVERPOOL TO LEGEND	NO LABEL	NO #	LP-12"	1991

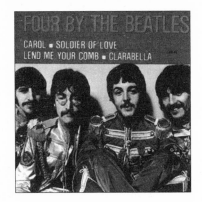

ALBUM TITLE	LABEL	CATALOG #	FORMAT	YEAR
FROM MATHEW ST. TO ABBEY RD. SESSIONS	CHTHONIAN	AEBCD-100	CD	1991
FROM ME../SHE LOVES../TILL../TWIST &...	DECCAGONE	PRO-1108	EP-7"	1981
FROM PENNY LANE TO ABBEY ROAD	LUNA	UNK	CD	1993
FROM SESSION TO SESSION	ALTERNATIVE	ARC-0072	LP-12"	1983
FROM THE VAULT	NO LABEL	NO #	5LP-CV	1987
FROM THEN TO YOU (THE XMAS ALBUM)	CHRISTMAS MEMORIES	BFC-6370	CD	1989
FROM US TO YOU	THE SWINGIN' PIG	TSP-015	3LP-CV	1989
FROM US TO YOU	THE SWINGIN' PIG	TSP-015-2	2CD	1989
FROM US TO YOU	THE SWINGIN' PIG	TSP-015	3LP-12"	1989
FROM US TO YOU-A PARL. REHEARS.SESS.	RUTHLESS RHYMES LTD	LMW 28 IF	EP-10"	1978
FROM US TO YOU-A PARL. REHEAR. SESS.	NO LABEL	LMW 28 IF	EP-10"-CV	1971
FROM YESTERDAY FOREVER	NEVEREND	NE/2 PIC	CD-PD	1992
FROM YESTERDAY FOREVER	NEVEREND	NE/2	2LP-CV	1992
FROM YESTERDAY FOREVER	AULICA/NEVEREND	NE/2	2LP-12"	1991
FROM YESTERDAY FOREVER	AULICA/NEVEREND	NE/2	CD	1991
FROM YESTERDAY FOREVER	NEVEREND	NE/2	CASS	1992
FUCK!	APPLE	SAPCOR-33	2LP-12"	1987
GARAGE TAPES/FOR SALE BY AUCTION	KREMO MUSIC PROD.	SEL-CD-18	CD	1992
GET BACK	RUTHLESS RHYMES LTD	BGD-111	LP-12"	1978
GET BACK	AMAZON ETCETERA	637	LP-12"	'70s
GET BACK	LEMON	LRS-123	LP-12"	1970
GET BACK	APPLE	PCS-7080-2	CD	1988
GET BACK	TONTO	TO-643	LP-12"	'80s
GET BACK	CHAMELION	9019	CD	1990
GET BACK	IMACULATE CONCEPTION	VAR-101	LP-12"	'70s
GET BACK	OIL WELL	RSC-008	CD	1994
GET BACK	WIZARDO	WRMB-315	LP-12"	1975
GET BACK	LEMON	BHB-111	LP-12"	1970
GET BACK	WIZARDO	WRMB-320	LP-12"	1975
GET BACK	APPLE GHOST	CD-53-43	CD	1991
GET BACK AND 22 OTHER SONGS	YELLOW DOG	YD-014	CD	1992
GET BACK AND MORE	ADAM VIII LTD.	9TX-014	CD	1991
GET BACK AND MORE	JSJ	1313	LP-12"	1970
GET BACK AND MORE	TB	TB-002	CD	1991
GET BACK JOURNALS	SUMA	80818089	11LP-12"	1987
GET BACK JOURNALS	BLACKBIRD	PCS-7080-2	11LP-12"	1987
GET BACK JOURNALS	TMOQ	2R-78	11LP-CV	1987
GET BACK JOURNALS, THE	VIGOTONE	VIGO/101-108	8CD-BX	1993
GET BACK JOURNALS, THE	VIGATONE	UNK	10-LP-BX	1994
GET BACK JOURNALS, THE	VIGOTONE	VIGO/101-108	8CD	1993
GET BACK SESSION	AMSTERDAM FAN CLUB	DISCO-2	LP-12"	'70s
GET BACK SESSION, THE	TMOQ	BGB-111	LP-12"	1974
GET BACK SESSIONS	DITTOLINO DISCS	NO #	LP-12"	1970
GET BACK SESSIONS	EARLY YEARS	CD-3322-PD	CD-PD	1989
GET BACK SESSIONS	TMOQ	1801	LP-12"	1974
GET BACK SESSIONS	EARLY YEARS	02-CD-3322	CD	1989
GET BACK SESSIONS	BLUE KANGAROO	BK-007	2CD	1992
GET BACK SESSIONS	DIG A BEATLE	DAB-5	LP-12"	1971
GET BACK SESSIONS	TMOQ	71024	LP-12"-CV	1972
GET BACK SESSIONS	PINE TREE	X-10069	LP-12"	1970
GET BACK SESSIONS	NO LABEL	CLH-105	LP-12"	1972
GET BACK SESSIONS	LEMON	X-10069	LP-12"	1970
GET BACK SESSIONS	WIZARDO	WRMB-320	LP-12"	1975
GET BACK SESSIONS	NO LABEL	CLH-105	LP-12"	'70s
GET BACK SESSIONS	MICHAEL & ALLYSON	2131/2132	LP-12"	1970

ALBUM TITLE	LABEL	CATALOG #	FORMAT	YEAR
GET BACK SESSIONS 2	K & S	018	LP-12"-CV	1974
GET BACK SESSIONS 2	TMOQ	71068	LP-12"	1971
GET BACK SESSIONS AND VIRGIN + THREE	TMOQ/IMP	71068/71024	LP-12"	1976
GET BACK SESSIONS ONE AND TWO	MARC	OG-#	LP-12"	1976
GET BACK SESSIONS VOL. 2	TMOQ	1892-A/B	LP-12"	1974
GET BACK SESSIONS VOL. 2	AMAZON ETCETERA	638	LP-12"	'70s
GET BACK SESSIONS VOL. 2	TMOQ	BHB-118	LP-12"	1974
GET BACK SESSIONS VOL. I	AMAZON ETCETERA	637	LP-12"	'70s
GET BACK SESSIONS (I)	BOX TOP	NO #	LP-12"-CV	1986
GET BACK SPECIAL	MIDO ENTERPRISE	ZS-9107	CD	1991
GET BACK TO TORONTO	IPF	2143	LP-12"	1971
GET BACK TO TORONTO	CBM/COMET	WEC-3519	LP-12"	1975
GET BACK TO TORONTO	CBM	WEC-3519	LP-12"	1973
GET BACK TO TORONTO	TORONTO	23	LP-12"	'70s
GET BACK TO TORONTO	IPF	IPF-1	LP-12"	1971
GET BACK TO TORONTO	IPF	RP-23	LP-12"	1971
GET BACK TO TORONTO	BC	V36766	LP-12"	'70s
GET BACK W/DON'T LET ME DOWN & 9...	GHOST	CD 53-43	CD	1991
GET BACK W/DON'T LET ME DWN & 11...	TONTO	TO-643	LP-12"	'80s
GET BACK W/DON'T LET ME DWN & 15...	EMI	CDPCS-87080-2	CD	1989
GET BACK W/DON'T LET ME DWN & 9...	EMI/BLACKBIRD	PCS-7080	LP-12"-CV	1989
GET BACK W/DON'T LET ME DWN & 9...	EMI/BLACKBIRD	PCS-7080	LP-12"	1989
GET BACK W/DON'T LET ME DWN & 9...	EMI/PARLOPHONE	CDP-7-480032	CD	1988
GET BACK (COLLECTOR'S ED.)	NO LABEL	UNK	LP-12"	'80s
GET BACK (PRESS KIT)	APPLE	PCS-7080	LP-12"	1986
GET BK.W/LET IT BE & 11 OTHER SONGS	DISQUES DU MONDE	6B871969	CD	1987
GET BK.W/LET IT BE & 11 OTHER SONGS	APPLE	UNK	LP-12"	1988
GET TOGETHER	TOBE MILO	4Q-1/2	EP-7"	1976
GET TOGETHER	TOBE MILO	4Q-1/2	EP-CV	1977
GET YER YEAH-YEAH'S OUT	WIZARDO	WRMB-316	LP-12"	1975
GET YER YEAH-YEAH'S OUT	BERKELEY	N2027	2LP-12"	1976
GET YER YEAH-YEAH'S OUT	WIZARDO	WRMB-316	2LP-12"	1975
GIRL/ YOU'RE GOING TO LOSE THAT GIRL	CAPITOL	4506	45-7"	1977
GOLDEN BEATLES	OVERSEAS	30-LP-561Y4A	CD	1988
GOLDEN SLUMBERS	MAX HAMMER	7001-7012	12LP-12"	1987
GOLDEN SLUMBERS/ BEST OF MCCARTNEY	NO LABEL	OVL 2-1/1	LP-12"	'70s
GOLDMINE	SUMA	8086591	2LP-CV	1987
GOOD OLD DAYS, THE	TMOQ	UNK	LP-12"	'70s
GOOD OLD DAYS, THE	SHEA	S-2531	LP-12"	'70s
GRAVE POSTS	APPLE	SAPCOR-NZ1964	2LP-12"	1987
GREAT TO HAVE YOU WITH US	MAIDENHEAD	MHR-JET-909-3	2LP-12"	1986
GREATEST HITS BY J, P, G, AND R	NO LABEL	FL-1178	LP-12"	'70s
GREATEST HITS: COLLECTOR'S EDITION	SUNSHINE MUSIC	501-4	4LP-12"	1973
GREATEST SHOW ON EARTH, THE	EAGLE	1832	LP-12"	'70s
HAHST AZ SON	TAKRL	2950	2LP-12"	1976
HAHST AZ SON	PHOENIX	44784	2LP-12"	1978
HAIL, HAIL ROCK 'N ROLL	OCTOPUS	OCT-001	CD	1993
HAPPY BIRTHDAY	CBM	5030	LP-12"	1974
HAPPY BIRTHDAY	WIZARDO	WRMB-345	LP-12"	1976
HAPPY BIRTHDAY	BLACK PANTHER	BP-024	CD	1989
HAPPY BIRTHDAY/SOLDIER OF LOVE	WIZARDO	WRMB-345	LP-12"	1976
HAPPY MICHAELMAS	A. GROUP	8146	LP-12"	1981
HARRISON TRACKS	OVERSEAS	30-CP-314	CD	1990
HARRISON TRACKS (GOLD)	TEICHIKU	TECP-35121	CD	1990
HAVE YOU HEARD THE WORD	CBM	WEC-3620	LP-12"	1975

ALBUM TITLE	LABEL	CATALOG #	FORMAT	YEAR
HAVE YOU HEARD THE WORD	KUSTOM	#002	LP-12"	1970
HAVE YOU HEARD THE WORD	SLIPPED DISC	SXTT-979	LP-12"	1978
HAVE YOU HEARD THE WORD	BERKELEY	UNK	LP-12"	1976
HAVE YOU HEARD THE WORD	CBM	WEC-3624	LP-12"	1975
HAVE YOU HEARD THE WORD	KING KONG	WEC-3624	LP-12"	1975
HAVE YOU HEARD THE WORD	AMAZON ETCETERA	600	LP-12"	'70s
HEADLINES	ROCK SOLID	RSR-1001	2LP-12"	1987
HEADLINES	ROCK SOUND	358	2LP-12"	1987
HEADLINES	ROCK SOLID	RSR-1001	2LP-CV	1987
HELLO LITTLE GIRL (+ 3)	BEACON	508	EP-7"	1978
HELP SPECIAL	MIDO ENTERPRISE	ZS-9102	CD	1991
HELP!	B4 RECORDS	CT-004	CD	1994
HELP! SOUNDTRACK	WIZARDO	WRMB-102/202	2LP-12"	1976
HELP/YESTERDAY	NEMS/ODEON	NR-101	45-7"	1986
HELTER SKELTER	ORANGE	SAPCOR-1000	CD	1993
HER MAJESTY	FAB FOUR RARITIES	FFR-9113	CD	1991
HER MAJESTY	NO LABEL	P-0002	LP-12"	1982
HERE WE GO	GREAT DANE	GDRCD-9326/10	CD	1995
HERE'S TO VETERANS	NO LABEL	EP-72196	LP-12"	1972
HEY JUDE SPECIAL	MIDO ENTERPRISE	ZS-9106	CD	1991
HEY JUDE & TOP OF THE POPS	TIP	#45	LP-12"	'70s
HEY JULIAN	APPLE	SAPCOR-41	2LP-12"	1987
HI HO SILVER	KING KONG	4438/GT-8410	LP-12"	1973
HI HO SILVER	SHALOM	8410	LP-12"	1978
HI HO SILVER	CBM	4438	LP-12"	1973
HIGH VOLTAGE	BLACK PANTHER	BP-CD-045	CD	1989
HISTORY OF THE BEATLE YEARS 1967–70	NO LABEL	UNK	9LP-12"	1987
HODGE-PODGE	BLACK DOG	BD-001	CD	1992
HOLD ME TIGHT	CONDOR/TOASTED	1990	CD	1989
HOLLAND/ SWEEDEN SUPER LIVE ...I	SHALOM/KING KONG	8430/3795 A	LP-12"	1975
HOLLAND/ SWEEDEN SUPER LIVE ...I	CBM	101	LP-12"	1973
HOLLYWOOD BOWL	TMOQ	71065	LP-12"	1971
HOLLYWOOD BOWL	MUSHROOM	S-2531/32	LP-12"	1976
HOLLYWOOD BOWL	BERKELEY	2027	LP-12"	1976
HOLLYWOOD BOWL 1964	WIZARDO	205	LP-12"	1976
HOLLYWOOD BOWL 1964	TMOQ	BHB-115	LP-12"	1974
HOLLYWOOD BOWL COMPLETE	YELLOW DOG	YD-034	CD	1993
HOLLYWOOD BOWL '64	NO LABEL	NO #	2EP-7"	1970
HOLLYWOOD BOWL '64	DITTOLINO DISCS	NO #	LP-12"	1970
HOMOGENIZED BEATLES	AVOCADO	2812	LP-12"	1970
HOT AS SUN	INSTANT ANALYSIS	4216/4217	2LP-12"	1975
HOT AS THE SUN	ADO	OG-593	LP-12"	1976
HOT WAX	ROCK SOLID	RSR 7005/6	2LP-12"	1987
HOUSTON AUGUST 19, 1965	BULLDOG	BGCD-034	CD	1988
HOW DO YOU DO IT	CBM	WEC-381	LP-12"	1973
HOW DO YOU DO IT	WIZARDO	WRMB-381	LP-12"	1975
HOW DO YOU DO IT/ KOMM, GIB MIR...	SWAN	S-4197	45-7"	1976
HOW DO YOU DO IT/ REVOLUTION	STRWB FLDS 4-EVER	SFF/SOK21-B-2	45-7"-CV	1976
HOWDY, YA'LL!	MELVIN	MM-15-UNREL	LP-12"	1981
I HAD A DREAM	KING REC LTD	MLK-001	LP-12"	1983
I SHOULD HAVE KNOWN BETTER	ORFH	276	EP-7"	1964
ILLEGAL BEATLES #7	D. SULPY	0007	CASS.	1987
IN A PLAY ANYWAY	CIRCUIT	TWK-2262	2LP-12"	1981
IN A PLAY ANYWAY	ROCK SOUND	2262	2LP-12"	1988
IN ABBEY ROAD	ABBEY ROAD STUDIOS	BFR PRO-003	LP-12"	1983

ALBUM TITLE	LABEL	CATALOG #	FORMAT	YEAR
IN ATLANTA WHISKEY FLATS	TMOQ	OPD-67	LP-12"	1975
IN ATLANTA WHISKEY FLATS	TMOQ	S-201	LP-12"	1975
IN ATLANTA WHISKEY FLATS	TMOQ	71007-8/70-417	LP-12"	1972
IN ATLANTA WHISKEY FLATS	RUTHLESS RHYMES LTD	OPD-19/67-2	LP-12"	1978
IN BUDOKAN 1966.6.30/7.1	BLACK DISC	S-3	2LP-PD	1981
IN CASE YOU DON'T KNOW	SPANK	SP-110	CD	1995
IN CONCERT AT WHISKEY FLAT	TMOQ	OPD-19/67-2	LP-12"	1975
IN CONCERT AT WHISKEY FLAT	NO LABEL	OPD-19/67-2	LP-12"	1975
IN CONCERT ATLANTA	JAP	UNK	LP-12"	'80s
IN PERSON SAM HOUSTON COLISEUM	TOBE MILO	5Q1/2-VC4835	EP-7"	1978
IN PERSON SAM HOUSTON COLISEUM	WAGEN LTD	WA-1919	LP-12"	'80s
IN PERSON SAM HOUSTON COLISEUM	TOBE MILO	10Q-3/4	LP-12"	1978
IN THE '70s	MELVIN	12-S	LP-12"	1980
IN THE BEGINNING	PULSAR	PULS 005	CD	1991
IN THE LAP OF THE GODS...	WIZARDO	WRMB-325	LP-12"	1975
INCREDIBLE	NO LABEL	AR-7039	LP-12"	'70s
INCREDIBLE!	OVERDONE PROD	EP 12/45-7039	EP-CV	'70s
INDIAN ROPE TRICK	FAN	BEAT-1	LP-12"	1978
INDIAN ROPE TRICK	DRAGONFLY	BEAT-1	LP-12"	1977
INDIAN ROPE TRICK	RUTHLESS RHYMES LTD	BEAT-1	LP-12"	1977
INDIAN ROPE TRICK	IDLE MIND	1162	LP-12"	1976
INTRODUCING THE BEATLES/FROM ME...	SWAN	S-4182-1	45-7"	1976
IT WAS 20 YEARS AGO TODAY	TMOQ	NO #	LP-12"	1987
IT WAS 25 YRS...BEATLES CAME TO GER.	BEATLES MUSEUM	BMIC/TR-002	45-7"	1992
ITALY	INSTANT ANALYSIS	4178	LP-12"	1975
ITALY/ PARIS	SHALOM	4178A/3688A	2LP-12"	1976
IT'S ALL TOO MUCH	NO LABEL	B-6	LP-12"	1985
IT'S ALL TOO MUCH	WORLD PRODUCTIONS	WPOCM-011	CD	1989
IT'S ALL TOO MUCH	SEX	3533	LP-12"	1985
I'LL BE ON MY WAY	NO LABEL	SON-115831	45-7"	1973
JIMI HENDRIX TAKES ON THE BEATLES	TORONTO	723LP23	LP-12"	'70s
JOHN, PAUL, GEORGE AND JIMMY	WIZARDO	WRMB-501	LP-12"	1976
JOHN, PAUL, GEORGE & RINGO	ORANGE	OR-20	CD	1995
JOHN, PAUL, GEORGE, RINGO IN THE '70S	MELVIN	MR-12-S	LP-12"	1980
JOHN & THE BEATLES LOST IN THE STUDIO	MONGOOSE	MONG-CD-028	CD	1992
JUDY	KUSTOM	ASC-003	LP-12"	1970
JUDY	KUSTOM	103	LP-12"	1970
J. POPE'S STRWB FLDS 4-EVER XMAS REC.	STRWB FLDS 4-EVER	#27:3	EP-7"-FLX	1977
J. POPE'S STRWB FLDS 4-EVER XMAS REC.	STRWB FLDS 4-EVER	#40:6	EP-7"-FLX	1980
J. POPE'S STRWB FLDS 4-EVER XMAS REC.	STRWB FLDS 4-EVER	#36:5	EP-7"-FLX	1979
J. POPE'S STRWB FLDS 4-EVER XMAS REC.	STRWB FLDS 4-EVER	#32:4	EP-7"-FLX	1978
J. POPE'S STRWB FLDS 4-EVER XMAS REC.	STRWB FLDS 4-EVER	#18:1	EP-7"-FLX	1975
J. POPE'S STRWB FLDS 4-EVER XMAS REC.	STRWB FLDS 4-EVER	#24:2	EP-7"-FLX	1976
KALEIDOSCOPE	DREAM LAB	007	LP-12"	'70s
KAMIKAZE ONE 85	PARLOPHONE	12R6272	EP-12"	1991
KARAOKE-THE R. STONES & THE BEATLES	YELLOW DOG	YD-033	CD	1993
KENNY EVERETT COTTONFIELDS INTERVIEW	NO LABEL	CORE 1	LP-12"-PD	1990
KFWB	KUSTOM	2637/8	LP-12"	1970
KITANUS DEMO, THE	UNK	JPGR-1234	CD	1994
KNIGHT'S HARD DAY, A	APPLE	SAPCOR-31	2LP-12"	1987
KOM, GIB MIR DEINE HAND/SIE LIEBT DICH	CAPITOL	AS-444	45-12"	1980
KOM, GIB MIR DEINE HAND/SIE LIEBT DICH	CAPITOL	AS-444	45-12"-CV	1980
KOMM, GIB MIR DEINE HAND + ONE	CAPITOL	AS-444	45-12"-CV	1980
KOOL WAX	SHOGUN	13111	2LP-12"	1987
KUM BACK	NO LABEL	KB-10	LP-12"	1969

184

ALBUM TITLE	LABEL	CATALOG #	FORMAT	YEAR
KUM BACK	KUM BACK #1	WCF	LP-12"	1969
KUM BACK	KING KONG	15A	LP-12"	1973
KUM BACK	THE WORLD'S GRTST	15/1-2	LP-12"	1971
KUM BACK	M.A.K.	S-1/2	LP-12"	'70s
KUM BACK	CBM	CBM-15A	LP-12"	1973
KUM BACK	KUM	KB-A/B	LP-12"	1971
KUM BACK STEREO	KUM	KB-10	LP-12"	1971
LAST ALBUM, THE	NO LABEL	01971	LP-12"	1971
LAST BEETLE RECORD	WIZARDO	WRMB-393	LP-12"	1976
LAST LIVE LIVE SHOW	TMOQ	1800-RI	LP-12"	1971
LAST LIVE SHOW	LIVE	LR #7001	LP-12"	1972
LAST LIVE SHOW	TMOQ	LLS-101	LP-12"	1971
LAST LIVE SHOW	SHEA	1/2	LP-12"-PD	1980
LAST LIVE SHOW	DITTOLINO DISCS	0009	LP-12"	1970
LAST LIVE SHOW	TMOQ	1800	LP-12"	1971
LAST LIVE SHOW	LIVE	501-WCF	LP-12"	1972
LAST LIVE SHOW (III)	TMOQ	71012	LP-12"	1972
LAST LIVE SHOW (IV)	TMOQ	S-202	LP-12"	1975
LEAVE MY KITTEN ALONE	LUNA	UNK	CD	1993
LEGENDARY	TEICHIKU	50CP-361/2	CD	1988
LEGENDARY BEATLES, THE	TEICHIKU	50CP-361-2	2CD	1988
LENNON TRACKS	OVERSEAS	30CP-312	CD	1990
LENNON TRACKS (GOLD)	TEICHIKU	TECP-35119	CD	1990
LES BEATLES A PARIS	KTS	FU-201	CD	1994
LES BEATLES A PARIS	NEON	2C006-1956	2LP-12"	1988
LET IT BE	NO LABEL	315	LP-12"	1975
LET IT BE	OASIS	OLE-170	LP-12"	'80s
LET IT BE	UNDERGROUND SOUNDS	101	LP-12"	1969
LET IT BE 315	WIZARDO	WRMB-315	LP-12"	1975
LET IT BE ACETATE	WIZARDO	WRMB-315	LP-12"	1975
LET IT BE AND 10 OTHER SONGS	APPLE	1-33-30	LP-12"	1987
LET IT BE LIVE	NO LABEL	LB-1	LP-12"	1976
LET IT BE LIVE	WIZARDO	WRMB-315	LP-12"	1975
LET IT BE LIVE	BERKELEY	LB-11	LP-12"	1976
LET IT BE LIVE	AMAZON ETCETERA	659	LP-12"	'70s
LET IT BE LIVE	SILVER GREATEST	WCF	LP-12"	1975
LET IT BE PERFORMANCE, THE	WIZARDO	WRMB-315	2LP-12"	1975
LET IT BE REHEARSALS VOL. 3 (PART 2)	YELLOW DOG	YD-053	CD	1994
LET IT BE REHEARSALS VOL. 4 (R'N'R)	YELLOW DOG	YD-054	CD	1994
LET IT BE REHEARSALS VOL. 5 (AUCTION)	YELLOW DOG	YD-055	CD	1994
LET IT BE SESSION	ANF	ANF-7004	CD	1990
LET IT BE SESSIONS	CHAPTER ONE	CO-144	CD	1991
LET IT BE SESSIONS VOL. 2	CHAPTER ONE	CO-188	CD	1992
LET IT BE SESSIONS VOL. III	CHAPTER ONE	CO-206	CD	1993
LET IT BE SPECIAL	MIDO ENTERPRISE	ZS-9108	CD	1991
LET IT BE (I)	APPLE	JS-17499	LP-12"	1983
LET IT BE: BEFORE PHIL SPECTOR	WIZARDO	WRMB-315	LP-12"	1975
LET IT END	APPLE	SAPCOR-42	2LP-12"	1987
LET THEM BEATLES BE	NO LABEL	NO #	2LP-12"	'70s
LIFTING MATERIAL FORM THE WORLD	APPLE	SAPCOR-43	2LP-12"	1987
LIKE DREAMERS DO	NO LABEL	BACK-1111	LP-12"-PD	'80s
LISTEN TO THIS/PROMO & REGARDS	BEATLES MUSEUM	BMIC/TR-001	45-7"	1992
LITTLE RED ALBUM, THE	APPLE	SAPCOR-38	2LP-12"	1987
LIVE	NO LABEL	BE-1001	LP-12"	1970
LIVE, LIVE, LIVE	YELLOW DOG	YDB-201	CD	1994

Black Market Beatles

ALBUM TITLE	LABEL	CATALOG #	FORMAT	YEAR
LIVE AT ABBEY ROAD STUDIOS	NO LABEL	ARS-2-9083	2LP-12"	1984
LIVE AT ATL. WHISKEY FLAT 65 & D.C. 64	ADAM VIII LTD.	CD 49-017	CD	1991
LIVE AT HOLLYWOOD BOWL	MUSHROOM	4	LP-12"	1976
LIVE AT HOLLYWOOD BOWL	TMOQ	115	LP-12"	1974
LIVE AT HOLLYWOOD BOWL	CBM	WEC-1103	LP-12"	1973
LIVE AT HOLLYWOOD BOWL	TMOQ	71065	LP-12"	1973
LIVE AT HOLLYWOOD BOWL	TMOQ	1704	LP-12"	1974
LIVE AT NASSAU COLOSSEUM	ZAPPLE	999	LP-12"	1974
LIVE AT SHEA	PEACE	1/2,3/4	2EP-7"	1974
LIVE AT SHEA	WIZARDO	WRMB-406	LP-12"	1976
LIVE AT SHEA 1964 1	NO LABEL	112	EP-10"	1971
LIVE AT SHEA 1964 2	NO LABEL	NO #	EP-10"	1971
LIVE AT SHEA STADIUM	BERKELEY	01	LP-12"	1976
LIVE AT SHEA STADIUM	FIGA	3	LP-12"	1972
LIVE AT SHEA STADIUM (I)	BENBECULA	P242813	LP-12"	1972
LIVE AT SHEA-STADIUM	MARC	OG-802	LP-12"	1976
LIVE AT SHEA-STADIUM	MARC	OG-718	LP-12"	1976
LIVE AT S.F. CANDLESTICK PARK	NO LABEL	1/2	LP-12"	1971
LIVE AT THE BBC 1962–65	RSR INTERNATIONAL	RSR 252	2LP-12"	1986
LIVE AT THE CIRCUS CRONE	FABULOUS FOUR	L-30157	LP-12"	'80s
LIVE AT THE HOLLYWOOD BOWL	POD	BHB-115	LP-12"	1980
LIVE AT THE HOLLYWOOD BOWL 1964	TMOQ	71065	LP-12"	1974
LIVE AT THE HOLLYWOOD BOWL 1964	TMOQ	S-208	LP-12"	1975
LIVE AT THE JUDO ARENA	IMAGE DISC	2043/DW 426	LP-12"-PD	1979
LIVE AT THE ROCK & ROLL HALL OF FAME	LIVING LEGEND	LLRCD-101	CD	1991
LIVE AT THE SHEA STADIUM	FIGA	3	LP-12"	1972
LIVE AT THE STAR CLUB	OVERSEAS	38CP-44	CD	1990
LIVE AT THE STAR CLUB, 1962	OVERSEAS	38-CP-44	CD	1985
LIVE AT THE WHISKEY FLAT	TMOQ	OPD-67-2	LP-12"	1975
LIVE AT THE WHISKEY FLAT	TMOQ	OPD-19	LP-12"	1975
LIVE AT THE WHISKEY FLAT	AMAZON ETCETERA	619	LP-12"	'70s
LIVE AT THE WHISKEY FLAT	TMOQ	70418F	LP-12"-CV	'70s
LIVE BEATLES	DOCUMENT	DR-005	LP-12"-PD	1988
LIVE BEATLES, THE: AUSTRALIA 1964	BULLDOG/CROCODILE	BGCD-156	2CD	1990
LIVE BEATLES, THE: HOUSTON, 8/19/65	BULLDOG	BGCD-034	CD	1988
LIVE BEATLES, THE: PARIS 6/20/65	BULLDOG	BGCD-005	CD	1989
LIVE BEATLES, THE: S. F., 8/29/66	BULLDOG	BGCD-016	CD	1988
LIVE BEATLES, THE: TOKIO, 7/2/66	BULLDOG	BGCD-002	CD	1989
LIVE BEATLES SAM HOUSTON COLISEUM, THE	BULLDOG	BGP-904	LP-PD	1987
LIVE BEATLES SAM HOUSTON COLISEUM, THE	BULLDOG	BGP-903	LP-PD	1987
LIVE BEATLES SINGLES COLLECTION, THE	BULLDOG	BGS-14	13-45-7"	1987
LIVE BEATLES SINGLES COLLECTION, THE	BULLDOG	BGS-14	13-7"-CV	1987
LIVE BEATLES: THE, MUNICH, 6/24/66	DOCUMENT	DR-005	LP-12"	1988
LIVE CONCERT AT WHISKEY FLATS	LEMON	510	LP-12"	1970
LIVE CONCERT AT WHISKEY FLATS	BERKELEY	510	LP-12"	1976
LIVE CONCERT ATLANTA	CBM	WEC-3552	LP-12"	1975
LIVE CONCERT ATLANTA	KING KONG	RI-3552	LP-12"	1975
LIVE CONCERT ATLANTA GA.	CBM	WEC-3552	LP-12"	1975
LIVE FROM GERMANY	NO LABEL	999	LP-12"	1975
LIVE FROM GERMANY	NO LABEL	01971	LP-12"	'70s
LIVE FROM THE LIVE	NO LABEL	LTTPR	LP-12"-PD	'70s
LIVE FROM THE SAM HOUSTON COLOSSEUM	BOX TOP	NO #	2LP-CV	1986
LIVE FROM THE SAM HOUSTON COLOSSEUM	BLACK DISC	ZAP-1049/50	LP-12"	1980
LIVE FROM THE SAM HOUSTON COLOSSEUM	ZAP	1049/50	2LP-12"	1976
LIVE FROM THE SAM HOUSTON COLOSSEUM	HOHRWEITE STEREO...	BV-006	LP-12"	1980

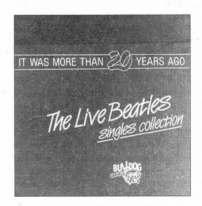

ALBUM TITLE	LABEL	CATALOG #	FORMAT	YEAR
LIVE FROM THE SAM HOUSTON COLOSSEUM	BOX TOP	NO #	2LP-12"	1986
LIVE FROM THE SAM HOUSTON COLOSSEUM	AUDIFON	BVP-006	2LP-12"	1979
LIVE FROM THE SAM HOUSTON COLOSSEUM	WAGEN	WA-1919	LP-12"	'80s
LIVE GERM. CONCERTS & US TELECASTS	CBM	WEC-1002	LP-12"	1973
LIVE IN ADELAIDE AND HOUSTON, TEXAS	STARLIFE	HRCD-52026	CD	1991
LIVE IN ANYTOWN	HIGHWAY HIGH FI	HHCER-110	LP-12"	1974
LIVE IN ATLANTA WHISKEY FLAT	WHISKEY	510	LP-12"	1976
LIVE IN ATLANTA WHISKEY FLAT	TMOQ	OPD-79	LP-12"	1975
LIVE IN ATLANTA WHISKEY FLAT	TMOQ	1704	LP-12"	1974
LIVE IN AUSTRALIA AND WASHINGTON	WIZARDO	WRMB-314	LP-12"	1975
LIVE IN ESSEN	DOCUMENT	DR-005	LP-12"	1988
LIVE IN EUROPE AND US T.V. CASTS	CBM	WEC-3571	LP-12"	1975
LIVE IN EUROPE & U.S. T.V. CASTS	PIRATE	3571	LP-12"	'70s
LIVE IN GERMANY	MARC	TB-75112	EP-7"	1979
LIVE IN GERMANY 1966	DOCUMENT	DR-005	LP-12"-PD	1988
LIVE IN GERMANY 1966	NO LABEL	NO #	LP-12"-PD	1989
LIVE IN GERMANY AND TOP OF THE POPS	BERKELEY	206	LP-12"	1976
LIVE IN HAMBURG '62	TEICHIKU	TECP-28435	CD-PD	1990
LIVE IN HAMBURG '62	TEICHIKU	TECP-25005	CD	1990
LIVE IN HAMBURG '62	TEICHIKU	TECP-30172	CD-BX	1990
LIVE IN HOLLYWOOD	CBM	WEC-110	LP-12"	1973
LIVE IN HOUSTON	BULLDOG	BGCD-034	CD-PD	1990
LIVE IN HOUSTON	ANF	ANF-7002	CD	1988
LIVE IN HOUSTON BOTH SHOWS	BOX TOP	BV-006	LP-12"	1986
LIVE IN ITALY	INSTANT ANALYSIS	IT-1038	LP-12"	1975
LIVE IN ITALY	KING KONG	4178	LP-12"	1973
LIVE IN ITALY	TOBE MILO	ITA-128	EP-7"	1980
LIVE IN JAPAN	RICKENBACKER/ODEON	RICEM 1A/2A	2LP-12"	1987
LIVE IN JAPAN	STARLIFE	HRCD-52024	CD	1991
LIVE IN JAPAN 1966	CONTACT	CDCN-116	CD	1987
LIVE IN JAPAN 1966	WIZARDO	WRMB-318	LP-12"	1975
LIVE IN LONDON 1963	DOCUMENT	DR-011	EP-10"-PD	1988
LIVE IN LONDON '63	DOCUMENT	DOC-011	EP-12"-PD	1989
LIVE IN MALMO	NO LABEL	NO #	LP-12"	'70s
LIVE IN MELBOURNE 1964 & PARIS 1965	PYRAMID	RFT-CD-001	CD	1988
LIVE IN MELBOURNE AUSTRALIA 7/16/64	INSTANT ANALYSIS	MB-1034	LP-12"	1975
LIVE IN MELBOURNE AUSTRALIA 7/16/64	CBM	WEC-4162	LP-12"	1975
LIVE IN MUNICH 1966	ZAP	7870	LP-12"	1977
LIVE IN PALAIS DE SPORTS - PARIS	STARLIFE	HRCD-52023	CD	1991
LIVE IN PARIS	RICKENBACKER/ODEON	RICEM-22	LP-12"	1987
LIVE IN PARIS 1964 AND S.F. 1966	PYRAMID	RFT-CD-002	CD	1988
LIVE IN PARIS 1964 AND S.F. 1966	PYRAMID	RFT-CD-002	LP-12"	1988
LIVE IN PARIS 1965	BULLDOG	BGCD-005	CD-PD	1990
LIVE IN PARIS 1965	THE SWINGIN' PIG	TSP-008	CD	1989
LIVE IN PARIS 1965	ANF	ANF-7003	CD	1990
LIVE IN PARIS 1965	THE SWINGIN' PIG	TSP-008	2LP-12"	1988
LIVE IN PARIS '65	THE SWINGIN' PIG	TSP-008	2LP-CV	1989
LIVE IN PHILADELPHIA	WIZARDO	WRMB-357	LP-12"	1976
LIVE IN PHILADELPHIA 1964	ANF	ANF-7005	CD	1988
LIVE IN PHILADELPHIA 1964	BULLDOG	BGCD-005	CD	1988
LIVE IN THE NETHERLANDS	WHY NOT	WN 3002	2CD-PD	1990
LIVE IN THE UNITED KINGDOM 1962–65	BULLDOG	BGCD-11112	2CD	1990
LIVE IN THE UNITED KINGDOM 1962–65	BULLDOG	BGCP-90512	2CD-PD	1990
LIVE IN THE U.K. 1963–65	GREAT DANE	UNK	2CD	1990
LIVE IN TOKYO	MARC	OG-545	LP-12"	1978

190

ALBUM TITLE	LABEL	CATALOG #	FORMAT	YEAR
LIVE IN TOKYO	MARC	OG-733	LP-12"	1978
LIVE IN TOKYO	MARC	OG-640	LP-12"	1978
LIVE IN TOKYO	MARC	OG-569	LP-12"	1978
LIVE IN TOKYO, JULY 1, 1966	WIZARDO	501	LP-12"	1976
LIVE IN TOKYO 1966	ANF	ANF-7001	CD	1988
LIVE IN TOKYO '66	MUSHROOM	12	LP-12"	1976
LIVE IN U.S.A. 1964–1965	LIVING LEGEND	LLRCD-007	CD	1988
LIVE IN VANCOUVER	CBM	WEC-4164	LP-12"	1975
LIVE IN VANCOUVER, CANADA	INSTANT ANALYSIS	VN-1032	LP-12"	1975
LIVE IN WASHINGTON D.C.	CBM	WEC-3571/3795	LP-12"	1974
LIVE ON SILVER	SILVER GREATEST	LB-1	LP-12"	1976
LIVE ON STAGE 1962–1966	UNK	SC-12620	5LP-12"	1992
LIVE ON STAGE IN JAPAN	DUCK	PE-JAP-I/II	LP-12"	'70s
LIVE PARIS OLYMPIA	CBM	WEC-3688	LP-12"	1975
LIVE PARIS OLYMPIA	SHALOM	WEC-3688	LP-12"	1974
LIVE PARIS OLYMPIA/ AT SHEA STAD.	NO LABEL	APO/ASS-6506/08	2LP-12"	'70s
LIVE SOMEWHERE	MELVIN	MS-18-UNREL	LP-12"	1982
LIVE TRACKS-PREVIOUSLY ITALIAN E.P.	NO LABEL	EPB-1967	EP-12"	'70s
LIVE VARIOUS LOCATIONS	DVMOR	CD-5500	CD	1991
LIVERPOOL FLASH - SIXTH AMENDMENT	ZAP	7869	LP-12"	1977
LIVERPOOL MAY 1960	INDRA	M5-6001	2LP-12"	1987
LIVERPOOL MAY 1960	STEMRA	TNT-4067/68	2LP-12"	1987
LIVERPOOOL MAY 1960	KTS	FU-207	CD	1994
LONDON, MELBOURNE, MUNCHEN	KOINE	K881101	CD	1988
LONDON PALLADIUM	KING KONG	WEC-3687	LP-12"	1974
LONG AND WINDING ROAD, THE/MY SWEET L.	BEAT-L	009	45-7"	1980
LONG LOST ALBUM, THE	MONGOOSE	MONG-CD-019	CD	1992
LONG LOST DEMOS, THE	MONGOOSE	MONG-CD-020	CD	1992
LONG LOST LEFTOVERS, THE	MONGOOSE	MONG-CD-021	CD	1992
LONG TALL SALLY/A HARD DAY'S NIGHT	BEAT	BE-12-142	45-7"-CV	1977
LOOK BACK	BOX TOP	LB72-7985	2LP-12"	1986
LOOK WHAT WE FOUND	LIVING LEGEND	LLRCD-029	CD	1989
LOOKING BACK ON ABBEY ROAD	APPLE WRECORDS	CX-320	LP-12"	'80s
LOST BEATLES TAPES VOL. 1	FAB GEAR	FGC-92001/2	2CD	1993
LOST BEATLES TAPES VOL. 2	FAB GEAR	FGC-92003/4	2CD	1993
LOST BEEB TAPES, THE	STARLIGHT/TIGER BEAT	TBR/LP-2	LP-12"	1988
LOST BEEBS, THE	ADAM VIII LTD.	CD 49-034	CD	1991
LOST MASTERS	STARLIGHT	SL-87049	LP-12"-CV	1991
LOST MASTERS	STARLIGHT	SL-87049	LP-12"	1989
LOST PEPPERLAND REEL, THE	VIGOTONE	VT-132	CD	1995
LOVE ME DO/TWIST/THERE'S A/P.S. I	VEE JAY	VJ-103	EP-7"	'70s
LOVE OF THE LOVED	DECCAGONE	PRO-1100	EP-45-7"	1976
LOVE OF THE LOVED/ REUNION	CLUB	NO. 3	45-7"	'70s
L.B. IN TORONTO	CUMBAT	UNK	LP-12"	'70s
L.S. BUMBLE BEE	CBM	WEC-3626	LP-12"	1975
L.S. BUMBLE BEE	BERKELEY	3626	LP-12"	1976
MACH SHAU	SAVAGE	L-20819	LP-12"	1985
MACH SHAU!	BEATLES MUSEUM	NO #	EP-7"	1992
MAGICAL MYSTERY DEMOS	CHAPTER ONE	CO-25197	CD	1992
MAGICAL MYSTERY TOUR PLUS	WIZARDO	WRMB-310	2LP-12"	1975
MAGICAL TOUR, THE	LUNA	UNK	CD	1993
MAGTRAX	SUMA	8084250	2LP-CV	1987
MAILMAN BLUES	APPLE GHOST	JET-3	LP-12"	'80s
MAL EVANS CHRISTMAS 1988	WHITE WALRUS	MEFC-12188	CASS	1988
MAL EVANS CHRISTMAS 1989	WHITE WALRUS	MEFC-12189	CASS	1989

ALBUM TITLE	LABEL	CATALOG #	FORMAT	YEAR
MAL EVANS TAPES, THE	UNK	UNK	CD	1993
MAN OF THE DECADE	TOBE MILO	MOTD-1269	LP-12"	1978
MANUAL EXCITATIONS	AN AFTERMATH	AM-12	LP-12"	1975
MARCH 5, 1963 PLUS THE DECCA TAPE	VIGATONE	VT-123	CD	1994
MARY JANE	CBM	WEC-3585	LP-12"	1975
MARY JANE	TMOQ	MJ-543	LP-12"	1973
MARY JANE	NO LABEL	93	LP-12"	1971
MARY JANE	GREAT LIVE CONCERTS	GLCR-93	LP-12"	'70s
MARY JANE	TMOQ	71076	LP-12"	1974
MARY JANE (SPICY SONGS)	TMOQ	MJ-543	LP-12"-CV	1973
MAX HAMMER COLLECTION, THE	NO LABEL	NO #	5LP-12"	1987
MAYBE YOU CAN DRIVE MY CAR	ORANGE	OR-19	CD	1995
McCARTNEY TRACKS	OVERSEAS	30CP-313	CD	1990
McCARTNEY TRACKS (GOLD)	TEICHIKU	TECP-35120	CD	1990
MEAN MR. MUSTARD	NO LABEL	NO #	LP-12"	'70s
MEET THE BEEB	BEEB TRANSCRIPTION	BB-2190/S	LP-12"	1988
MELBOURNE AND WASHINGTON	WIZARDO	WRMB-314	LP-12"	1975
MELBOURNE/VANCOUVER SUPER LIVE #4	INSTANT ANALYSIS	1032A/1034A	LP-12"	1975
MELLOW YELLOW	APPLE	SAPCOR-39	2LP-12"	1987
MEMPHIS/LOVE OF THE LOVED	DECCAGONE	PRO 1102	45-7"-CV	1976
MEMPHIS/LOVE OF THE LOVED	PYE	406	45-7"	1978
MERRY CHRISTMAS THROUGH THE YEARS	NATIONAL RADIO	UNK	CD	1990
MISCELLANEOUS	SPEED	MI-3001	LP-12"	'70s
MISCELLANEOUS TRACKS	YELLOW DOG	YDB-103	CD	1994
MIXED BLESSING	BOX TOP	GN-70077	2LP-CV	1986
MONEY/ SURE TO FALL	DECCAGONE	PRO-1104	45-7"-CV	1976
MONKEY BUSINESS	AMAZING	7000-1/2	LP-12"	1988
MONKEY BUSINESS	ROCK SOLID	RSR 76001-2	2LP-12"	1987
MORE BEATLES	BRS	BRS-71160	LP-12"	1989
MORE BEATLES	BRS	BRSCD-73160	CD	1990
MORE BY FOUR	STARLIGHT/TIGER BEAT	TBR/URT-516	2-7"-CV	1988
MORE FROM THE FAB FOUR	WIZARDO	WRMB-390	LP-12"	1976
MORE GET BACK SESSIONS	MUSHROOM	13	LP-12"	1976
MORE GET BACK SESSIONS	HIWAY HIFI	HH1/2	LP-12"	1974
MORE GET BACK SESSIONS	TMOQ	71068	LP-12"	1974
MORE GET BACK SESSIONS	MICHAEL & ALLYSON	MA-001	LP-12"	1970
MORE GET BACK SESSIONS	TMOQ	1893	LP-12"	1974
MORE GET BACK SESSIONS	OLD GLORY	KO-407	LP-12"	'70s
MUNICH AT LAST- 7TH AMENDMENT	ZAP	7870	LP-12"	1977
MUSIC CITY/ KFW BEATLES	CUSTOM	RB-2637/8	45-7"	'70s
MY BONNIE/ MEIN BONNIE	DECCA	31382	45-7"	'70s
NATURE SCAPES	HIGHWAY HIGH FI	HHCER-116	LP-12"	1974
NEVER RELEASED MARY JANE, THE	CBM	WEC-3585	LP-12"	1975
NEW 21, THE	MELVIN	MM06	LP-12"-CV	1978
NEXT TO LAST RECORD'G SESS.-5TH AM.	ZAP	7866	LP-12"	1977
NIPPON BUDOKAN HALL	GREAT DANE	UNK	CD	1990
NIPPON BUDOKAN HALL 1966	THE SWINGIN' PIG	TSP-002	CD	1989
NIPPON BUDOKAN HALL TOKIO 7/2/66	BULLDOG	BGLP-002	LP-12"	1989
NO OBVIOUS TITLE-1ST AMENDMENT	ZAP	7853	LP-12"	1976
NORTHERN SONGS	MAGIC DWARF	MDR-45-1/S	CD-PD	1990
NORTHERN SONGS	MAGIC DWARF	MDR-45-1	EP-7"	1989
NOT FOR SALE	ADAM VIII LTD.	CD 49-032	CD	1991
NOT FOR SALE	CONDOR/TOASTED	1986	CD	1989
NOT FOR SALE	NEMS	MOP-910	LP-12"	1985
NOT FOR SALE	STRAWBERRY	NO #	LP-12"-CV	1988

ALBUM TITLE	LABEL	CATALOG #	FORMAT	YEAR
NOT FOR SALE	TMOQ/ 1/4 APPLE	WABD-3561A	LP-12"	'80s
NOT FOR SALE	TMOQ/ 1/4 APPLE	JQWX-1003A	LP-12"	'80s
NOT GUILTY	CONDOR/TOASTED	1989	CD	1989
NOT GUILTY	E.H.M.V.	NO #	LP-12"	1986
NOTHING BUT AGING	VIGATONE	VT-LP68	LP-12"	1992
NOTHING BUT AGING	UNK	UNK	CD	1992
NOTHING IS REAL	WILBUR	W-3-86	LP-12"-PD	1986
NOTHING IS REAL	CHAPTER ONE	CO-25193	CD	1992
NOTHING IS REAL	NEMS	BUD-280	LP-12"	1986
NOW OR NEVER	NO LABEL	AT-88E	LP-12"	1988
NO. 3 ABBEY ROAD NW8	ADAM VIII LTD.	CD 49-033	CD	1991
NO. 3 ABBEY ROAD N.W. 8	VIGATONE	VT-116	CD	1994
NO. 3 ABBEY ROAD N.W. 8	BOX TOP	NO #	LP-12"	1986
NO. 3 ABBEY ROAD N.W. 8	AUDIFON	AR-8-69	LP-12"	1979
OB-LA-DI, OB-LA-DA	THAMES	LG3301	LP-12"	1987
OB-LA-DI, OB-LA-DA	STARLIGHT/FAT MAN	ML 1612-9386	EP-7"	1987
OFF THE BEATLES TRACK	CHAPTER ONE	CO-171	CD	1992
OFF WHITE	NML	WHT-868	CD	1988
OFF WHITE	MACLEN MUSIC	WHT-868	LP-12"	1988
OFF WHITE VOL. 2	RED PHANTOM	RPCD-1137	CD	1993
OFF WHITE VOL. 3	RED PHANTOM	RPCD-1138	CD	1993
ON STAGE	WIZARDO	WRMB-328	LP-12"	1975
ON STAGE IN EUROPE	WIZARDO	WRMB-328	LP-12"	1975
ON STAGE IN GERMANY	WIZARDO	WRMB-328	LP-12"-CV	1975
ON STAGE IN JAPAN	TAKRL	1900	LP-12"	1976
ON STAGE IN JAPAN	PIG'S EYE	PE-1	LP-12"	1975
ON STAGE IN JAPAN 1966 TOUR	NO LABEL	TB-1966T	LP-12"	'80s
ON STAGE IN JAPAN THE 1966 TOUR	MUSHROOM	PE-S VOL. 12	LP-12"	1976
ON STAGE IN JAPAN THE 1966 TOUR	WIZARDO	WRMB-318	LP-12"	1975
ON STAGE IN MELB. AUS. & WASH. D.C.	WIZARDO	WRMB-314	LP-12"	1975
ON THE BBC, VOLS. 1 & 2	TASK FORCE	T-1961/2	2CD	1989
ONCE UPON A TIME A FAROUT SOUND..	NAPOLEAN	11044	LP-12"	'70s
ONE, TWO, THREE, FOUR	BIG JOLLY	BJR-008	2LP-12"	1983
ONLY LIVE RECORDING, THE	KUSTOM	ASC-002	LP-12"	1970
OPERATION BIG BEATLE	CAPITOL	OM-1	LP-12"	'80s
ORIGINAL AUDITION TAPE	WIZARDO	WRMB-308	LP-12"	1975
ORIGINAL BEATLES LIVE, THE	NO LABEL	HRCD 52023,4,6	3CD-BX	1990
ORIGINAL BEATLES LIVE, THE	NO LABEL	ST-3605	3CD	1991
ORIGINAL BEATLES SPECIAL, THE	WORLD MUSIC	WM-2778	2LP-12"	1989
ORIGINAL DEMO SESSIONS	WIZARDO	WRMB-308	LP-12"	1975
ORIGINAL GET BACK ACETATE, THE	WIZARDO	WRMB-315	LP-12"	1975
ORIGINAL GREATEST HITS	GREATEST	GRC-1001	LP-12"	1964
ORIGIONAL GREATEST HITS, THE	SUTRA	LP-6667	LP-12"	1967
ORIG. DECCA TAPES & CAVERN CLUB..,THE	YELLOW DOG	YD-011	CD	1991
ORIG. ST. ACETATE FOR LET IT BE...	WIZARDO	WRMB-315	LP-12"	1975
OUTTAKES 1 & 2	TMOQ	7508	2LP-12"	1975
OUTTAKES VOLS. 1 & 2	TMOQ	D-207	LP-12"	1975
OUTTAKES VOL. 1	TMOQ	BO-519	LP-12"-CV	1975
OUTTAKES VOL. 1	TMOQ	71048	LP-12"	1974
OUTTAKES VOL. 2	TMOQ	BO-520	LP-12"-CV	1975
OUTTAKES VOL. 2	TMOQ	71049	LP-12"	1974
PALAIS DES SPORTS 1965	BULLDOG	BGCD-005	CD	1989
PARIS 1965	WIZARDO	WRMB-335	LP-12"	1976
PARIS AGAIN	CBM	WEC-3688	LP-12"	1975
PARIS MATCH, PARIS 1965, THE	FAB FOUR RARITIES	FFR-9117	CD	1991

ALBUM TITLE	LABEL	CATALOG #	FORMAT	YEAR
PARIS MATCH, THE	BEAT RIFF	MNS-54007	LP-12"	1985
PARIS SPORTS PALAIS	CBM	LLPA-77	LP-12"	1977
PARIS SPORTS PALAIS	RUTHLESS RHYMES LTD	LPPA-77	LP-12"	1977
PARIS SPORTS PALAIS 1965	WIZARDO	WRMB-335	LP-12"-CV	1976
PARIS '65	WIZARDO	WRMB-335	LP-12"	1976
PARIS '65	STARLIGHT/BIRD BRAIN	UNK	LP-12"	1987
PARIS '65	INSTANT ANALYSIS	BBR-007	LP-12"	1975
PAST MASTERS & SELECTIONS	PRIME	AEBCD-301	CD	1993
PAST MASTERS (MONO MIXES)	VARIO	VARIO-301	CD	1992
PEACE OF MIND	CBM	WEC-3670	LP-12"	1975
PEACE OF MIND	BERKELEY	2009	LP-12"	1976
PERFECT BEAT	WORLD PRODUCTIONS	WPOCM-019	CD	1989
PERFECT COLLECTION, VOL. 1	TASK FORCE	T-1811	CD	1989
PERFECT COLLECTION, VOL. 2	TASK FORCE	T-1812	CD	1989
PERFECT COLLECTION, VOL. 3	TASK FORCE	T-1813	CD	1989
PERFECT COLLECTION, VOL. 4	TASK FORCE	T-1814	CD	1989
PERFECT COLLECTION, VOL. 5	TASK FORCE	T-1815	CD	1989
PERFECT COLLECTION, VOL. 6	TASK FORCE	T-1816	CD	1989
PERFECT COLLECTION, VOL. 7	TASK FORCE	T-1817	CD	1989
PERFECT COLLECTION, VOL. 8	TASK FORCE	T-1963	CD	1989
PERFECT COLLECTION, VOL. 9	TASK FORCE	T-1964	CD	1989
PETE BEST STORY, THE	NO LABEL	NO #	LP-12"-CV	'70s
PETER SELLERS TAPE, THE	SPANK	SP-104	CD	1993
PICTURE THIS	SEA HORSE	NO #	5LP-PD	'80s
PISS OFF PETE!	BELGIUM	B-5	LP-12"	1987
PLAYING BEATLES 2:HOUSTON CONCERT, THE	GREAT DANE	GDRCD-9304/A-B	2CD-BX	1993
PLAYING BEATLES-LIVE BEATLES, THE	GREAT DANE	GDR-9235	2CD	1992
PLAYING BEATLES-LIVE BEATLES, THE	GREAT DANE	GDR-CD-9235/A-B	2CD-BX	1992
PLEASE PLEASE ME	PDL DISQUES	PDL 5001	CD-EP	1991
PLEASE RELEASE ME	DOCUMENT	DR-017	LP-12"	1988
PLEASE RELEASE ME	APPLE	SAPCOR-29	2LP-12"	1987
PLEASE RELEASE ME	DOCUMENT	DR-017	CD	1989
PLOP PLOP, FIZZ FIZZ	SEANMARK	HAR-170	LP-12"	'70s
POP GO THE BEATLES	THE EARLY YEARS	02-CD-3301	CD	1989
POP GO THE BEATLES	THE EARLY YEARS	02-CD-3305	CD-PD	1989
POP GO THE BEATLES/YOUNGBLOOD	NO LABEL	BVP-005	2LP-12"	1979
POP GOES THE BEATLES	TEDDY BEAR	TB-CD-01/02	2CD	1993
POP GOES THE BEATLES	WIZARDO	WRMB-345	LP-12"	1976
POP GOES THE RADIO	UNK	UNK	2CD	1992
POSTERS, INCENSE, AND STROBE CANDLES	VIGATONE	70	LP-12"	1993
POSTERS, INCENSE, AND STROBE CANDLES	VIGATONE	70	LP-DLX	1993
POSTERS, INCENSE AND STROBE CANDLES	VIGOTONE	VIGO-109	CD	1993
POWER BROKERS	STRAWBERRY	NO #	LP-12"-CV	1988
POWER BROKERS	WIZARDO	WRMB-392	LP-12"	1976
PSYCHEDELIC YEARS II (VOL. 4)	LSD	LSD-004	CD	1994
PSYCHEDELIC YEARS II (VOL. 5)	LSD	LSD-005	CD	1994
PSYCHEDELIC YEARS II (VOL. 6)	LSD	LSD-006	CD	1994
PSYCHODELIC YEARS VOL. 1	LSD	LSD-001	CD	1993
PSYCHODELIC YEARS VOL. 2	LSD	LSD-002	CD	1993
PSYCHODELIC YEARS VOL. 3	LSD	LSD-003	CD	1993
QUARRYMEN, THE: 58–62	MIDDLE	QMCD-593	CD	1993
QUARRYMEN AT HOME, THE	NML	CD-947	CD	1989
QUARRYMEN AT HOME, THE	DOCUMENT	DR-008	CD	1988
QUARRYMEN AT HOME REMIXES	CHAPTER ONE	CO-190	CD	1992
QUARRYMEN AT HOME: LIVERPOOL...	BLACKSHOP	BS-007	LP-12"	1987

ALBUM TITLE	LABEL	CATALOG #	FORMAT	YEAR
QUARRYMEN REHEARSE 1960	UNK	UNK	LP-12"	1990
QUARRYMEN: JOHN, PAUL, GEORGE & STU	LOST GOLD	UNK	CD	1990
Q-MEN REHEARSE W/STU SUT. SPR., '60	PRE-BEATLES	VD-15/16	LP-12"	1987
RABBI SAUL	APPLE	SAPCOR-34	LP-12"	1987
RADIO ACTIVE VOL. 1	PYRAMID	RFT-CD-005	CD	1989
RADIO ACTIVE VOL. 1	PYRAMID	RFT-CD-005	LP-12"	1989
RADIO ACTIVE VOL. 10	PYRAMID	RFT-CD-024	CD	1990
RADIO ACTIVE VOL. 10	PYRAMID	RFT-CD-024	LP-12"	1990
RADIO ACTIVE VOL. 11	PYRAMID	RFT-CD-025	LP-12"	1990
RADIO ACTIVE VOL. 11	PYRAMID	RFT-CD-025	CD	1989
RADIO ACTIVE VOL. 12	PYRAMID	RFT-CD-032	CD	1990
RADIO ACTIVE VOL. 12	PYRAMID	RFT-CD-032	LP-12"	1990
RADIO ACTIVE VOL. 13	PYRAMID	RFT-CD-033	LP-12"	1990
RADIO ACTIVE VOL. 13	PYRAMID	RFT-CD-033	CD	1990
RADIO ACTIVE VOL. 2	PYRAMID	RFT-CD-006	LP-12"	1989
RADIO ACTIVE VOL. 2	PYRAMID	RFT-CD-006	CD	1989
RADIO ACTIVE VOL. 3	PYRAMID	RFT-CD-007	LP-12"	1989
RADIO ACTIVE VOL. 3	PYRAMID	RFT-CD-007	CD	1989
RADIO ACTIVE VOL. 4	PYRAMID	RFT-CD-018	LP-12"	1989
RADIO ACTIVE VOL. 4	PYRAMID	RFT-CD-018	CD	1989
RADIO ACTIVE VOL. 5	PYRAMID	RFT-CD-014	LP-12"	1989
RADIO ACTIVE VOL. 5	PYRAMID	RFT-CD-014	CD	1989
RADIO ACTIVE VOL. 6	PYRAMID	RFT-CD-015	LP-12"	1989
RADIO ACTIVE VOL. 6	PYRAMID	RFT-CD-015	CD	1989
RADIO ACTIVE VOL. 7	PYRAMID	RFT-CD-019	CD	1989
RADIO ACTIVE VOL. 7	PYRAMID	RFT-CD-019	LP-12"	1989
RADIO ACTIVE VOL. 8	PYRAMID	RFT-CD-016	CD	1989
RADIO ACTIVE VOL. 8	PYRAMID	RFT-CD-016	LP-12"	1989
RADIO ACTIVE VOL. 9	PYRAMID	RFT-CD-017	CD	1989
RADIO ACTIVE VOL. 9	PYRAMID	RFT-CD-017	LP-12"	1989
RADIO PROMO SPOTS	NO LABEL	LP-001	LP-12"-CV	1990
RADIO YEARS AT THE BEEB, THE	YELLOW DOG	YDB-301	CD	1994
RARE BEATLES	CBM	TB-5030	LP-12"	1974
RARE SESSIONS	CBM	B-213	LP-12"	1975
RARE TRACKS VOL. 1	RELME	RR45-11412	EP	'70s
RARER THAN RARE	WHITE KNIGHT	WK-271	2LP-12"	1978
RARETIES	NO LABEL	CRA-001	LP-12"	'80s
RARITIES 2: WE CAN WORK IT OUT	BEAT	CD-009	CD	1994
RARITIES 3: THE FINAL MIXES	BEAT	CD-010	CD	1994
READY STEADY GO!	WIND	001	LP-12"	1987
REAL CASE HAS JUST BEGUN, THE	CORE LTD	RAS 8611-1	LP-12"	1988
REAL EARLY BEATLES, THE	STARLIGHT	SL-87050	LP-12"-BX	1990
REAL EARLY BEATLES, THE	STARLIGHT	SL-87050	LP-EP-CAS	1991
REAL EARLY BEATLES, THE	STARLIGHT	SL-87050	LP-12"-CV	1991
REALLY BIG SHEW, THE	CBS	SP-910	EP-7"	1982
RECORDING SESSIONS, VOL. 1	EARLY YEARS	02-CD-3305	CD	1989
RECORDING SESSIONS, VOL. 1	EARLY YEARS	02-CD-3305	CD-PD	1989
RECORDING SESSIONS, VOL. 2	EARLY YEARS	02-CD-3306	CD	1989
RECORDING SESSIONS, VOL. 2	EARLY YEARS	02-CD-3306	CD-PD	1989
RECORDING SESSIONS, VOL. 3	EARLY YEARS	02-CD-3307	CD-PD	1989
RECORDING SESSIONS, VOL. 3	EARLY YEARS	02-CD-3307	CD	1989
RECORDING SESSIONS, VOL. 4	EARLY YEARS	02-CD-3308	CD-PD	1991
RECORDING SESSIONS, VOL. 4	EARLY YEARS	02-CD-3325	CD	1989
RECORDING SESSIONS, VOL. 5	EARLY YEARS	TEY-039	CD-PD	1991
RECOVERED TRACKS	BORNOBY	FF-9	2LP-12"	1980

ALBUM TITLE	LABEL	CATALOG #	FORMAT	YEAR
REINTRODUCING THE BEATLES	APPLE	SAPCOR-28	2LP-12"	1987
RENAISSANCE	TOASTED	2S-911	2LP-12"	'80s
RENAISSANCE MINSTRELS 1	NO LABEL	KO-401	LP-12"	'70s
RENAISSANCE MINSTRELS 1	RENAISSANCE	WCF-725	LP-12"	1972
RENAISSANCE MINSTRELS 1	TMOQ	73001	LP-12"	1973
RENAISSANCE MINSTRELS 1	TMOQ	71025	LP-12"	1973
RENAISSANCE MINSTRELS 1	RENAISSANCE	RR-1002	LP-12"	1973
RENAISSANCE MINSTRELS 2	TMOQ	71026	LP-12"	1973
RENAISSANCE MINSTRELS 2	RUTHLESS RHYMES LTD	PR-1001	LP-12"	1978
RENAISSANCE MINSTRELS 2	NO LABEL	KO-402	LP-12"	'70s
RENAISSANCE MINSTRELS 2	MID	RR 2022	LP-12"-CV	1990
RENAISSANCE MINSTRELS 2	RENAISSANCE	WCF-726	LP-12"	1973
RENAISSANCE MINSTRELS 2	TMOQ	73002	LP-12"	'80s
RENAISSANCE MINSTRELS 3	TMOQ	73032	LP-12"-CV	1990
RENAISSANCE MINSTRELS 3	BERKELEY	2033	LP-12"	1976
RENAISSANCE MINSTRELS 4	CBM/CUMQUAT	TB-5020	LP-12"	1975
RENAISSANCE MINSTRELS 4	NO LABEL	KO-405	LP-12"	'70s
RENAISSANCE MINSTRELS VOL. 1–4	STRAWBERRY	NO #	4LP-CV	1988
RENAISSANCE MINSTRELS VOL. I	UNK	NO #	LP-12"-CV	'70s
RENAISSANCE MINSTRELS VOL. I	NO LABEL	RRGM-725	LP-12"	1972
RENAISSANCE MINSTRELS VOL. I	AMAZON ETCETERA	612	LP-12"	'70s
RENAISSANCE MINSTRELS VOL. I	TMOQ	1852	LP-12"	1973
RENAISSANCE MINSTRELS VOL. II	AMAZON ETCETERA	613	LP-12"	'70s
RENAISSANCE MINSTRELS VOL. II	NO LABEL	RRGM-726	LP-12"	1972
RENAISSANCE MINSTRELS VOL. II	WIZARDO	WRMB-358	LP-12"	1976
RENAISSANCE MINSTRELS VOL. III	AMAZON ETCETERA	625	LP-12"	'70s
RENAISSANCE MINSTRELS VOL. III	OLD GLORY	KO-404	LP-12"	'70s
RENAISSANCE MINSTRELS VOL. IV	OLD GLORY	KO-405	LP-12"	'70s
RETURN TO ABBEY ROAD	EMI	NW-8	LP-12"	'80s
REUNION NONSENSE- 9TH AMEND.	ZAP	7873	LP-12"	1977
REUNIONS '74 & '92, THE	VARIO	VARIO-1486	CD	1992
REVOLTING	APPLE	SAPCOR-35	2LP-12"	1987
REVOLUTION	VIGATONE	VT-117	CD	1994
REVOLUTION	M.I.A.	ACT-3	CD	1992
REVOLUTION/HOW DO YOU DO IT	SOK PROD.	UNK	45-7"-CV	'80s
REVOLVER SPECIAL	MIDO ENTERPRISE	ZS-9104	CD	1991
RE-INTRODUCING THE BEATLES	APPLE	SAPCOR-28	2LP-12"	1987
ROAD TO FAME, THE	STAR CLUB	HADCD-241	CD	1994
ROCK AND ROLL MUSIC	PYRAMID	PY-CD-027	CD	1989
ROCK AND ROLL MUSIC	BRS	BRSCD-73161	CD	1990
ROCK N' ROLL MUSIC	BRS	BRS-71161	LP-12"	1989
ROCK & ROLL HALL OF FAME	ROCK	112-HOF 003	LP-12"	1988
ROCK 'N' ROAD	STRWB FLDS 4-EVER	CX-320-A/B	LP-12"-CV	'80s
ROCKIN' MOVIE STARS VOL. 1	ORANGE	OR-3	CD	1994
ROCKIN' MOVIE STARS VOL. 2	ORANGE	OR-4	CD	1994
ROCKIN' MOVIE STARS VOL. 3	ORANGE	OR-7	CD	1994
ROCKIN' MOVIE STARS VOL. 4	ORANGE	OR-8	CD	1994
ROCKIN' MOVIE STARS VOL. 5	ORANGE	OR-9	CD	1994
ROCKIN' MOVIE STARS VOL. 6	ORANGE	OR-10	CD	1994
ROCKIN' MOVIE STARS VOL. 7	ORANGE	OR-11	CD	1994
ROCKIN' MOVIE STARS VOL. 8	ORANGE	OR-12	CD	1994
ROCK'N'ROLL BEATLES	OVERSEAS	30CP-112	CD	1990
ROCK-A-BILLY BEATLES	OVERSEAS	30CP-164	CD	1990
ROMA	TRANS	158	2LP-12"	1987
ROMA	ROCK SOLID	RSR 62765	2LP-12"	1987

ALBUM TITLE	LABEL	CATALOG #	FORMAT	YEAR
ROME, ITALY 1965	CLEAN SOUND	CS-1008	LP-12"	1985
ROUGH CUT APPLE	JAP	UNK	2LP-12"	'80s
ROUGH NOTES	POD	L-2408	LP-12"	1981
ROUGH NOTES	HEEVER	SR-73941	LP-12"	1982
ROUGH NOTES	AUDIFON	SR-73941	LP-12"	1980
ROUGH NOTES	DOUBLE-TIME	DTD-001	2CD	1990
ROYAL COMMAND PERF. PRINCE OF WALES...	DECCAGONE	PRO-1108	45-7"-CV	1976
ROYAL VARIETY PERFORMANCE 1963, THE	NO LABEL	UK-2826	LP-12"	'70s
RUBBER SOUL SPECIAL	MIDO ENTERPRISE	ZS-9103	CD	1991
RUMI TAPE & MORE	JAP-1	CD-JAP-1	CD	1993
SAM HOUSTON COLISEUM	BEAT	BE-01-101	LP-CV	1977
SAM HOUSTON COLISEUM	BULLDOG	BG-016	2LP-12"	1988
SAM HOUSTON COLISEUM 1965	GREAT DANE	GDR-016	CD	1990
SAM HOUSTON LIVE	BEAT RIFFS	NO #	LP-CV	1989
SAM HOUSTON LIVE	CONTROL	T-2350	2LP-12"	1986
SAN FRANCISCO 66	NO LABEL	NO #	LP-12"	'80s
SAN FRANCISCO AUG. 29, 1966 C. PARK	BULLDOG	BGCD-016	CD-PD	1988
SAVAGE YOUNG BEATLES	TEICHIKU	TECP-28437	CD-PD	1990
SAVAGE YOUNG BEATLES	TEICHIKU	TECP-30220	CD-CAN	1990
SAVAGE YOUNG BEATLES	TEICHIKU	TECP-18008	CD	1990
SCRAPS	REIGN	001	LP-12"	'70s
SEARCHIN'/ LIKE DREAMERS DO	PYE	306	45-7"	1978
SEARCHIN'/LIKE DREAMERS DO	DECCAGONE	PRO-1103	45-7"-CV	1976
SECOND TO NONE	SODD	009	2LP-12"	1976
SECRET	WIZARDO	WRMB-359	LP-12"	1976
SECRET SONGS FROM PEPPERLAND	RED ROBIN	UNK	CD	1995
SECRET SONGS IN PEPPERLAND	MASTERDISC	MDCD-006	CD	1994
SESSIONS	CONDOR/TOASTED	1991	CD	1989
SESSIONS	UNK	AEBCD-10	CD	1992
SESSIONS	SPANK	SP-103	CD-BX	1993
SESSIONS	DISQUES DU MONDE	SS-87-1967	CD	1988
SESSIONS	EMI/PARLOPHONE	CDP-7-480012	CD	1988
SESSIONS	ADAM VIII LTD.	CD 49-020	CD	1991
SESSIONS	MASTERDISC	MDCD-002	CD	1993
SESSIONS	EMI/PARL./ODEON	064-2402701	LP-12"	1985
SFF 1976 2ND ANNUAL CHRISTMAS	EVA-TONE	12877	LP-12"	1976
SFF 1977 A HARD DAY'S NIGHT B/4 XMAS	EVA-TONE	1123772	LP-12"	1977
SFF 1978 CHRISTMAS RECORD	EVA-TONE	128781	LP-12"	1978
SGT. PEPPER 25TH ANNIV. MEMORIAL BOX	JAP	UNK	2CD-BX	1992
SGT. PEPPER SPECIAL	MIDO ENTERPRISE	ZS-9105	CD	1991
SGT. PEPPER'S GROOVE	BEATLES MUSEUM	BMIC/TR-003	45-7"	1993
SGT. P:A HISTORY OF THE BEATLES 62–70	NO LABEL	BN-87	9LP-12"	1987
SHADES OF ORANGE	DECCA	RS-2597	LP-12"	'70s
SHE LOVES YOU	BRS	BRSCD-73166	CD	1992
SHE LOVES YOU/I'LL GET YOU	SWAN	S-4152	45-7"	1976
SHE LOVES YOU/I WANT TO HOLD..(GER.)	CAPITOL	ST-100	45-12"-CV	1980
SHEA AT LAST	LXXXIV	SERIES #44	LP-12"-CV	'70s
SHEA AT LAST!	STRAWBERRY	NO #	LP-12"-CV	1988
SHEA STADIUM	BLACK DISC	ZAP-1071	LP-12"	1981
SHEA THE GOOD OLD DAYS	KUSTOM	ASC-002	LP-12"	1970
SHEA THE GOOD OLD DAYS	DITTOLINO DISCS	SHEA 1/2	LP-12"	1971
SHEA THE GOOD OLD DAYS	NO LABEL	J-41	LP-12"	'70s
SHEA THE GOOD OLD DAYS	TMOQ	4178	LP-12"	1975
SHEA THE GOOD OLD DAYS	PINE TREE	S-2531/2	LP-12"	1970
SHEA THE GOOD OLD DAYS	CBM	WEC-2315	LP-12"	1972

ALBUM TITLE	LABEL	CATALOG #	FORMAT	YEAR
SHEA THE GOOD OLD DAYS	WIZARDO	207	LP-12"	1976
SHEA!	TMOQ	LLS-101	LP-12"	1975
SHEA-THE GOOD OLD DAYS	WIZARDO	116-207	LP-12"	1976
SHEA... AT LAST!	RUTHLESS RHYMES LTD	71012	LP-12"	1978
SHEA... AT LAST!	TMOQ	T-102	LP-12"	1975
SHEA/CANDLESTICK PARK	SPANK	SP-109	CD	1995
SHEIK OF ARABY/SEPT. IN THE RAIN	PYE	206	EP	1978
SHEIK OF ARABY/SEPT. IN THE RAIN	DECCAGONE	PRO-1101	45-7"-CV	1976
SHOUT	NO LABEL	526.404.251	LP-12"	'70s
SHOUT	MANTO	NO #	LP-12"	1988
SHOUT/I FORGOT TO REMEMBER TO FORGET	MELVIN	MM6-2/MM6-3	45-7"	1980
SID BARRETT'S P. FLOYD LAST SCREAMS	D.I.Y.E.	DIYE-CD-15	CD-PD	1991
SILVER ALBUM OF WORLD'S GREATEST	JARRIS	0020	LP-12"	'70s
SILVER BEATLES	OVERSEAS	30CP-48342	CD	1986
SILVER BEATLES	TEICHIKU	TECP-30219	CD-CAN	1990
SILVER BEATLES	WORLD MUSIC	WM-31003	LP-12"	1989
SILVER BEATLES	NO LABEL	HIS-11182	LP-12"-PD	'80s
SILVER BEATLES	TEICHIKU	TECP-28436	CD-PD	1990
SILVER DAYS	STRAWBERRY	NO #	LP-12"-CV	1988
SILVER LINING	NO LABEL	IAH-21	LP-12"	1980
SILVER LINING	MIDWEST	MM-08	LP-12"	1979
SING THIS ALL TOGETHER	NO LABEL	R-55/66	2LP-CV	1977
SING THIS ALL TOGETHER	SMILIN' EARS	SE-7700-2	2LP-12"	1977
SING THIS ALL TOGETHER	NO LABEL	R-55/66	2LP-12"	1977
SINGING THE BLUES	KING	MLK-003	LP-12"	1984
SNAP SHOTS	GNAT	GN 70083-4	2LP-12"	1984
SNAPS 'N' TRAX	GERITOL	ST-208	LP-12"	1979
SNAPSHOTS	BOX TOP	NO #	LP-12"-CV	1986
SO MUCH YOUNGER THEN	DEMOCRATIC	DC7577-5	5LP-PD	1977
SOLDIER OF LOVE	KING KONG	TB-1022	LP-12"	1973
SOLDIER OF LOVE	CBM	WEC-1022	LP-12"	1973
SOLDIER OF LOVE/CLARABELLA	MERSEY BEAT	VMMFP-5471	45-7"	1981
SOME LIKE IT HOT	MARC	OG-595	LP-12"	1976
SOME LIKE IT HOT	ADO	OG-595	LP-12"	1976
SOME OTHER GUY	BERKELEY	2008	LP-12"	1976
SOME OTHER GUY	CBM	WEC-3813	LP-12"	1975
SOME OTHER GUY/CAVERN CLUB	CBM	B215	LP-12"	1975
SOMETHING EXTRA	GENUINE PIG	TGP-CD-107	CD	1990
SOMETHING TO HIDE	CONDOR/TOASTED	1992	CD	1989
SONGS FOR OTHERS	REE BEN	DH-3780	45-7"	1988
SONGS FROM THE PAST	DISQUES DU MONDE	RC-871968	CD	1989
SONGS FROM THE PAST 1	BLUE KANGAROO	BK-007	CD	1992
SONGS FROM THE PAST 2	BLUE KANGAROO	BK-008	CD	1992
SONGS FROM THE PAST VOL. 2	SIDEWALK MUSIC	LM-871968	CD	1988
SONGS FROM THE PAST VOL. 3	SIDEWALK MUSIC	LM-89001	CD	1989
SONGS FROM THE PAST VOL. 4	SIDEWALK MUSIC	LM-89002	CD	1989
SONGS FROM THE PAST VOL. 5	SIDEWALK MUSIC	LM-89003	CD	1989
SONGS THE BEATLES GAVE AWAY, THE	ADAM VIII LTD.	CD 49-035	4CD	1991
SOUNDCHECK	ROCK SOLID	RSR 256	2LP-12"	1987
SOUVENEIR OF THEIR VISIT TO AMERICA	VEE JAY	VJEP1-903	EP-7"-PD	1980
SP 602	WIZARDO	WRMB-316	2LP-12"	1976
SPARE PARTS	STARLIGHT/BIRD BRAIN	BBR-001	LP-12"	1987
SPICY BEATLES SONGS	TMOQ	71076	LP-12"	1974
SPICY BEATLES SONGS	TMOQ	1848	LP-12"	1983
SPICY BEATLES SONGS	K & S	051	LP-12"	1974

ALBUM TITLE	LABEL	CATALOG #	FORMAT	YEAR
SPICY BEATLES SONGS	LXXXIV	SERIES #15	LP-12"	'70s
SPICY BEATLES SONGS	TMOQ	S-210	LP-12"	1975
SPICY BEATLES SONGS	K & S	051	LP-12"-CV	1974
SPICY BEATLES SONGS/MARY JANE	BOX TOP	NO #	LP-12"	1986
SPICY BEATLES SONGS/MARY JANE	AMAZON ETCETERA	635	LP-12"	'70s
SPORTS PALACE FRANCE - SECOND SHOW	CBM	WEC-1101	LP-12"	1973
STARS OF '63	CBM	WEC-4779/4750	LP-12"	1975
STARS OF '63	SHALOM/GAMMA ALPHA	CBM-4749/4750	2LP-12"	1974
STARS OF '63	GAMMA ALPHA	4749/4750	2LP-12"	1975
STARS OF '63	THE SWINGIN' PIG	TSP-005	LP-CV	1989
STARS OF '63	THE SWINGIN' PIG	TSP-005	LP-12"	1989
STARS OF '63	THE SWINGIN' PIG	TSP-CD-005	CD	1989
STATE FAIR TO HOLLYWOOD	GREAT DANE	GDRCD-9315	CD	1993
STEREO WALK, THE	RUBBER SOUL	B4A/B4B	LP-12"	1985
STOCKHOLM	CBM	WEC-1040	LP-12"	1973
STOCKHOLM	INSTANT ANALYSIS	4179	LP-12"	1975
STOCKHOLM 1963/BLACKPOOL 1965	LIQUID	UNK	LP-12"	'80s
STOCKHOLM & BLACKPOOL	SAVAGE	PLD-6365	LP-12"	1985
STOCKHOLM/ BLACKPOOL	BOX TOP	NO #	LP-12"	1986
STRAWBERRY FIELDS FOREVER	NO LABEL	NO #	LP-12"-PD	'80s
STRAWBERRY FIELDS FOREVER	CONDOR/TOASTED	1988	CD	1989
STRAWBERRY FIELDS FOREVER	RUFF 'N' REDDY	P 5810	LP-12"	1987
STRAWBERRY FIELDS FOREVER	NEMS	CLUE-9	LP-12"	1985
STUDIO OUTTAKE RECORDINGS 1962–1964	WIZARDO	WRMB-326	LP-12"	1975
STUDIO OUTTAKES	TOBE MILO	4Q11/12-VC4646	EP-7"	1977
STUDIO SESSIONS, 1964	YELLOW DOG	YDB-302	CD	1994
STUDIO SESSIONS, 1965–66	YELLOW DOG	YDB-303	CD	1994
STUDIO SESSIONS, FEB. 11, 1963	YELLOW DOG	YDB-202	CD	1994
STUDIO SESSIONS, MARCH 5, SEPT. 12	YELLOW DOG	YDB-203	CD	1994
STUDIO SESSIONS ONE	KING KONG	WEC-3640	LP-12"	1974
STUDIO SESSIONS TWO	KING KONG	WEC-3641	LP-12"	1974
STUDIO SESSIONS VOLUME ONE	CBM	ZAP-1061	LP-12"	1974
STUDIO SESSIONS VOLUME ONE	CBM	WEC-3640	LP-12"	1974
STUDIO SESSIONS VOLUME TWO	CBM	ZAP-1062	LP-12"	1974
STUDIO SESSIONS VOLUME TWO	CBM	WEC-3641	LP-12"	1974
SUNDAY NIGHT AT THE LONDON PALLADIUM	CBM	WEC-3687	LP-12"	1975
SUNDAY NIGHT @ THE LONDON PALLADIUM	SHALOM	WEC-3687	LP-12"	1974
SUNSHINE SUPERMEN	STRWB FLDS 4-EVER	CX296 A/B	LP-12"-CV	'70s
SUPER LIVE CONCERT SERIES 1	SHALOM	3795/S4449	LP-12"	1978
SUPERTRACKS 1	CBM	WEC-3922	LP-12"	1975
SUPERTRACKS 2	CBM	WEC-3923	LP-12"	1976
SUPERTRACKS 2	CBM	TB-1018	LP-12"	1976
SUPERTRACKS 2	HIGHWAY HIGH FI	HHCER-102	LP-12"	1974
SUPERTRACKS 2	TMOQ	TB-1018	LP-12"	1974
SUPERTRACKS I	STRAWBERRY	NO #	LP-12"-CV	1988
SURE TO FALL/MONEY	DECCAGONE	PRO-1103	45-7"-CV	1976
SWEDEN, WASHINGTON, SWEEDEN	KING KONG	WEC-3795	LP-12"	1975
SWEDEN 1963	CBM	WEC-3795/3571	LP-12"	1975
SWEET APPLE TRACKS VOL. 3	GLC	15803	2LP-12"	1980
SWEET APPLE TRAX	TWK	1YHO-10	2LP-12"	1981
SWEET APPLE TRAX	JAP	UNK	2CD	1992
SWEET APPLE TRAX	WIZARDO	WRMB-343	2LP-12-CV	1976
SWEET APPLE TRAX	NEWSOUND	NR-909-1	2LP-12"	1973
SWEET APPLE TRAX	TWK	0169A	2LP-12"	1981
SWEET APPLE TRAX	OLD GLORY	KO-406	3LP-CV	'70s

ALBUM TITLE	LABEL	CATALOG #	FORMAT	YEAR
SWEET APPLE TRAX 3	BLACK DISC	BL-8106	LP-12"	1981
SWEET APPLE TRAX I	BERKELEY	05	2LP-12"	1976
SWEET APPLE TRAX III	SWEET SOUND	W909	2LP-12"	1980
SWEET APPLE TRAX III	SWEET SOUND	SA-3909 C/D	2LP-PD	1980
SWEET APPLE TRAX VOL. 1	BLACK DISC	ZAP-1055	LP-12"-PD	1981
SWEET APPLE TRAX VOL. 2	BLACK DISC	ZAP-1055	LP-12"-PD	1981
SWEET APPLE TRAX VOL. I	NO LABEL	APP-001	LP-12"	'70s
SWEET APPLE TRAX VOL. ONE	BLANK	4182	2LP-12"	1975
SWEET APPLE TRAX VOL. ONE	INSTANT ANALYSIS	WEC-4182	2LP-12"	1973
SWEET APPLE TRAX VOL. ONE	IMAGE DISC	909-1A/1B	LP-12"-PD	1979
SWEET APPLE TRAX VOL. THREE	IMAGE DISC	909-1E/1F	LP-12"-PD	1979
SWEET APPLE TRAX VOL. TWO	INSTANT ANALYSIS	WEC-4181	2LP-12"	1973
SWEET APPLE TRAX VOL. TWO	IMAGE DISC	909-1C/1D	LP-12"-PD	1979
SWEET APPLE TRAX VOL. TWO	BLANK	4181	2LP-12"	1975
SWEET APPLE TRAX VOL.II	NO LABEL	APP-002	LP-12"	'70s
TAKE GOOD CARE OF MY BABY	DEMODISC	L-1389	45-7"	1979
TALKING ABOUT	NO LABEL	MHT-1984	LP-12"	1984
TELEVISION OUTTAKES	TOBE MILO	4Q-3/4	EP-7"	1977
TEXAN TROUBADOURS	TX	VC-5280	2LP-12"	1980
TEXAN TROUBADOURS	NO LABEL	VC-5280	2LP-12"	1980
TEXAN TROUBADOURS	NO LABEL	TX	2LP-12"	1980
THANK YOU MEMBERS	BFR/SLP	BLP-198303	LP-12"	1983
THAT'LL BE THE DAY	KING HORN	BO-1958	2LP-12"	1986
THE ROAD TO FAME	STAR-CLUB	HADCD-241	CD	1994
THEIR BIGGEST HITS	TOLLIE	EP1-8091	EP-7"	1975
THEIR COMPLETE XMAS COLLECTION '63-'69	CBM	WEC-206	LP-12"	1973
THEIR GREATEST UNRELEASED	MELVIN	MM01	LP-12"	1974
THINGS WE SAID...YESTERDAY!	BFR/SLP	BLP-198303	LP-12"	1983
THIRTY NOSTALGIA HITS	WIZARDO	102-232	2LP-12"	1978
THIS BOY/ CAN'T BUY ME LOVE	NO LABEL	1806	45-7"	'80s
THIS IS THE SAVAGE YOUNG BEATLES	SAVAGE	BM-69	LP-12"	1964
THOSE WERE THE DAYS	CBM	WEC-3907	LP-12"	1976
THREE COOL CATS/HELLO LITTLE GIRL	PYE	106	45-7"	1978
THREE COOL CATS/HELLO LITTLE GIRL	DECCAGONE	PRO-1100	45-7"-CV	1976
THROUGH THE YEARS	FAB FOUR RARITIES	FFR-9112	CD	1991
TICKET TO RIDE	BACK TRAX	CD04-88088	CD	1988
TICKET TO RIDE	OIL WELL	RSC-009	CD	1994
TITLES UNKNOWN - POLAND	B & H	PUR 000284-392	45-7"	'80s
TO KNOW HER.../BESAME MUCHO	DECCAGONE	PRO-1106	EP-7"-CV	1991
TO KNOW HIM.../BESAME MUCHO	DECCAGONE	PRO-1106	45-7"-CV	1976
TOKYO 66	WIZARDO	116-206	LP-12"	1976
TOKYO DAYS	TEICHIKU	SVX-301-V	LP-12"	1986
TOKYO SIXTY-SIX	CBM	JAPAN-1900	LP-12"	1975
TOKYO '66	WIZARDO	206	LP-12"	1976
TOP OF THE POPS	HIGHWAY HIGH FI	HHCER-111	LP-12"	1974
TOP OF THE POPS	MELVIN	NO #	EP-7"	1981
TOP OF THE POPS	CAPITOL	P9431	EP-7"	1978
TOP OF THE POPS/LIVE IN GERMANY	BERKELEY	999	LP-12"	1976
TOUR ALBUM, THE- 3RD AMENDMENT	ZAP	7861	LP-12"	1976
TOUR YEARS 63-66	HONEYSUCKLE PROD	ENG-4001	2LP-12"	1982
TRAGICAL HISTORY TOUR/DR. PEPPER	APPLE	SAPCOR-36/37	2LP-12"	1987
TUESDAY NIGHT AT THE WASHINGTON...	NO LABEL	1070	LP-12"	1970
TV APPEARANCES (ED SULLIVAN SHOWS)	YELLOW DOG	YDB-102	CD	1994
TV CASTS & WASHINGTON, D.C.	NO LABEL	3795,CI3571B	LP-12"	'70s
TWENTY-ONE BIG ONES	MELVIN	MM06	LP-12"	1978

ALBUM TITLE	LABEL	CATALOG #	FORMAT	YEAR
TWICE IN A LIFETIME	NO LABEL	B7	LP-12"	1988
TWICKENHAM JAMS	SMILIN' EARS	SE-7702	LP-12"	1977
TWICKENHAM JAMS	STRWB FLDS 4-EVER	PRO-909	EP-7"-CV	1977
TWIST & SHOUT	BRS	BRSCD-73163	CD	1992
T'ANKS FOR THE MAMMARIES	TAKRL	BOZO-1	2LP-12"	1978
ULTIMATE COLLECTION VOL. 1, THE	YELLOW DOG	YDB-1001/4	4CD-BX	1994
ULTIMATE COLLECTION VOL. 2, THE	YELLOW DOG	YDB-2001/4	4CD-BX	1994
ULTIMATE COLLECTION VOL. 3, THE	YELLOW DOG	YDB-3001/4	4CD-BX	1994
ULTIMATE LIVE COLLECTION VOL. 1, THE	YELLOW DOG	YD-038/39	2CD	1993
ULTIMATE ULTRA RARE TRACKS VOL. 1, THE	GREEN BUDGIE	GBCD-909.1	CD	1993
ULTIMATE UNRELEASED COLLECT. VOL. 1	ADAM VIII LTD.	CD 49-012	CD	1991
ULTIMATE UNRELEASED COLLECT. VOL. 2	ADAM VIII LTD.	CD 49-013	CD	1991
ULTRA RARE TRAX VOL. 1	THE SWINGIN' PIG	TSP-001	CD	1988
ULTRA RARE TRAX VOL. 1	THE SWINGIN' PIG	TSP-001	LP-12"-CV	1989
ULTRA RARE TRAX VOL. 1 & 2	STASH	STASH-637	2LP-12"	1988
ULTRA RARE TRAX VOL. 2	THE SWINGIN' PIG	TSP-002	LP-12"-CV	1989
ULTRA RARE TRAX VOL. 2	THE SWINGIN' PIG	TSP-002	CD	1988
ULTRA RARE TRAX VOL. 3	THE SWINGIN' PIG	TSP-003	LP-12"-CV	1989
ULTRA RARE TRAX VOL. 3	THE SWINGIN' PIG	TSP-025	CD	1989
ULTRA RARE TRAX VOL. 3 & 4	THE SWINGIN' PIG	TR-2190-S	2LP-12"	1988
ULTRA RARE TRAX VOL. 3 & 4	CONDOR	UNK	2LP-12"	1989
ULTRA RARE TRAX VOL. 4	THE SWINGIN' PIG	TSP-026	CD	1989
ULTRA RARE TRAX VOL. 4	THE SWINGIN' PIG	TSP-004	LP-12"-CV	1989
ULTRA RARE TRAX VOL. 5	SWINGING PIG	TSP-CD-035	CD	1991
ULTRA RARE TRAX VOL. 5	THE SWINGIN' PIG	TSP-035	CD	1990
ULTRA RARE TRAX VOL. 5 & 6	THE SWINGIN' PIG	TR-2191-S	2LP-12"	1988
ULTRA RARE TRAX VOL. 5 & 6	CONDOR	UNK	2LP-12"	1989
ULTRA RARE TRAX VOL. 6	SWINGING PIG	TSP-CD-036	CD	1991
ULTRA RARE TRAX VOL. 6	THE SWINGIN' PIG	TSP-036	CD	1990
ULTRA RARE TRAX VOL. 7	GENUINE PIG	TGP-111	CD	1990
ULTRA RARE TRAX VOL. 8	GENUINE PIG	TGP-112	CD	1990
UNA SENSAZIONALE INTERVISTA	APPLE	DPR-108	EP-7"	'70s
UNFINISHED MUSIC (VOLUME NO. ONE)	NO LABEL	V-1	LP-12"	1981
UNFINISHED MUSIC (VOLUME NO. TWO)	NO LABEL	V-2	LP-12"	1981
UNHEARD MELODIES	CHAPTER ONE	C0-25198-99	2CD	1993
UNRELEASED TRACKS, THE	BLACK PANTHER	BP-062	CD	1992
UNRELEASED TRACKS 1	LIVING LEGEND	LLRCD-062	CD	1990
UNRELEASED TRACKS 2	LIVING LEGEND	LLRCD-063	CD	1990
UNRELEASED TRACKS VOL. 1	GREAT DANE	UNK	CD	1990
UNRELEASED TRACKS VOL. 2	GREAT DANE	UNK	CD	1990
UNSURPASSED DEMOS	YELLOW DOG	YD-008	CD	1991
UNSURPASSED MASTERS 1	SPHINX	003	CD	1990
UNSURPASSED MASTERS 1	YELLOW DOG	YD-001	CD-MO	1989
UNSURPASSED MASTERS 1	YELLOW DOG	YD-001	CD-ST	1990
UNSURPASSED MASTERS 2	YELLOW DOG	YD-002	CD-ST	1990
UNSURPASSED MASTERS 2	YELLOW DOG	YD-002	CD-MO	1989
UNSURPASSED MASTERS 2	SPHINX	004	CD	1990
UNSURPASSED MASTERS 3	SPHINX	005	CD	1990
UNSURPASSED MASTERS 3	YELLOW DOG	YD-003	CD-ST	1990
UNSURPASSED MASTERS 3	YELLOW DOG	YD-003	CD-MO	1989
UNSURPASSED MASTERS 4	YELLOW DOG	YD-004	CD	1990
UNSURPASSED MASTERS 5	YELLOW DOG	YD-005	CD	1991
UNSURPASSED MASTERS 6	YELLOW DOG	YD-012	CD	1992
UNSURPASSED MASTERS 7	YELLOW DOG	YD-013	CD	1992
UNSURPASSED MASTERS VOL. 1	UNIQUE TRACKS	UTCD-001	CD	1990

ALBUM TITLE	LABEL	CATALOG #	FORMAT	YEAR
UNSURPASSED MASTERS VOL. 2	UNIQUE TRACKS	UTCD-002	CD	1990
UNSURPASSED MASTERS VOL. 3	UNIQUE TRACKS	UTCD-003	CD	1990
UNSURPASSED MASTERS VOL. 4	UNIQUE TRACKS	UTCD-004	CD	1990
UPON US ALL	ZAP	7864	LP-12"	1976
UPON US ALL	ZAP	7864	LP-12"	1976
VALENTINE BOX	TEICHIKU	TECP-28082	CD	1990
VALENTINE BOX II	TEICHIKU	TECP-28570	CD	1991
VANCOUVER 1964	NO LABEL	BV-562	2LP-12"	1980
VANCOUVER 1964	TMOQ	72012	2LP-12"	1972
VANCOUVER 1964	TMOQ	D-211	2LP-12"	1975
VANCOUVER 1964	TMOQ	BV-562	2LP-12"	1983
VANCOUVER 1964	BOX TOP	BV-562	2LP-CV	1986
VANCOUVER 1964	K & S	BV-562	2LP-12"	1983
VANCOUVER 1964	WIZARDO	WRMB-340	LP-12"	1976
VANCOUVER '64/ WASHINGTON '64	WHY NOT	WNR-3001	CD	1989
VANCOUVER/ CHICAGO 64	ADAM VIII LTD.	CD 49-031	CD	1991
VEGIMITE	NO LABEL	BT-6896	2LP-12"	1982
VERY BEST OF THE BEATLES VOL 1, THE	TKRWM	1985	LP-12"	1976
VERY BEST OF THE BEATLES VOL 2, THE	TKRWM	1986	LP-12"	1976
VERY BEST OF THE BEATLES VOL 3. THE	TKRWM	1987	LP-12"	1976
VERY BEST OF THE BEATLES VOL 4, THE	TKRWM	1988	LP-12"	1977
VERY BEST OF THE BEATLES VOL 5, THE	TKRWM	1989	LP-12"	1977
VERY BEST OF THE BEATLES VOL 6, THE	TKRWM	1995	LP-12"	1977
VERY BEST OF THE BEATLES VOL 7, THE	TKRWM	1998	LP-12"	1977
VINTAGE GOLD II	UNK	CDR-16	CD	1991
VINTAGE GOLD (GOLD)	OVERSEAS	35DN-11	CD	1991
VIRGIN PLUS THREE	TMOQ	71068	LP-12"	1974
VIRGIN + 3	K & S	018	LP-12"	1983
VIRGIN + 3	TMOQ	S-209	LP-12"	1975
VISIT TO MINNEAPOLIS	MELVIN	MMEP-001	EP-7"	1979
VOL. III-LIVE IN FRANCE 1965	BANANA	UNK	CD	1994
VOL. II-LIVE IN AUSTRALIA 1964	BANANA	UNK	CD	1994
VOL. IV-LIVE IN JAPAN 1966	BANANA	UNK	CD	1994
VOL. I-LIVE IN EUROPE 1964	BANANA	UNK	CD	1994
WATCHING RAINBOWS	RUTHLESS RYMES	L-7/RE-1	LP-12"	1978
WATCHING RAINBOWS	NO LABEL	77-132M/3	EP-7"-CV	1977
WBCN GET BACK REFERNCE ACETATE	YELLOW DOG	YD-035	CD	1993
WBCN GET BACK REF. ACETATE 9/22/69	YELLOW DOG	YD-035	CD	1993
WELCOME 1985	NO LABEL	NO #	3LP-PD	1985
WELCOME THE BEATLES	MARC	TB-76057	LP-12"	1979
WHAT A SHAME MARY JANE...THE PARTY	NO LABEL	F82001	45-12"	1979
WHAT A SHAME MARY JANE...THE PARTY	NO LABEL	R-8028	45-12"	1979
WHAT A SHAME MARY JANE...THE PARTY	EMI	R8028	45-12"	1979
WHEN EVERYBODY COMES TO TOWN	DEATH	529	LP-12"	'70s
WHEN IT SAYS BEATLES BEATLES BEATLES...	MELVIN	MM04	LP-12"	1978
WHISKEY RECORDS 1	WHISKEY	WH-1	LP-12"	1970
WHISKEY RECORDS 2	WHISKEY	WH-X-1/2	LP-12"	1970
WHISKEY RECORDS 3	WHISKEY	WH-XX-1/2PY	LP-12"	1970
WHITE ALBUM DEMOS	EARLY YEARS	02-CD-3314	CD-PD	1989
WHITE ALBUM DEMOS	EARLY YEARS	TEY014/CD3314	CD	1989
WHITE ALBUM DEMOS VOL. 2	CHAPTER ONE	CO-25194	CD	1992
WHITE ALBUM SESSIONS	CHAPTER ONE	CO-151/152	2CD-BX	1991
WHITE ALBUM SESSIONS	CHAPTER ONE	CO-151/152	2CD	1992
WHITE BEATLES '91	TEICHIKU	TECP-28617	CD	1991
WHITE EP	APPLE	EP-1	2EP-7"	1990

ALBUM TITLE	LABEL	CATALOG #	FORMAT	YEAR
WHITE (CANNED) BEATLES	TEICHIKU	TECP-30112	CD	1990
WHO'S SHOUTING IN MY EARS?	BEST TAPES	BTA-002	LP-12"	1987
WITH LOVE FROM US TO YOU	ORO	6365	LP-12"	1982
WITHERED BEATLES	APPLE	SAPCOR-30	2LP-12"	1987
WIZARDO'S GREATEST HITS	WIZARDO	WRMB-391	LP-12"	1976
WONDERFUL PICTURE OF YOU	CIRCLE	SKI-5430	2LP-12"	1985
WORDS OF LOVE	WIZARDO	WRMB-326	LP-12"	1975
WORDS OF LOVE	BRS	BRSCD-73164	CD	1992
WORDS OF LOVE	STRAWBERRY	NO #	LP-12"-CV	1988
WORDS OF LOVE	WIZARDO	WRMB-326	LP-12"-CV	1975
WORLDWIDE	CBM	3795	LP-12"	1975
XMAS DISC COLLECTION, THE	JANSON	CX-96295	45-7"-PD	1991
YELLOW MATTER CUSTARD	TMOQ	1858	LP-12"	1973
YELLOW MATTER CUSTARD	NO LABEL	YMC-101/102	LP-12"	1975
YELLOW MATTER CUSTARD	BLACK GOLD CONCERTS	BFG-2102	LP-12"	1981
YELLOW MATTER CUSTARD	STARLIGHT	SL-87016	LP-12"	1988
YELLOW MATTER CUSTARD	TMOQ	71032	LP-12"	1973
YELLOW MATTER CUSTARD	SHALOM	3316C/D	LP-12"	1976
YELLOW MATTER CUSTARD	RUTHLESS RYMES	BBL-513	LP-12"	1978
YELLOW MATTER CUSTARD	TMOQ	BBL-513	LP-12"	1983
YELLOW MATTER CUSTARD	TMOQ	S-205	LP-12"	1975
YELLOW MATTER CUSTARD	NO LABEL	J-11/12	LP-12"	1975
YELLOW MATTER CUSTARD	CBM	WEC-2 C1/D1	LP-12"	1973
YER BLUES/LUCILLE	NEMS	103-A/B	45-7"-PD	1988
YESTERDAY	BRS	BRSCD-73165	CD	1992
YESTERDAY AND TODAY	PDL DISQUES	PDL 1001	CD	1991
YESTERDAY AND TODAY	NO LABEL	SHEA-1	LP-12"-PD	1980
YESTERDAY AND TODAY	PDL DISQUES	PDL 1001	CD+45-BX	1991
YESTERDAY AND TODAY	BERKELEY	2043	LP-12"	1976
YESTERDAY TODAY AND FOREVER	NO LABEL	P-2	LP-12"-PD	1980
YESTERDAY TODAY AND FOREVER	BLACK DISC	UNK	LP-12"	1981
YESTERDAY & TODAY	BEATLES CONV.	NO #	EP-7"	1980
YOUNGBLOOD	RUTHLESS RHYMES LTD	BVP-005	LP-12"	1979
Y'ORITE WACK	SHOGUN	13113	2LP-CV	1987

214

APPENDIX A
GLOSSARY

ACETATE A one-sided disc which is heavier than commercially pressed records. The disc lasts for only a dozen plays before damage to the grooves creates a distorted sound. Distribution is usually restricted to the artists, producers, management and publishing sectors of the industry.

AUCTION A formal sale of recordings whereby the price is determined by bidding. The highest bidder purchases the item or lot.

ALTERNATE Refers to a *different* version, take, or mix of a song that is commercially released.

BLANK LABEL A record label that lacks a title, record company name, catalog/matrix number or artist designation. A blank, handwritten, or typed label usually indicates an acetate or bootleg disc.

BOOTLEG Bootlegs or underground recordings include the body of unreleased material of an artist, such as demonstration and rehearsal tapes, studio outtakes and alternate takes, TV/ radio performances and concerts.

BOOTLEGGER A person or company that makes unauthorized recordings, manufactures and/or distributes bootlegs.

COUNTERFEIT Unauthorized recordings that attempt to completely reproduce an officially released album, including the music, album artwork and label graphics.

DEMO A demonstration disc or tape used by artists, producers, music publishers and record companies for a variety of purposes. Usually consists of a rough version of a song yet to be formally recorded and produced.

DISCOGRAPHY   An organized listing of the recordings of a particular artist. Discographies usually contain album title, record label, catalog number and the year of release.

INSERT   A sheet included with an LP, 45 rpm, EP or CD, that provides graphics, lyrics or other identifiable information about the release.

LABEL VARIATIONS   Printing differences and other variants that may occur between different issues of identical music, usually seen on LPs and 45 rpm discs.

MATRIX NUMBER   The number used by either the manufacturer or the pressing plant, to identify the disc or its sequential place in a catalog. These numbers are usually located on a record label, a disc, the run-out wax of vinyl records and on the disc packaging.

MIX   The blending of different tape tracks containing vocal and instrumental performances. Mixes are often changed and varied to achieve a complete overall sound.

OUTTAKE   Refers to a finished track that is usually left off of a commercial release—relegated to the studio vaults.

PIRATE DISC   Unauthorized recordings that reproduce legitimately released music, with no attempt made to reproduce the legitimate album cover artwork or labels.

PROMO   A copy of a disc furnished by record companies at no charge to the media or record stores, in hopes of achieving heavy radio airplay and enhancing sales.

APPENDIX B
LIST OF BEATLES BOOTLEGS
ORGANIZED BY MAJOR MANUFACTURER

BULLDOG

ALBUM TITLE	CATALOG #	YEAR
CANDLESTICK PARK	BGCD-0016-PD	1990
HOUSTON AUGUST 19, 1965	BGCD-034	1988
LIVE BEATLES, THE: HOUSTON, 8/19/65	BGCD-034	1988
LIVE BEATLES, THE: PARIS 6/20/65	BGCD-005	1989
LIVE BEATLES, THE: S. F., 8/29/66	BGCD-016	1988
LIVE BEATLES, THE: TOKIO, 7/2/66	BGCD-002	1989
LIVE BEATLES SINGLES COLLECTION, THE	BGS-14	1987
LIVE BEATLES SINGLES COLLECTION, THE	BGS-14	1987
LIVE IN HOUSTON	BGCD-034	1990
LIVE IN PARIS 1965	BGCD-005	1990
LIVE IN PHILADELPHIA 1964	BGCD-005	1988
LIVE IN THE UNITED KINGDOM 1962-65	BGCD-11112	1990
LIVE IN THE UNITED KINGDOM 1962-65	BGCP-90512	1990
NIPPON BUDOKAN HALL TOKIO 7/2/66	BGLP-002	1989
PALAIS DES SPORTS 1965	BGCD-005	1989
SAM HOUSTON COLISEUM	BG-016	1988
SAN FRANCISCO AUG. 29, 1966 C. PARK	BGCD-016	1988

BULLDOG/CROCODILE

AUSTRALIA 1964	BGCD-156	1990
LIVE BEATLES, THE: AUSTRALIA 1964	BGCD-156	1990

CBM

20 NEVER PUBLISHED SONGS	WEC-3030	1972
ABBEY ROAD REVISITED	WEC-3907	1973
AS SWEET AS YOU ARE	WEC-3316	1973
AT THE CAVERN CLUB	WEC-3906	1973
BACK IN '64 AT THE HOLLYWOOD BOWL	4178	1973
BATTLE	N-2027	1973
BEATLES IN ATLANTA WHISKEY FLAT	1001	1973
BEATLES!, THE	WEC-3609	1974
BEST OF THE BEATLES & JETHRO TULL	WEC-2A/B	1973
BUDO KAN HALL	JAPAN-1900	1975
BYE BYE BYE SUPER TRACKS 1	WEC-3922	1974
CAVERN CLUB	WEC-3906	1974
CINELOGUE I (LET IT BE)	TB-4020	1973
CINELOGUE II (YELLOW SUBMARINE)	YSA-1/450-4	1973
CINELOGUE VI	WEC-3665	1975
CINELOGUE VI	TB-635	1975

CBM continued

COMPLETE CHRISTMAS COLLECTION 1963–69	WEC-3316	1973
COMPLETE CHRISTMAS COLLECTION 63–69	2 C1/01	1973
DECCA AUDITION OUTTAKES	WEC-3640/41	1974
DISTRICT OF COLUMBIA	WEC-3571	1972
DISTRICT OF COLUMBIA	WEC-3795	1973
DON'T PASS ME BY	WEC-RI-3316	1975
GET BACK TO TORONTO	WEC-3519	1973
HAPPY BIRTHDAY	5030	1974
HAVE YOU HEARD THE WORD	WEC-3624	1975
HAVE YOU HEARD THE WORD	WEC-3620	1975
HI HO SILVER	4438	1973
HOLLAND/ SWEEDEN SUPER LIVE ...I	101	1973
HOW DO YOU DO IT	WEC-381	1973
KUM BACK	CBM-15A	1973
LIVE AT HOLLYWOOD BOWL	WEC-1103	1973
LIVE CONCERT ATLANTA	WEC-3552	1975
LIVE CONCERT ATLANTA GA.	WEC-3552	1975
LIVE GERM. CONCERTS & US TELECASTS	WEC-1002	1973
LIVE IN EUROPE AND US T.V. CASTS	WEC-3571	1975
LIVE IN HOLLYWOOD	WEC-110	1973
LIVE IN MELBOURNE AUSTRALIA 7/16/64	WEC-4162	1975
LIVE IN VANCOUVER	WEC-4164	1975
LIVE IN WASHINGTON D.C.	WEC-3571/3795	1974
LIVE PARIS OLYMPIA	WEC-3688	1975
L.S. BUMBLE BEE	WEC-3626	1975
MARY JANE	WEC-3585	1975
NEVER RELEASED MARY JANE, THE	WEC-3585	1975
PARIS AGAIN	WEC-3688	1975
PARIS SPORTS PALAIS	LLPA-77	1977
PEACE OF MIND	WEC-3670	1975
RARE BEATLES	TB-5030	1974
RARE SESSIONS	B-213	1975
SHEA THE GOOD OLD DAYS	WEC-2315	1972
SOLDIER OF LOVE	WEC-1022	1973
SOME OTHER GUY	WEC-3813	1975
SOME OTHER GUY/ CAVERN CLUB	B215	1975
SPORTS PALACE FRANCE - SECOND SHOW	WEC-1101	1973
STARS OF '63	WEC-4779/4750	1975
STOCKHOLM	WEC-1040	1973
STUDIO SESSIONS VOLUME ONE	WEC-3640	1974
STUDIO SESSIONS VOLUME ONE	ZAP-1061	1974
STUDIO SESSIONS VOLUME TWO	ZAP-1062	1974
STUDIO SESSIONS VOLUME TWO	WEC-3641	1974
SUNDAY NIGHT AT THE LONDON PALLADIUM	WEC-3687	1975
SUPERTRACKS 1	WEC-3922	1975
SUPERTRACKS 2	TB-1018	1976
SUPERTRACKS 2	WEC-3923	1976
SWEDEN 1963	WEC-3795/3571	1975
THEIR COMPLETE XMAS COLLECTION '63–'69	WEC-206	1973
THOSE WERE THE DAYS	WEC-3907	1976
TOKYO SIXTY-SIX	JAPAN-1900	1975
WORLDWIDE	3795	1975
YELLOW MATTER CUSTARD	WEC-2 C1/D1	1973

CBM/COMET

DON'T PASS ME BY	WEC-RI-3316	1975
GET BACK TO TORONTO	WEC-3519	1975

CBM/CUMQUAT

RENAISSANCE MINSTRELS 4	TB-5020	1975

INSTANT ANALYSIS

BACK IN '64 AT THE HOLLYWOOD BOWL	1032	1975
BEATLES INVADE EUROPE	BBR-008	1987
BUMBLE WORDS- SUPER STUDIO SERIES 3	3624/3626	1975
CINELOGUE III (A HARD DAY'S NIGHT)	HD-1024	1975
CINELOGUE IV (HELP!)	1026	1975
CINELOGUE V (MAGICAL MYSTERY TOUR)	MM-1028	1975
CLASSIFIED DOCUMENT	BBR-014	1987
CONFIDENTIAL DOCUMENT	BBR-014	1988
FOREST HILLS TENNIS STADIUM	FH-1058	1975
HOT AS SUN	4216/4217	1975
ITALY	4178	1975
LIVE IN ITALY	IT-1038	1975
LIVE IN MELBOURNE AUSTRALIA 7/16/64	MB-1034	1975
LIVE IN VANCOUVER, CANADA	VN-1032	1975
MELBOURNE/ VANCOUVER SUPER LIVE #4	1032A/1034A	1975
PARIS '65	BBR-007	1975
STOCKHOLM	4179	1975
SWEET APPLE TRAX VOL. ONE	WEC-4182	1973
SWEET APPLE TRAX VOL. TWO	WEC-4181	1973

KING KONG

BACKTRAX SESSIONS	WEC-3922	1988
BACKTRAX SESSIONS	3922	1988
CINELOGUE VI	TB-4022	1975
CINELOGUE VI	TB-4022	1975
CINELOGUE: MAGICAL MYSTERY TOUR	634	1974
DAY TRIPPER JAM	NO #	'70s
FIRST UNITED STATES PERFORMANCE	1070	1973
FOREST HILLS TENNIS STADIUM	FH-1058/4228	1973
HAVE YOU HEARD THE WORD	WEC-3624	1975
HI HO SILVER	4438/GT-8410	1973
KUM BACK	15A	1973
LIVE CONCERT ATLANTA	RI-3552	1975
LIVE IN ITALY	4178	1973
LONDON PALLADIUM	WEC-3687	1974
SOLDIER OF LOVE	TB-1022	1973
STUDIO SESSIONS ONE	WEC-3640	1974
STUDIO SESSIONS TWO	WEC-3641	1974
SWEDEN, WASHINGTON, SWEEDEN	WEC-3795	1975

PYRAMID

AT THE BEEB VOL. 1	RFT-CD-005	1989
AT THE BEEB VOL. 10	RFT-CD-024	1990
AT THE BEEB VOL. 11	RFT-CD-025	1990
AT THE BEEB VOL. 12	RFT-CD-032	1990
AT THE BEEB VOL. 13	RFT-CD-033	1990

PYRAMID continued

AT THE BEEB VOL. 2	RFT-CD-006	1989
AT THE BEEB VOL. 3	RFT-CD-007	1989
AT THE BEEB VOL. 4	RFT-CD-018	1989
AT THE BEEB VOL. 5	RFT-CD-014	1989
AT THE BEEB VOL. 6	RFT-CD-015	1989
AT THE BEEB VOL. 7	RFT-CD-019	1989
AT THE BEEB VOL. 8	RFT-CD-016	1989
AT THE BEEB VOL. 9	RFT-CD-017	1989
LIVE IN MELBOURNE 1964 & PARIS 1965	RFT-CD-001	1988
LIVE IN PARIS 1964 AND S.F. 1966	RFT-CD-002	1988
LIVE IN PARIS 1964 AND S.F. 1966	RFT-CD-002	1988
RADIO ACTIVE VOL. 1	RFT-CD-005	1989
RADIO ACTIVE VOL. 1	RFT-CD-005	1989
RADIO ACTIVE VOL. 10	RFT-CD-024	1990
RADIO ACTIVE VOL. 10	RFT-CD-024	1990
RADIO ACTIVE VOL. 11	RFT-CD-025	1989
RADIO ACTIVE VOL. 11	RFT-CD-025	1990
RADIO ACTIVE VOL. 12	RFT-CD-032	1990
RADIO ACTIVE VOL. 12	RFT-CD-032	1990
RADIO ACTIVE VOL. 13	RFT-CD-033	1990
RADIO ACTIVE VOL. 13	RFT-CD-033	1990
RADIO ACTIVE VOL. 2	RFT-CD-006	1989
RADIO ACTIVE VOL. 2	RFT-CD-006	1989
RADIO ACTIVE VOL. 3	RFT-CD-007	1989
RADIO ACTIVE VOL. 3	RFT-CD-007	1989
RADIO ACTIVE VOL. 4	RFT-CD-018	1989
RADIO ACTIVE VOL. 4	RFT-CD-018	1989
RADIO ACTIVE VOL. 5	RFT-CD-014	1989
RADIO ACTIVE VOL. 5	RFT-CD-014	1989
RADIO ACTIVE VOL. 6	RFT-CD-015	1989
RADIO ACTIVE VOL. 6	RFT-CD-015	1989
RADIO ACTIVE VOL. 7	RFT-CD-019	1989
RADIO ACTIVE VOL. 7	RFT-CD-019	1989
RADIO ACTIVE VOL. 8	RFT-CD-016	1989
RADIO ACTIVE VOL. 8	RFT-CD-016	1989
RADIO ACTIVE VOL. 9	RFT-CD-017	1989
RADIO ACTIVE VOL. 9	RFT-CD-017	1989
ROCK AND ROLL MUSIC	PY-CD-027	1989

THE SWINGIN' PIG

A SLICE OF SWINGIN' PIG VOL. 1	TSP-PRO-001	1989
A SLICE OF SWINGIN' PIG VOL. 2	TSP-PRO-002	1989
FIVE NIGHTS IN A JUDO ARENA	TSP-011	1989
FIVE NIGHTS IN A JUDO ARENA	TSP-011	1989
FROM US TO YOU	TSP-015	1989
FROM US TO YOU	TSP-015	1989
FROM US TO YOU	TSP-015-2	1989
LIVE IN PARIS 1965	TSP-008	1988
LIVE IN PARIS 1965	TSP-008	1989
LIVE IN PARIS '65	TSP-008	1989
NIPPON BUDOKAN HALL 1966	TSP-002	1989
STARS OF '63	TSP-CD-005	1989
STARS OF '63	TSP-005	1989
STARS OF '63	TSP-005	1989

THE SWINGIN' PIG continued

ULTRA RARE TRAX VOL. 1	TSP-001	1988
ULTRA RARE TRAX VOL. 1	TSP-001	1989
ULTRA RARE TRAX VOL. 2	TSP-002	1989
ULTRA RARE TRAX VOL. 2	TSP-002	1988
ULTRA RARE TRAX VOL. 3	TSP-003	1989
ULTRA RARE TRAX VOL. 3	TSP-025	1989
ULTRA RARE TRAX VOL. 4	TSP-026	1989
ULTRA RARE TRAX VOL. 4	TSP-004	1989
ULTRA RARE TRAX VOL. 5	TSP-035	1990
ULTRA RARE TRAX VOL. 6	TSP-036	1990
ULTRA RARE TRAX VOL. 3 & 4	TR-2190-S	1988
ULTRA RARE TRAX VOL. 5 & 6	TR-2191-S	1988

TAKRL

BACK IN THE SADDLE - 8TH AMENDMENT	ZAP-7872	1977
BACK UPON US ALL	#1969	1977
BACK UPON US ALL - 4TH AMENDMENT	ZAP-7864	1977
EMI OUTTAKES	1374	1975
HAHST AZ SON	2950	1976
ON STAGE IN JAPAN	1900	1976
T'ANKS FOR THE MAMMARIES	BOZO-1	1978

TMOQ

20 NEVER PUBLISHED SONGS	73030	1973
ALIVE AT LAST IN ATLANTA	71007	1972
AT THE HOLLYWOOD BOWL	S-208	1974
AT THE HOLLYWOOD BOWL	S-208	1975
BATTLE	RP-24	'70s
BEATLES, THE	73030	1973
BEATLES AT SHEA	UNK	'70s
BEATLES COMPLETE XMAS COLL. 63-69, THE	BCC-104	1973
BEATLES IN ATLANTA WHISKEY FLAT	71007	1972
BUG CRUSHER 'LIVE'	TMQ-71076	1976
COMPLETE CHRISTMAS COLLECTION 63-69	71015	1972
FAB RAVER SHOW	2	1974
GET BACK JOURNALS	2R-78	1987
GET BACK SESSION, THE	BGB-111	1974
GET BACK SESSIONS	1801	1974
GET BACK SESSIONS	71024	1972
GET BACK SESSIONS 2	71068	1971
GET BACK SESSIONS VOL. 2	1892-A/B	1974
GET BACK SESSIONS VOL. 2	BHB-118	1974
GOOD OLD DAYS, THE	UNK	'70s
HOLLYWOOD BOWL	71065	1971
HOLLYWOOD BOWL 1964	BHB-115	1974
IN ATLANTA WHISKEY FLATS	OPD-67	1975
IN ATLANTA WHISKEY FLATS	71007-8/70-417	1972
IN ATLANTA WHISKEY FLATS	S-201	1975
IN CONCERT AT WHISKEY FLAT	OPD-19/67-2	1975
IT WAS 20 YEARS AGO TODAY	NO #	1987
LAST LIVE LIVE SHOW	1800-RI	1971
LAST LIVE SHOW	1800	1971
LAST LIVE SHOW	LLS-101	1971
LAST LIVE SHOW (III)	71012	1972

TMOQ continued

LAST LIVE SHOW (IV)	S-202	1975
LIVE AT HOLLYWOOD BOWL	115	1974
LIVE AT HOLLYWOOD BOWL	71065	1973
LIVE AT HOLLYWOOD BOWL	1704	1974
LIVE AT THE HOLLYWOOD BOWL 1964	S-208	1975
LIVE AT THE HOLLYWOOD BOWL 1964	71065	1974
LIVE AT THE WHISKEY FLAT	OPD-67-2	1975
LIVE AT THE WHISKEY FLAT	70418F	1970s
LIVE AT THE WHISKEY FLAT	OPD-19	1975
LIVE IN ATLANTA WHISKEY FLAT	OPD-79	1975
LIVE IN ATLANTA WHISKEY FLAT	1704	1974
MARY JANE	71076	1974
MARY JANE	MJ-543	1973
MARY JANE (SPICY SONGS)	MJ-543	1973
MORE GET BACK SESSIONS	1893	1974
MORE GET BACK SESSIONS	71068	1974
OUTTAKES 1 & 2	7508	1975
OUTTAKES VOLS. 1 & 2	D-207	1975
OUTTAKES VOL. 1	BO-519	1975
OUTTAKES VOL. 1	71048	1974
OUTTAKES VOL. 2	71049	1974
OUTTAKES VOL. 2	BO-520	1975
RENAISSANCE MINSTRELS 1	73001	1973
RENAISSANCE MINSTRELS 2	73002	1980s
RENAISSANCE MINSTRELS 3	73032	1990
RENAISSANCE MINSTRELS VOL. I	1852	1973
SHEA THE GOOD OLD DAYS	4178	1975
SHEA!	LLS-101	1975
SHEA...AT LAST!	T-102	1975
SPICY BEATLES SONGS	71076	1974
SPICY BEATLES SONGS	S-210	1975
SPICY BEATLES SONGS	1848	1983
SUPERTRACKS 2	TB-1018	1974
VANCOUVER 1964	BV-562	1983
VANCOUVER 1964	D-211	1975
VANCOUVER 1964	72012	1972
VIRGIN PLUS THREE	71068	1974
VIRGIN + 3	S-209	1975
YELLOW MATTER CUSTARD	1858	1973
YELLOW MATTER CUSTARD	BBL-513	1983
YELLOW MATTER CUSTARD	71032	1973
YELLOW MATTER CUSTARD	S-205	1975
RENAISSANCE MINSTRELS 1	71025	1973
RENAISSANCE MINSTRELS 2	71026	1973

TMOQ/ 1/4 APPLE

NOT FOR SALE	JQWX-1003A	'80s
NOT FOR SALE	WABD-3561A	'80s

TMOQ/IMP

GET BACK SESSIONS AND VIRGIN + THREE	71068/71024	1976

TOBE MILO

ACROSS THE UNIVERSE	5Q-3VC4946	1978
AROUND THE BEATLES	10Q9/10	UNREL
BEATLES IN PERSON AT SAM HOUSTON	XMILO-10Q3/4	1978
BEATLES LIVE IN HOUSTON	XMILO-5Q-1/2	1978
BEATLES LIVE IN SEATTLE 1964, THE	10Q7/8	UNREL
BEATLES STUDIO OUTTAKES	4Q-11/12	1979
BEATLES '66	4Q7-10VC46234	1977
BEATLES '66	4Q-7-10	1977
BEST OF TOBE MILO PRODUCTIONS	10Q-1/2	1978
BRUNG TO EWE BY	4Q5/6VC4589	1977
GET TOGETHER	4Q-1/2	1976
GET TOGETHER	4Q-1/2	1977
IN PERSON SAM HOUSTON COLISEUM	5Q1/2-VC4835	1978
IN PERSON SAM HOUSTON COLISEUM	10Q-3/4	1978
LIVE IN ITALY	ITA-128	1980
MAN OF THE DECADE	MOTD-1269	1978
STUDIO OUTTAKES	4Q11/12-VC4646	1977
TELEVISION OUTTAKES	4Q-3/4	1977

WIZARDO

ABBEY ROAD REVISITED	WRMB-353	1976
ABBEY ROAD REVISITED	WRMB-353	1976
ABC MANCHESTER 1964	WRMB-361	1976
AROUND THE BEATLES	WRMB-349	1976
AS SWEET AS YOU ARE	208	1976
AS SWEET AS YOU ARE	116-208	1976
AWAY WITH WORDS	WRMB-505	1976
A/B SINGLE ACETATE	WRMB-315	1975
BEATLES LIVE AT ABC MANCHESTER	WRMB-361	1976
BEATLES TOUR: THE GREAT TAKE OVER	502	1976
BOTTOM OF THE APPLE TAPES	WRMB-404	1976
BRITISH COLUMBIA '64	WRMB-340	1976
BRITISH COLUMBIA '64	WRMB-340	1976
COMPLETE CHRISTMAS COLLECTION 63-69	WRMB-400	1976
COMPLETE LET IT BE SESSIONS	WRMB-315	1975
COMPLETE SOUNDTRACK TO HELP!	WRMB-317	1975
COMPLETE UNCUT SOUNDTRACK TO A.H.D.N.	WRMB-303	1975
DO IT NOW	WRMB-381	1976
DR. ROBERT	WRMB-378	1976
DR. ROBERT	WRMB-378	1976
FIRST UNITED STATES PERFORMANCE	WRMB-360	1976
FOUR YOUNG NOVICES	WRMB-361	1976
GET BACK	WRMB-320	1975
GET BACK	WRMB-315	1975
GET BACK SESSIONS	WRMB-320	1975
GET YER YEAH-YEAH'S OUT	WRMB-316	1975
GET YER YEAH-YEAH'S OUT	WRMB-316	1975
HAPPY BIRTHDAY	WRMB-345	1976
HAPPY BIRTHDAY/SOLDIER OF LOVE	WRMB-345	1976
HELP! SOUNDTRACK	WRMB-102/202	1976
HOLLYWOOD BOWL 1964	205	1976
HOW DO YOU DO IT	WRMB-381	1975
IN THE LAP OF THE GODS...	WRMB-325	1975
JOHN, PAUL, GEORGE AND JIMMY	WRMB-501	1976

WIZARDO continued

LAST BEETLE RECORD	WRMB-393	1976
LET IT BE 315	WRMB-315	1975
LET IT BE ACETATE	WRMB-315	1975
LET IT BE LIVE	WRMB-315	1975
LET IT BE PERFORMANCE, THE	WRMB-315	1975
LET IT BE: BEFORE PHIL SPECTOR	WRMB-315	1975
LIVE AT SHEA	WRMB-406	1976
LIVE IN AUSTRALIA AND WASHINGTON	WRMB-314	1975
LIVE IN JAPAN 1966	WRMB-318	1975
LIVE IN PHILADELPHIA	WRMB-357	1976
LIVE IN TOKYO, JULY 1, 1966	501	1976
MAGICAL MYSTERY TOUR PLUS ...	WRMB-310	1975
MELBOURNE AND WASHINGTON	WRMB-314	1975
MORE FROM THE FAB FOUR	WRMB-390	1976
ON STAGE	WRMB-328	1975
ON STAGE IN EUROPE	WRMB-328	1975
ON STAGE IN GERMANY	WRMB-328	1975
ON STAGE IN JAPAN THE 1966 TOUR	WRMB-318	1975
ON STAGE IN MELB. AUS. & WASH. D.C.	WRMB-314	1975
ORIGINAL AUDITION TAPE	WRMB-308	1975
ORIGINAL DEMO SESSIONS	WRMB-308	1975
ORIGINAL GET BACK ACETATE, THE	WRMB-315	1975
ORIG. ST. ACETATE FOR LET IT BE...	WRMB-315	1975
PARIS 1965	WRMB-335	1976
PARIS SPORTS PALAIS 1965	WRMB-335	1976
PARIS '65	WRMB-335	1976
POP GOES THE BEATLES	WRMB-345	1976
POWER BROKERS	WRMB-392	1976
RENAISSANCE MINSTRELS VOL. II	WRMB-358	1976
SECRET	WRMB-359	1976
SHEA THE GOOD OLD DAYS	207	1976
SHEA-THE GOOD OLD DAYS	116-207	1976
SP 602	WRMB-316	1976
STUDIO OUTTAKE RECORDINGS 1962-1964	WRMB-326	1975
SWEET APPLE TRAX	WRMB-343	1976
THIRTY NOSTALGIA HITS	102-232	1978
TOKYO 66	116-206	1976
TOKYO '66	206	1976
VANCOUVER 1964	WRMB-340	1976
WIZARDO'S GREATEST HITS	WRMB-391	1976
WORDS OF LOVE	WRMB-326	1975
WORDS OF LOVE	WRMB-326	1975

YELLOW DOG

ACETATES	YD-009	1991
ALL THINGS MUST PASS (PT. 1: ELECTRIC)	YD-016	1992
ALL THINGS MUST PASS (PT. 2: ACOUSTIC)	YD-053	1994
AUCTION TAPES	YD-055	1994
BEATLES COMPLETE X-MASs'63-66,THE	YD-031	1992
CELLULOID ROCK	YD-006	1991
COMPLETE ROOFTOP CONCERT, THE	YD-015	1992
CONTROL ROOM MONITOR MIXES, THE	YD-032	1993
GET BACK AND 22 OTHER SONGS	YD-014	1992
HOLLYWOOD BOWL COMPLETE	YD-034	1993

YELLOW DOG continued

KARAOKE-THE R. STONES & THE BEATLES	YD-033	1993
ORIG. DECCA TAPES & CAVERN CLUB..,THE	YD-011	1991
ROCK AND ROLL	YD-054	1994
ULTIMATE COLLECTION VOL. 1, THE	YDB-1001/4	1994
ULTIMATE COLLECTION VOL. 2, THE	YDB-2001/4	1994
ULTIMATE COLLECTION VOL. 3, THE	YDB-3001/4	1994
ULTIMATE LIVE COLLECTION VOL. 1, THE	YD-038/39	1993
UNSURPASSED DEMOS	YD-008	1991
UNSURPASSED MASTERS 1	YD-001	1990
UNSURPASSED MASTERS 1	YD-001	1989
UNSURPASSED MASTERS 2	YD-002	1989
UNSURPASSED MASTERS 2	YD-002	1990
UNSURPASSED MASTERS 3	YD-003	1989
UNSURPASSED MASTERS 3	YD-003	1990
UNSURPASSED MASTERS 4	YD-004	1990
UNSURPASSED MASTERS 5	YD-005	1991
UNSURPASSED MASTERS 6	YD-012	1992
UNSURPASSED MASTERS 7	YD-013	1992
WBCN GET BACK REFERENCE ACETATE	YD-035	1993

APPENDIX C
PHOTO SURVEY OF BOOTLEG
TRADEMARKS AND LOGOS

227

SODD Records

The Amazing
Kornyphone Label

Savage Records

BIRD
BRAIN
RECORDS

WHITE KNIGHT
RECORDS
WK 20

Vigotone

TIGER BEAT
RECORDS

Ze Anonym Plattenspieler

Phony Graf

Old Glory

TMOQ

TMOQ

ORO

Cat 'n' Dog

De Wentraub

Dittolino

Kustom

Wizardo

Slipped Disc

Instant Analysis

Highway High-Fi

Ruthless Rhymes

Melvin

Audifon

POD

Amazing Kornyfone

Shalom

Godzilla

Oh Boy!

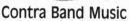

Contra Band Music

CBM Label

IMP Records

TAKRL Records

Magic Dwarf

Melvin

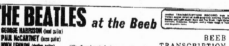

TMOQ

APPENDIX D
BOOTLEGGER'S FAMILY TREES

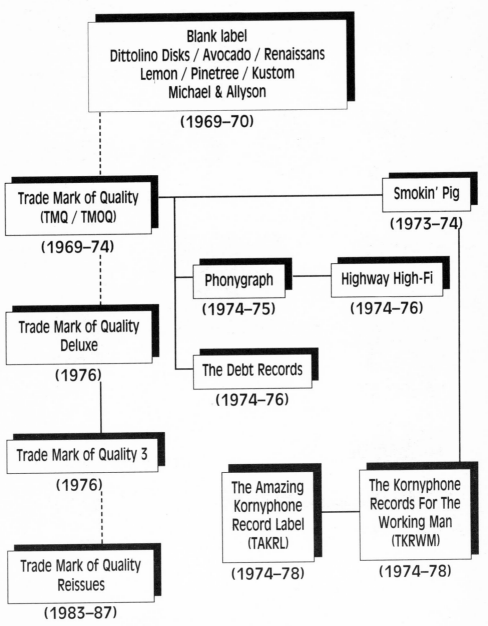

Blank label
Dittolino Disks / Avocado / Renaissans
Lemon / Pinetree / Kustom
Michael & Allyson
(1969–70)

Trade Mark of Quality
(TMQ / TMOQ)
(1969–74)

Smokin' Pig
(1973–74)

Phonygraph
(1974–75)

Highway High-Fi
(1974–76)

Trade Mark of Quality
Deluxe
(1976)

The Debt Records
(1974–76)

Trade Mark of Quality 3
(1976)

The Amazing
Kornyphone
Record Label
(TAKRL)
(1974–78)

The Kornyphone
Records For The
Working Man
(TKRWM)
(1974–78)

Trade Mark of Quality
Reissues
(1983–87)

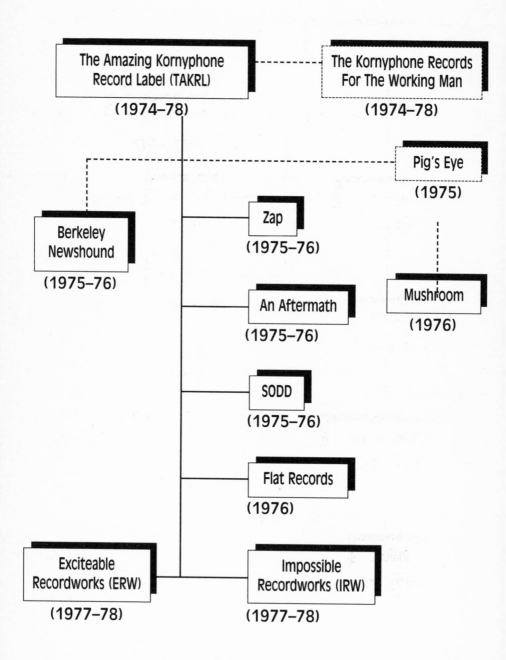

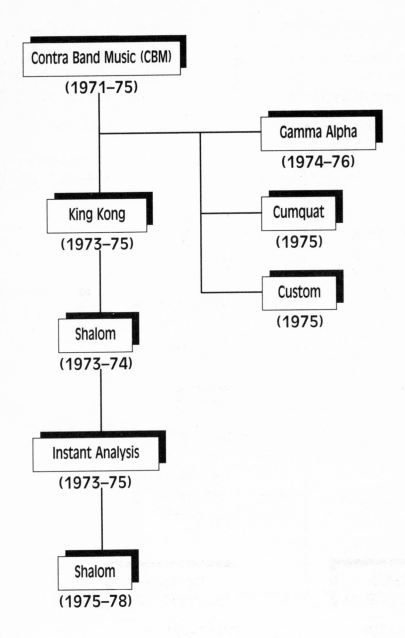

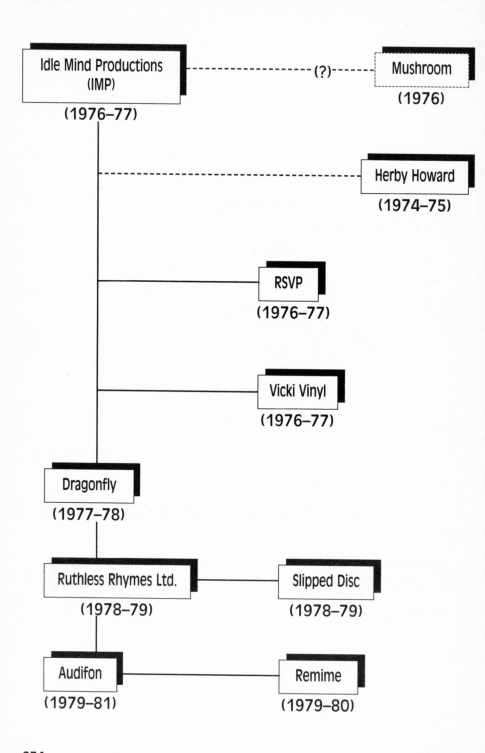

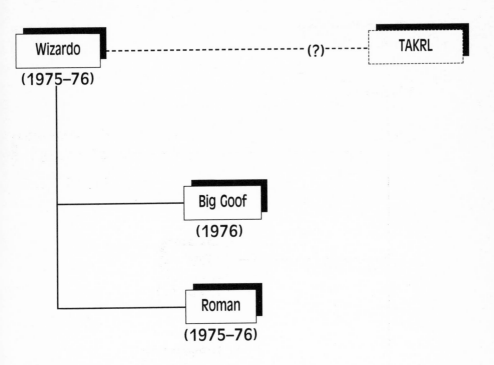

BEATLES SPECIALTY LABELS

REFERENCE BOOKS

Castleman, Harry and Podrazik, Walter J. *All Together Now*. Ballantine Books, 1975; now published by Popular Culture Ink.

Davis, Hunter. *The Beatles*, 2d rev. ed. McGraw-Hill, 1985.

Howlett, A. *The Beatles At The Beeb 1962-1965*. BBC, 1982.

King, LRE. *Do You Want To Know A Secret?*. Storyteller Productions, 1988.

_____. *Fixing A Hole*. Storyteller Productions, 1988.

_____. *Help! - A Companion to The Beatles Recording Sessions*. Storyteller Productions, 1989.

Lewisohn, Mark. *The Beatles Live!*. Henry Holt, 1986.

_____. *The Beatles Recording Sessions*. Harmony, 1988.

_____. *The Complete Beatles Chronicle*. Harmony, 1992.

_____. *The Beatles Day By Day*. Harmony, 1989.

Rehwagen, Thomas. *The Beatles From Session to Session*. Private, 1987.

Reinhart, Charles. *You Can't Do That*. Pierian Press, 1981; now published by Popular Culture Ink.

Robertson, John. *The Art & Music of John Lennon*. Birch Lane Press, 1990.

Schaffner, Nicholas. *The Beatles Forever*. McGraw-Hill, 1977.

Schultheiss, Tom. *A Day In The Life*. Pierian Press, 1980; now published by Popular Culture Ink.

Schwartz, David. *Listening To The Beatles*. Popular Culture Ink, 1990.

Voigts, Andreas. *The Official Bootleg Price Guide.* Self Published in Germany, 1990.

Walker, Bob. ed. *Hot Wacks Book XIV.* Hot Wacks Press, 1990.

Weiner, Allen J. *The Beatles: The Ultimate Recording Guide.* Facts On File, 1992.

REFERENCE PERIODICALS

Beatlefan
The Goody Press
P.O. Box 33515
Decatur, GA 30033

Beatles Book Monthly
Beat Publications
45 St. Mary's Road
Ealing, London, W5 5RQ
England

Beatles Unlimited magazine
P.O. Box 602, 3430 AP
The Nieuwegein
Netherlands

Beatletter
P.O. Box 13
St. Clair Shores, MI 48080

Belmo's Beatleg News
P.O. Box 17163
Ft. Mitchell, KY 41017

CD International
P.O. Box 22014
Milwaukee, OR 97222

Goldmine magazine
700 E. State Street
Iola, WI 54990

Good Day Sunshine
c/o Charles F. Rosenay
397 Edgewood Avenue,
New Haven, CT 06511

ICE The Monthly CD Newsletter
c/o Peter J. Howard
P.O. Box 3043
Santa Monica, CA 90408

Record Collector
Beat Publications
43-45 St. Mary's Road
Ealing, London W5 5RQ
England.

Rolling Stone
1290 Avenue of the Americas
New York, NY 10104-0298

Beatlefest
P.O. Box 436
Westwood, NJ 07675
Three U.S. National Beatles conventions per year in NY, Chicago and LA

ABOUT THE AUTHORS

Jim Berkenstadt has been a Beatles archivist/historian since 1964. His articles on The Beatles have been published or cited in *The Washington Post*; *Rolling Stone*; *Vox*; *Goldmine*; *ICE, the CD Newsletter*; *Good Day Sunshine*; *Belmo's Beatleg News*; *The Beatles Book Monthly* and *Beatlefan*. Berkenstadt produced a spoken-word documentary series of The Beatles for compact disc entitled *The Beatles Tapes*, featuring interviews and press conferences of the group, on Great Northwest Music's Jerden label. He has also appeared as a consultant on The Beatles for CBS-TV (WISC-TV affiliate) and ABC-TV (WKOW-TV affiliate), and has covered the Ringo Starr 1992 and Paul McCartney 1993 concert tours for CBS. Berkenstadt, who was the first to break the national story on The Beatles' Reunion of 1994, has also served as a consultant to Rykodisc Record Company and Dick Clark Productions.

Belmo, a.k.a. Scott Belmer, is the founding publisher and editor of the international newsletter, *Belmo's Beatleg News*. This publication, now seen as the premier authority on unreleased and unauthorized Beatles' recordings, has been quoted in *Rolling Stone*; *Goldmine*; *Beatlefan*; *ICE, the CD Newsletter* and others. Belmo has written a number of articles on The Beatles which have appeared in national publications. He is a contributing editor to *Beatlefan* magazine. He served as a consultant for an NBC-TV "Expose" news story on bootlegging. He authored *The Black Hole Handbook* in 1981 and *The Mystic Warrior* in 1991.

COLLECTOR'S GUIDE PUBLISHING
ORDER FORM

TITLE		PRICE (U.S.)	QTY.
The Hitchhiker's Guide To Elvis By Mick Farren		$12.95	_____
The Illustrated Collector's Guide To Kate Bush By Robert Godwin		$10.95	_____
The Illustrated Collector's Guide To Hawkwind By Robert Godwin (box set—w/ *Warriors On The Edge Of Time* CD)		$12.95 $28.98	_____ _____
The Illustrated Collector's Guide To Motorhead By Alan Burridge & Mick Stevenson (box set—w/ *The Best Of Motorhead* CD)		$12.95 $28.98	_____ _____
The Illustrated Collector's Guide To Led Zeppelin By Robert Godwin	paperbk. hardcvr.	$17.95 $21.95	_____ _____
Olivia: More Than Physical – A Collector's Guide By Gregory Branson-Trent (box set—w/ *Have You Never Been Mellow* CD)		$12.95 $28.98	_____ _____
Queens Of Deliria By Michael Butterworth (box set—w/ *Quark, Strangeness & Charm* CD)		$12.95 $28.98	_____ _____
Shipping & handling		+ <u>$5.00</u>, $3 each add. book	
Total		_____	

UPCOMING RELEASES FROM
COLLECTOR'S GUIDE PUBLISHING

The Illustrated Book Of Nazareth
By Michael D. Melton

A comprehensive guide to, and in appreciation of Nazareth, the band and their music. Every Nazareth album, from their 1971 self-titled debut to the recent release of Move Me, is included in this 172 page guide; numerous rarities, singles, solo material, special releases, and more are also included, documented in over 100 photos.

The Illustrated Collector's Guide To Wishbone Ash (w/ CD)
By Andy Powell

Written by Ash guitarist Andy Powell, this extensive book features over 100 photos, with a comprehensive discography of the group, along with complete listings of band line-ups, tours and concert dates, set lists, tour programs and posters, catalogue numbers, videos, songbooks, fanzines, memorabilia, and much more. Also included in the box set is the CD BBC Radio 1 Live In Concert, which was originally recorded at the Paris Theatre in 1972.

The Progressive Rock Book, Vol. 1 – North & South American Editon
By Ron Johnston

This incredibly exhaustive book contains complete single and album listings for hundreds of progressive rock bands hailing from North and South America. The listings include LPs, cassettes, CDs, EPs, 45s, bootlegs, imports, and so on, and extend to such diverse musical styles as jazz, new age, blues-rock, electronic, cosmic and space music, acid and psychedelic, and folk..

The Illustrated Collector's Guide To Ian Gillan (w/ CD)
By Mary Gear

Legendary Deep Purple frontman Ian Gillan is the subject of this extensive book about the man and his music. This guide features a full Gillan discography spanning his entire career, including his stints in Episode Six, Black Sabbath, along with his solo works. The book also has listings of rare imports, videos, tour dates and posters, postcards, magazines, and so on. Comes packaged in a box set with the CD Trouble: The Best of Ian Gillan.

The Alternative Rock Book
By Alan Cross

A guide to the most important genre of music to emerge in the last fifteen years. This book includes a complete analysis of hundreds of alternative bands, with full listings of albums, singles, band details, etc.